The
ENGLISH
PUBLIC
SCHOOL
—

Martin Stephen is only the second man in history to have occupied both High Master posts in UK public schools – at The Manchester Grammar School and St Paul's School London. Starting his career teaching in remand homes, he was also Headmaster of The Perse School, Cambridge. He and his wife Jenny were the first married couple ever both to be Heads of schools in membership of HMC (the Headmasters' and Headmistress's Conference), and at one stage could claim between them to have been Head of five schools in the top thirty of the A-level league tables. Martin was elected as Chairman of the HMC in 2004, despite being described as a 'dangerous maverick' at his first meeting. He is the author of twenty-one books on literature, military history and education, including the classic First World War poetry anthology *Never Such Innocence*, five novels in the 'Henry Gresham' series of historical crime thrillers, and the acclaimed *Educating the More Able Student* (with Ian Warwick, 2015). He is a founder-Governor of The London Academy of Excellence.

The

ENGLISH PUBLIC SCHOOL

—

A personal and
irreverent history

MARTIN STEPHEN

metro

Published by Metro Publishing,
an imprint of John Blake Publishing,
3 Bramber Court, 2 Bramber Road,
London W14 9PB, England

www.johnblakebooks.com

www.facebook.com/johnblakebooks ⬜
twitter.com/jblakebooks ⬜

First published in hardback in 2018

ISBN: 978-1-78606-877-4

British Library Cataloguing-in-Publication Data:

A catalogue record for this book is available from the British Library.

Design by www.envydesign.co.uk

Printed and bound in Great Britain by Clays Ltd, St Ives plc

1 3 5 7 9 10 8 6 4 2

Papers used by John Blake Publishing are natural, recyclable products made from
wood grown in sustainable forests. The manufacturing processes conform to the
environmental regulations of the country of origin.

Every attempt has been made to contact the relevant copyright-holders, but some were
unobtainable. We would be grateful if the appropriate people could contact us.

John Blake Publishing is an imprint of Bonnier Publishing
www.bonnierpublishing.com

CONTENTS

DEFINITIONS   IX

AUTHOR'S INTRODUCTION   I

PREFACE   PUBLIC SCHOOLS: A BRIEF HISTORY IN
                NINE HUNDRED WORDS   13

CHAPTER 1   THE BOARDING HOUSE, FAGGING
                AND CASUAL CRUELTY   23

CHAPTER 2   ALL BOYS TOGETHER: SEX AND THE
                PUBLIC SCHOOL   53

CHAPTER 3   WHITEWASH!: THE CLARENDON
                COMMISSION OF 1864, THE PUBLIC
                SCHOOLS ACT OF 1868 AND THE
                HEADMASTERS' CONFERENCE   75

CHAPTER 4   PLAY UP! PLAY UP! AND PLAY THE
                GAME!: PUBLIC SCHOOLS AND THE
                WORSHIP OF SPORT   95

CHAPTER 5   MUSCULAR CHRISTIANITY: PUBLIC
               SCHOOLS AND THE WORSHIP OF
               CHRISTIANITY   113

CHAPTER 6   SPARE THE ROD: THE PUBLIC-
               SCHOOL LOVE AFFAIR WITH
               CORPORAL PUNISHMENT   137

CHAPTER 7   SOME CORNER OF A FOREIGN
               FIELD: PUBLIC SCHOOLS, EMPIRE
               AND WORLD WAR ONE   149

CHAPTER 8   BILLY BUNTER AND FRIENDS   171

CHAPTER 9   MOST EXTRAORDINARY MEN:
               HEADMASTERS   193

CHAPTER 10   MUTINY!: DISSENT IN THE ENGLISH
               PUBLIC SCHOOL   233

CHAPTER 11   CHANGE AND DECAY: WHO NEEDS
               SCIENCE? AND DAISY PULLS IT OFF   245

CHAPTER 12   EVOLUTION   263

AFTERWORDS   281

SELECT BIBLIOGRAPHY   285

APPENDIX A   TEN WAYS TO IDENTIFY A PUBLIC-
               SCHOOL MAN   293

APPENDIX B   RANDOM EXAMPLES OF PUBLIC-
               SCHOOL SLANG, MOSTLY
               HISTORICAL   295

INDEX   299

'The youth of Eton are dissipated gentlemen; those at Westminster dissipated with a little of the blackguard; and those at St Paul's the most depraved of all'

– Schoolmaster, 1806

'I want your school to be a kind of minor religion with you, ranked by the side of patriotism. Make it a sort of bond, a freemasonry between you and all those who have been here'

– Desmond T. F. Cooke, *The Bending of a Twig* (1906)

'. . . partly due to habit and fashion and despite criticism and divided feelings . . . a public school came to be widely accepted in the course of the eighteenth century as the place where boys destined to be bred as gentlemen night most conveniently be initiated into the life of a community of their peers and contemporaries'

– John Chandos, *Boys Together* (1984)

'. . . the teacher's life . . . wrastles with vnthankfullnesse aboue all other measure . . . One displeased parent will do more harme upon a head . . . than a thousand of the thankfullest will euer do good'

– Richard Mulcaster, Head of Merchant Taylors' School, 1561–86

DEFINITIONS

Oceans of ink have been wasted on defining what is and what is not a 'public school'. Throughout this book I have used the term 'public school' (heartily disliked by the schools themselves because of its implications of social elitism) to refer to schools in membership of the Headmasters' and Headmistresses' Conference (HMC), which includes boarding and day schools, all-boy schools and coeducational schools, but not girls' schools, which need a separate history. I have concentrated on boarding schools, as these have done most to define and create the image of the public school. I have not included preparatory or junior schools, preferring to focus on the big beasts.

AUTHOR'S
INTRODUCTION

D id you know that, when William of Wykeham founded Winchester College in 1382, it was in the name of social mobility? Winchester would give the poor and disadvantaged the Latin grammar denied them by their poverty, and in so doing give them their only passport to a professional career. These empowered children would, of course, seal their success by proceeding on to Wykeham's version of a finishing school, New College, Oxford. Wykeham left enough money to educate seventy children free of all charge. He also left a time bomb in the cellar that would allow, in due course of time, his and all other public schools to ditch their duty to the poor and become finishing schools for the seriously rich. His statute allowed his college to take up to ten 'sons of noble and influential persons' at no cost to the college. In other words, they would have to pay fees.

It is not the least of ironies in the modern public-school world that Winchester, which is mindful of its Founder more than many, would in all probability be unrecognisable to him. Or perhaps not. There are those who believe that Wykeham ignored his own protestations and offered places at his college as patronage to increase his power and influence. In this case, Wykeham stands as one of the greatest hypocrites of all time. In either case – hypocrisy or transmogrification of the original idea– it shows there is nothing new in the story of the English public school.

And today? If you are English and reading this now, a public-school boy or girl is influencing your life. They may have been doing so obviously, as Prime Minister, Chancellor of the Exchequer, Foreign Secretary or Archbishop of Canterbury, or they may be the judge or barrister who will make or break your life. They may well be the person who decides whether you're sacked or promoted, and the surgeon who either botches the job and kills you, or gets it right and saves your life. There's a high probability that the young actor you so admire went to a public school, and a growing chance that your favourite rock band is peopled by public-school boys. When you cheer the next clutch of gold medals at the Olympics, it's likely that at least a third of the winners will have been public-school-educated. And, when you cheer the next royal wedding, it's inconceivable that the bride or groom won't have been to a public school. Only 7 per cent of children attend 'independent schools' in the UK, yet over a third of the entrants to the UK's top universities come from public schools. The products of these institutions dominate politics, the profession and almost every area of English life – and have been doing so for hundreds of years. For this reason alone, we need to know about and understand the English public school, as we need to understand all things that exert a major influence on all our lives.

The problem is that public schools are difficult enough to understand for those who attended or taught at them, never mind those who did not. They are the Japanese knotweed of education – extraordinarily difficult to eradicate and born survivors. Public schools, as with any other elite organisation, seek to exclude those not 'in the know'. Public-school boys can smell each other out over vast distances, and are equally sensitive to those who did not attend such a school. They have their own traditions and eccentricities, nonsense to outsiders but life blood to them. We are talking about schools that describe 'terms' as halves, and at times glory in apparent nonsense. This is the same wilful eccentricity, designed to fool foreigners, that calls the oldest college at Oxford 'New College', and it was there in 1766, in the *Account of Eton Discipline and Education*, which has the classic comment that boys '. . . go into the school a little before seven o'clock (this is called Six o'clock lesson) and stay till half an hour after seven.'[1]

Well of course, one would call a seven o'clock lesson the six o' clock lesson, wouldn't one? Just as one calls a game 'Fives' (Eton or Rugby) that cannot be played by more than four people. Schools had their own private language, none more so than Winchester, another feature that both defined the insider and excluded the outsider.

Much of the existing literature on the English public schools is hopelessly one-sided. In the one corner stand the sycophantic and dreary 'official' histories of the great and the not-so-great public schools. These are not good hunting grounds for the Booker or the Costa Prize. Their most exciting entries often read along the lines of:

---

1 Percival, *Very Superior Men*, p. 15.

Tobias Smegwick-Gorston was appointed as Head-master of St Cake's in 1738. Distinguished by being one of very few undergraduates to have been awarded the honour of becoming Chief Præposter Under The Privies of Balliol College in his first year, his Latin and Greek elegiacs were the envy of the nation. In his time academic standards increased greatly, and numbers tripled to 150 pupils.

Fascinating stuff, even though it leaves out that he was a sadist and a drunkard, distinguished mainly by his sycophancy to any member of the aristocracy who was misguided enough to ask him to dinner. At the other extreme are polemics that believe that public schools are the root of all evil, responsible for 'educational apartheid' and clear proof that the way to improve a whole education system is to abolish by force what independent agencies rank as some of the best schools in the world. The present author is a veteran of several Oxbridge or Cambridge Union debates in which, to all intents and purposes, the motion before the House might as well have been, 'This House Believes that Anyone Associated with Public Schools Should Be Shot, After Having Been Publically Castrated or Disembowelled in Front of His or Her Family'. Public schools produce strong feelings, for and against. After one such Oxford Union debate (which we won), I emerged from the Union to be soundly beaten over the head several times with a handbag, its owner a mature lady whose contribution to the debate was to shriek repeatedly, 'You're the reason our society's rotten!' Well, better to be infamous than not known at all . . .?

Wilfred Owen won an MC for bravery in World War One, which in effect meant he had killed Germans. He described himself as a 'pacifist with a very seared conscience'. I was a suicidally miserable public-school boy who vowed on leaving that he would never set foot inside a ****ing school again, and who never made it even to the lowliest level of House Prefect. I was deemed to have led a hunger strike at school when I was fourteen (Chiz! Chiz! Wasn't like that, as Molesworth might have said in *Down With Skool*) and was threatened with things unmentionable in my last term for the heinous crime of 'being seen talking to village girls'. It took me fifty years to find out that the problem wasn't being seen talking to village girls, but rather that it was feared I was buying drugs from them. Apart from the fact that I was far more excited by girls at sixteen than I was by drugs, at that time I wouldn't have known a drug from a pear drop. I suspect I was saved only by the kindness of my brilliant Housemaster. From this inauspicious start in education (the first report my mother kept read, 'Martin will never become a milk monitor until he learns to be responsible'), Fate decreed that I would land some of the better Milk Monitor posts in the public-school system that I had hated, namely Headmaster of The Perse School, Cambridge, and High Master of The Manchester Grammar School and St Paul's School, the bonus points or extra bottle of full-cream milk being elected Chairman of HMC, the Headmasters' and Headmistresses' Conference. As I used sometimes to tell the children entrusted to my care, it's unwise to assume one is ever in total control of one's life . . . As essentially a maverick and a rebel, and someone who throughout his life has managed to be at odds with the Establishment, I was a public-school Headmaster with a seared conscience, haunted throughout a succession of wonderfully privileged and enriching posts, which gave me a career and opportunities to die for, by the image of the 93 per cent of children who could not afford to come to these brilliant schools.

So perhaps I am unusually positioned to write a new book about institutions that have dominated English lives for centuries. I have been one with them, man and boy, but yet in my mind have always sat outside of them. Perhaps I can write the book that sits between craven sycophancy and hysterical envy. Public schools are like people, capable of being adorable and infuriating at the same time, misunderstood yet sometimes understood all too well, bastions of privilege yet for some children a ladder out of the ghetto, a drain on the national education system yet an inspiration for it, full of cant and humbug yet also full of common sense . . . Winchester College knew secrets of educating the gifted and talented before the rest of the world had invented the term, yet for much of its history it depended on whether a thing was a 'Good Notion' or a 'Bad Notion', the most crucial rule being that anything new was a Bad Notion. Here is a school whose pupils rebelled and smashed their new crockery because a Headmaster tried to improve conditions at breakfast.

Much scorn and even hatred has been poured on the public schools, and at times I have helped in that process. Yet, bizarrely, I've delayed writing this book for fear it might hurt my former Housemaster, so great is my respect and affection for him, and for his wife. There's another World War One comparison here. The poet and novelist Robert Graves castigated his old school, Charterhouse, in his autobiography, *Goodbye To All That*. Yet Graves's best man at his wedding was his Charterhouse Housemaster. Here again there is extraordinary contrast. As we shall see later, David Niven's public-school experience left such strong feelings that he went back to the school to ask some searching questions, in particular of one of his prep.-school teachers. This book contains plentiful references to vile public school teachers who were roundly loathed by their pupils and remembered as such well into adult life. Yet one of the very greatest things about public schools has been the extraordinarily enriching and warm relationship that public schools can create between the teacher and the pupil. Public schools throw up stark contrasts wherever you look, one reason why they're interesting. Terrible bullying occurred in public and all schools, and still does. Yet in my four years in Highfield House at Uppingham, for all my desperate unhappiness, I never experienced the faintest whiff of bullying, nor the faintest effort to interfere with the natural growth of my sexuality.

And the moral of my own and other people's stories? One is that the memories of any former public-school boys are deeply fallible and selective. What follows is not the definitive history of the English public school. It is an account of those schools from a slightly wounded product of what they were, as deeply personal, fallible and selective as all the rest.

I do not claim to solve the enigma of the English public schools. Yet I do believe that we are all the product of history, and that only by understanding the history of these extraordinary institutions can we understand them at all. Previous books have tended either to be sycophantic and excessively reverential (after all, when was the last time the honours system in the UK was not controlled by former public-school pupils?), or just plain boring. Others, occasionally hilariously, have been obsessed by the hotbed of sexuality these schools represented, and the ludicrous extremes of repression the schools resorted to (placing barbed wire between pupils' beds is one example). If this book has any conclusions, they are that we should take only a very few things seriously, and that the greatest claim to fame of the public schools is that they created nothing. Rather, they simply provided for the movers and shakers in the land what they wanted for their children. They are a mirror held up to the aspirational middle classes of England, and the most brilliant social history of pre- and post-industrial Britain. Public schools are frequently castigated for telling the rest of us what to do. This book suggests that their greatest crime in their history was to do what they were told.

It is also my intention to suggest that the public schools of England in their traditional form have had their day, and need to reinvent themselves. It is not a new idea, and they have survived as long as they have in no small measure through a capacity to change with the times. I worry they are not adapting fast enough. Eton has done more to reinvent itself than many other schools, as in the provision of bursaries, the sponsorship of the London Academy of Excellence and the taking-on of an Imam alongside the traditional School Chaplain. It is interesting to note, therefore, that it was a group of Eton schoolboys who managed to arrange a meeting with President Putin, and were subsequently granted a lengthy interview on Russian media. What's wrong with that? The boys organised it themselves, and it shows wonderful initiative. My problem was simply that I felt deeply uncomfortable at a group of schoolboys giving opinions that could be misconstrued as the views of the nation, and everyone in it, including me. My sense was that a manipulative regime was manipulating once again, in this case through the young people of one particular school. I am happy for any young person to speak for themselves on a topic they hold dear, and have always believed that if sometimes they get it wrong that is part of the price we pay for education. I am happy for a school to speak for itself. With a person such as Putin, I prefer dialogue to be entered into by elected politicians. It has been said of Eton that it encourages aspirations, with every stone imbued with the motto, 'Why not me?' The problem occurs if that motto erroneously translates into, 'It is mine by right.' If any of our young people have the chance to meet with one of the world's most influential figures, I would prefer it to be because of who and what they are, not because of the school they attended.

No one who stands for half an hour in Eton High Street and watches the beaks and the boys pass by can fail to smell the extraordinary sense of entitlement that fills the place. Eton has made noble efforts to spread the gospel, and it is a brilliant school, which I wish I had attended , but the fact remains that Eton puts a golden spoon in the mouths of its pupils, and in so doing reduces the pressure to give every child in the UK an equivalent. And that is the key to 'the public-school problem', which has not changed for hundreds of years. It is not to do away with the best things these schools do – to a standard bettered nowhere in the world – but rather to take them out as the sole preserve of the wealthy and privileged and offer them to the wider public. To its lasting credit, Eton was offering places to financially disadvantaged young people long before it became fashionable. Here, as so often in the history of the public schools, one comes across opposites that cannot be blended into any one simple answer.

We do not need to abolish the public schools of England. Rather, we need to make what they offer available to any child in the United Kingdom, regardless of race, colour, creed or the social and economic standing of their parents. This is the mantra I repeated at The Manchester Grammar School while leading the team (thank you, Ian Thorpe) that raised £13 million to subsidise free and supported places, and the mantra I tried to repeat at St Paul's School. It was behind the question I repeatedly asked of Gonville & Caius College, Cambridge, when I was Headmaster of The Perse School, Cambridge: what happened to the endowment entrusted by Stephen Perse to the Fellows of Caius to ensure the survival of the 'Cambridge Free School'? I received no answer, any more than I did when I asked the Mercers' Company what had happened to the John Colet Foundation, bequeathed to fund free education at St Paul's School. I await the answer.

As proof that there is nothing new in the world, the need for the state to fund places at independent schools is a very, very old idea. An integrated system was recommended by the Taunton Report in 1868. As long ago as 1919, Charterhouse, Eton and Marlborough offered to accept a percentage of elementary-school children if the government would subsidise them. In 1942 Rab Butler set up the Fleming Committee, which recommended gradual integration of the public schools into the state system. It was unanimously accepted by the Headmasters' Conference, but foundered largely because of lack of money to finance it. In the postwar period, independent schools have several times offered to accept state-school pupils for the same money it would cost the government to educate them in the state sector (most recently, at the time of writing, in 2016), but have been refused. The problem here was that the independent schools insisted on their right to select pupils. The problem with earlier schemes was that the government 'subsidy' would have to be set at the fee levels decided by the schools themselves. The Assisted Places Scheme introduced in 1980 foundered because it was a Cheat's Charter, and because government is obsessed with total control over anything that costs money, and did not have it with the scheme.

So it is that the public schools have been at the centre of controversy almost since their foundation, and almost every generation produces a movement to abolish them. It has always failed, mainly because of the power of the Establishment, but also because the best schools reach standards unmatched in the world and the poor standard of too many state schools gives the public schools an easy market. The situation has not been helped by the double thinking of those who oppose it. Tony Benn, the leading left-wing icon, was enabled by Westminster. Another leading left-winger, Diane Abbott, sent one of her children to a leading London independent school. Abbott later explained her dilemma in a *Daily Mirror* interview. Recognising that her decision was 'intellectually indefensible' she said, 'I had to choose between him [her son] and my career and I chose my son'. She has not been alone in facing that choice. I have spent a portion of my life concealing the fact that the son of a leading Labour MP attended the fee-paying school I worked for. And so on. 'Do as I say, not do as I do' has not helped the anti-public-schoolers, any more than their use of the politics of envy or their translation of the vital creed that every child should have an equal opportunity into the mindless chant that every child can have only the same opportunity.

I believe two things about England's public schools. The first is that they are pricing themselves out of reach of the parents and children who historically have been their bedrock foundation and security. My father was an ordinary GP. Yes, he became Sir Andrew Stephen, but the services to soccer and to medicine that brought his knighthood brought him no extra income. Certainly, his marriage brought him a house without the bother of a mortgage, but in essence, as a bog-basic GP, he was able to pay to put three sons through a boarding education. I forget how many times we were told any inheritance we might have hoped for was being spent instead on our education. Could the middle-of-the-road GP or the provincial lawyer afford boarding school for one son now, never mind three? I doubt it. It is not the blue-blood nobility that have sustained the public schools in England, but the middle class professionals who have been their bedrock. I was educated at public school, as were my sons. Their instinct is not to pay fees, even though they earn good salaries, but to move house to the catchment area of a good state school

The second thing I believe? It is that the public schools have survived as long as they have by taking a leaf out of the AIDS virus. They have shown both an extraordinary ability to defend themselves against any threat, but also an extraordinary ability to adapt in order to survive. They grew from tiny, local day schools to seething bear pits, then revolutionised themselves in line with Victorian morality, and changed yet again in the 1960s into academic hothouses. They are akin to Doctor Who's need to regenerate at intervals in order to survive. The problem? They seem to have forgotten how to regenerate. These are egalitarian times, yet at no time in their history have public schools been so unaffordable by the mass of the population.

Yet there is hope. It does not lie in Eton, Harrow, Westminster or Winchester, as it has done for so much of the history of the English public school, undoubted though it is that these 'great' schools and others like them will survive and no doubt flourish, but in the new kids on the block: Leicester Grammar School, the Grange School and the truly local day school, which either have been founded this century in simple response to parental need (as Marlborough, Wellington and Cheltenham were in their day) and are affordable, or are older schools that have served their local communities without delusions of grandeur since their foundation. In the case of the survival of public schools, it is the meek who shall inherit the earth.

MARTIN STEPHEN
NORFOLK

PREFACE

PUBLIC SCHOOLS: A BRIEF HISTORY IN NINE HUNDRED WORDS

'Public' schools were founded to educate poor local boys into a rudimentary knowledge of the classics, the word 'public' deriving from the simple fact that that was originally what they were meant to be: available to the public. Winchester claims to be oldest (1382). Other claims, such as those by the King's School, Canterbury, to have been founded as early as AD 60, are of dubious validity, in that they relate to preceding schools linked to the Church that have no real connection with the medieval foundations that are at the core of the English public schools. By the start of the nineteenth century, and sometimes earlier, these schools had begun to offer, in exchange for fees, places to non-local boys, satisfying a growing demand for education from the upper middle and upper classes that might or might not lead to university, but rapidly losing their commitment to educating poor boys, and not infrequently losing their endowments to corruption.

At the start of the nineteenth century the five best-known schools were Eton (1440), Winchester (1382), Westminster (1560), Harrow (1571) and Rugby (1567). By the end of the nineteenth century this list had expanded to include Charterhouse (1611), Shrewsbury (1552), and two day schools, St Paul's (1509) and Merchant Taylors' (1561). Over the course of the nineteenth century what had been poor grammar schools had turned themselves into supreme institutions for the wealthy and powerful fee-paying Establishment. Yet these schools were mad, bad bear pits, awash with violence, drunkenness and debauchery in a manner that made *Lord of the Flies* appear positively benign and liberal. More importantly, their unlicensed anarchy was increasingly out of touch with Victorian times, and the Clarendon Commission of the 1860s (see Chapter 3), prompted largely by the financial corruption endemic in the governance of Eton, marked a watershed. It was also one of the biggest whitewash jobs of all time, but it sent a clear warning out to the great and the not-so-great schools that they could not simply carry on as they had done. They changed then, and later history showed them capable of a miraculous Darwinian evolution, transforming themselves from institutions concerned mainly with social class and status and the training to be an English gentleman and a real man into today's academic powerhouses, something dating back to the 1960s, when all of a sudden those grammar-school boys started to take the Oxbridge places hitherto seen as the birthright of the public schools.

Boarding schools have traditionally held more snob value than day schools. Boarding schools are now very much the minority, but retain their mystique. For most of their history, the public schools were fiercely all-male, but most have adapted apparently effortlessly to at least a form of coeducation. For the duration of their existence they have been ranked, ranging historically from the nine great British public schools cited by the Clarendon Commission to the barely worthy 'minor public school', and to the schools highlighted for their academic success by these newfangled 'league tables'. Public schools have in the past dominated English society, and still do so, taking a lion's share of the places at top universities and in top jobs. The Premier League in England at the time of writing is probably, in no particular order, Eton, Harrow, Winchester, Westminster and St Paul's. Strong players in the next league down would include:

- Ampleforth
- Brighton College
- Charterhouse
- City of London
- Dulwich
- Haileybury
- Haberdashers' Aske's
- King's, Canterbury
- King Edward's, Birmingham
- King's College, Wimbledon
- Magdalen College School, Oxford
- Marlborough
- Merchant Taylors' Boys
- Oundle
- Radley
- RGS Guildford
- RGS, Newcastle
- Rugby
- The Manchester Grammar School
- The Perse School

- Shrewsbury
- Tonbridge
- Uppingham
- Wellington

Justifiably annoyed at not being in the above group would be:

- Barnard Castle
- Bedales
- Bedford (School and Bedford Modern School)
- Birkdale
- Blundell's
- Bradfield College
- Bryanston
- Canford
- Cheltenham
- Christ's Hospital
- Clifton
- Cranleigh
- Epsom
- Felsted
- Framlingham
- Grange, The
- Gresham's
- Highgate
- Hurstpierpoint
- King's, Chester
- Kingswood
- Lancing
- Latymer Upper School, London
- Leeds Grammar School

- Leicester Grammar School
- Malvern
- Oakham
- Repton
- Rossall
- Sedbergh
- Sevenoaks
- Sherborne
- Stonyhurst
- Stowe
- UCS, London
- Whitgift
- Yarm

I have not included here the leading girls' schools, which are a separate story.

Prior to the rise of the great public schools, school had been a painful necessity for children, exemplified in Shakespeare's urchin going 'unwillingly to school'. The public schools transformed this into a 'tribal mystic',[1] where schooldays were the happiest days of a chap's life, a 'mystical tenderness and romantic nostalgia'.[2] This was true in fact, and celebrated in fiction to perpetuate the legend, from *Tom Brown's Schooldays* to the jolly japes of the Remove at Greyfriars in the Billy Bunter stories. That in reality these schools were brutal, scholarship-free zones of unbridled and testosteroned masculinity has somehow run parallel with the image of jolly japes, the one not denying the other.

In one of the more remarkable transubstantiations in English social history the school of Billy Bunter transformed itself not only

---

1   Chandos, *Boys Together*, p. 20.
2   Ibid. p. 27.

into the most efficient way for a boy to get into the ferociously competitive Oxford and Cambridge, but for his sister to do so as well. And, just to show that they had not lost their traditional grip over the English Establishment and its seats of power, at one time in the second decade of the twenty-first century, the political leader of the United Kingdom, the Prime Minister, the spiritual leader, the Archbishop of Canterbury, and its leading local politician, the Mayor of London, had all been educated at the same public school. The public-school boy – and girl – is not an extinct species. It is alive and well, and influencing our lives even as you read these words.

And the personal bit . . .?

I know now that the public school I attended, Uppingham School, as a boarder between 1962 and 1966 – having changed little since the 1930s and facing declining numbers – was in crisis. In educational terms, I am one of the last generation of public-school boys to be the equivalent of the naturalist who was alive when dinosaurs roamed the earth. I have talked candidly with my three sons about almost every aspect of my life. I find it interesting that at no time have I even tried to tell them what it was like to be at a traditional English boarding school between 1962 and 1966. Why not? It's simply that I don't believe anything in their lives could give them a bridge into the quite extraordinary experience that Uppingham in the mid-sixties was.

It was a feature of many survivors of World War One that they rarely, if ever, talked about their experiences, even to their closest family. I suspect it was for the same reason. The intensity of warfare was so outside the experience of those who had not fought that many soldiers despaired of ever telling their loved ones what it was like. So with the experience of being at a public school in the old days. It is one reason why Old Boys' Societies flourish, as do the equivalent for old soldiers: only someone who actually went through it can understand. There is another link. The experience of warfare and a certain type of school pushed one to all sorts of extremes, emotional or physical. Love it or hate it, many people never felt so alive as they did when they were at war or at school, so much so that for many the rest of their lives were an anticlimax.

Something that worried me greatly was the impact of a public-school education on its pupils. One of the great unheralded results of the system was to indoctrinate its victims with passive acceptance. It was a system where one's popularity with one's peers, and acceptance by them, dominated one's quality of life. It tended to punish savagely any boy who was 'different', or out of step. To survive meant to conform. It is noticeable that there is a visible gap for many public schools in the attendance at old boys' dinners from those who attended the school in the age of rebellion, the 1960s and 1970s. The absentees are those who refused to conform.

My personal opinion, backed by no research or non-anecdotal findings, is that this addiction to conformity gave rise to two features that have bedevilled the English Establishment and hence the governance of our country. The first is the embedded unwillingness to countenance real change. The second is to run the country as if it were an enlarged gentlemen's club, one offshoot of which was starkly revealed in the Philby et al. spy crisis. Modern writing has shown that these Establishment spies at time telegraphed what they were and what they were doing, but were deemed incapable of treachery because they were members of the public-school club. It is interesting that left-wing politics has seemed to mirror the inward-looming, cabal-like cronyism of the right, seen in recent administrations but also in the secretive, sub-Masonic machinations of many a town hall in the North of England, where the sighting of a Tory was as common as the sighting of a fairy. We talk in our country about the 'official' opposition. In my experience, the unofficial opposition does far more good. It is the dissenting voice in the meetings for which there are no minutes, and it is precisely this voice that the internal life of many public schools sought to drive out.

There are honourable exceptions. Perhaps surprisingly, Eton is one, though it could be argued that it put unblinking personal ambition in the place of conformity. One Old Etonian commented privately, 'At Eton, you had to conform to the rules of nonconformity.' St Paul's and The Manchester Grammar School could never be accused of encouraging conformity or passive acceptance of anything, and I suspect they share this with a number of leading day schools. Also, public schools have changed and are ever-changing. It is part of the secret of their longevity. The product of the modern public school, those in their twenties and thirties, may well grow to challenge the Establishment that nurtured them, but for the next twenty years or so we are probably stuck with the old guard.

If Uppingham sought to impose conformity on me, it failed. Yet I am not sure that failure did me any good. It produced an intense stubbornness and resistance to being told what to do, which have held me back at times and I think are one of the lasting scars inflicted on me by my education. I do not claim to be a hero, but the 1960s' public school wielded terrible power over its inmates. In resisting it I learned not to fear it, yet, like a child's fear of fire, fear of authority is not all bad. Had I been a little more fearful I might not have taken on some opponents in adult life that hindsight tells me now were unbeatable not because they had the Establishment on their side, but because they *were* the Establishment.

The other thing I noted from my public-school experience was the necessity of putting a screen up around one's innermost thoughts:

- 'Never show your emotions here';[3]
- 'Keep your feelings to yourself – spare us the embarrassment';[4] and
- 'Thou shalt have a face for everybody.'[5]

This feature of boarding-school education, but also of the most competitive day schools, has two negative consequences. The first is the number of people I know who spent five years covering up their emotions and in so doing dried them up by starving them of oxygen and sunlight, the public school man who in emotional terms is a hollow shell. The second is the person who hides both malice and rank ambition beneath a cloak of charm, and thus becomes doubly dangerous. In fairness, it would be wrong to blame the public schools for this personality trait. It is as old as mankind, and was certainly present in the thirteenth century, when Chaucer warned us to beware 'The smylere with the knyf under the cloke'.[6]

---

3   Lambert, *Hothouse Society*, p. 225.
4   Ibid.
5   Ibid., p. 231.
6   Chaucer, The Knight's Tale, line 1999.

I

THE BOARDING HOUSE, FAGGING AND CASUAL CRUELTY

'A school house,' said C. H. P. Mayo, himself a popular Harrow master '. . . is, when you come to think of it, an anomaly, a collection of boys sent away from home at their most impressionable age to be educated by strangers.'[1]

It might seem strange that the English middle-, upper-middle- and upper-class parents, almost uniquely in the world, go to all the trouble of having children only to send them away at thirteen years of age. It becomes less so if you recognise that the English have a very long collective cultural memory, and well into medieval and Renaissance times these same classes were accustomed to sending their sons to serve as squires in distant noble houses, to learn all the better how it should be done. 'It', as all members of the ruling class know, is the secret of how to be a member of the ruling class. It's possible to argue that the

---

1   Lamb, The Happiest Days, pp. 66–7.

public schools were simply the natural evolution of landing a place for your son as a squire. These places were hard fought for, and almost as difficult to get as a place at as it is now to get into one of the top academic public schools.

As many commentators have noted, there is no such thing as a 'public school'. Independent, fee-paying schools in the UK comprise a huge variety of schools, of which the traditional, all-male boarding schools form nowadays only a tiny minority. Yet it is the traditional public school that is fixed in the popular imagination, took this country through the creation, management and loss of much of its Empire and two World Wars and helped to form the core ideology of many of its modern descendants, and any understanding of these schools must learn a lot from their past. That past is not only interesting in itself, frequently careering between hilarity and tragedy, but is a potted social history in miniature of the classes who ruled Britain.

There is a common misconception about these traditional public schools that needs to be dispelled from the outset.

To the outsider, the actual school is often the entity that matters most to pupils. Billy Bunter has a lot to answer for. The jolly set of chums in the wildly popular stories first printed in *The Magnet* comic identify themselves firstly by being pupils at Greyfriars School, and secondly by being in the Remove, or their form or class in that school. This is one of many areas where the Billy Bunter stories are a misrepresentation of actual public-school life. In history, and before the dominance of the day schools, it is to their boarding House, always shortened to 'House' by the cognoscenti, that pupils owed their extreme loyalty. Most people think of 'school'. Many boarders do not; they think of 'house'.

- '"It's house, house, house, nothing but the house, sir, it bores me stiff," writes a jaded fifth-former ..." It is the house which gives a boy character, not so much the school."[2]

- 'The house is both a physical building, a grouping of people, and an ideology. It is difficult to overemphasise the importance of the house to the experience of being in a public boarding school.'[3]

The House is the equivalent of the tribe. Listen to those red-nosed, bald old men as they are introduced for the first time to someone who went to the same school as they did. The first question is always, 'What House were you in?' At Eton, boys playing school teams still wear odd socks – one sock a 'school' sock, the other sock representing their House. Eton Houses are named after their Housemaster. One former Housemaster said he had resigned when he realised that winning the Cock House rugby final mattered more to him than winning World War Two. However, it is a moot point whether the real power in a boarding House lay with the Housemaster, or the Prefects who ran it. A House Captain writes to his successor in the 1960s in a tone remarkably similar to Sir Humphrey writing to his successor in *Yes, Minister*:

> The Housemaster has many new and pretty odd ideas which, no doubt, he will try and spring on you. If you don't like them, don't have them. Just be politely firm and he will gently fade away . . . don't let him interfere with the elections of deputies.[4]

---

2   Lambert, Hothouse Society, p. 132.
3   Walford, Life in Public Schools, p. 69.
4   Ibid., p. 156.

In the nineteenth and early twentieth centuries, the strength or otherwise of the Housemaster could not only exert a vast influence over a boy's quality of life, but even damn him by association. I am convinced that with a different and lesser Housemaster I would never have survived, or been allowed to survive, public school. One's House could be hugely positive. It could also be the reverse.

'About the same time, it could be said of a boy with a bad record at Rugby that 'if he had been at any different house but Birds he would have been one of the finest and most gentlemanly fellows at Rugby'.[5]

For most of their most recent history, the boarding House was by far and away the dominant unit for a public-school boy. It was not only where he slept, but usually where he ate (only a few schools such as Haileybury had a communal dining hall, and even then pupils ate at a House table), spent every evening and spent the majority of his time when not actually in a main school classroom or out on the school playing fields. He would leave for those playing fields from his House, come back to shower and change in his House. His social circle was defined not only by his House, but by the ten or twelve boys who joined the school in his year in that House. He would see his name creep up the hierarchy of the House every year as roll call was held at House Prayers.

My cousin, who is touching seventy as I write this, can still recite from memory the roll call of names read out at evening prayer in his and my boarding House. I've spent fifty-two years trying to forget it. The public-school boy would sit in a House block in the Chapel, or at the school play and school concert. The Cock House Rugby competition was more bitterly fought than any World Cup, and for many pupils the result of a House

---

5   Chandos, *Boys Together*, p. 97.

match was more important than the result of a school fixture. The Headmaster was God on a distant Olympus, the summons to him (and it always was a him) to be dreaded as signifying expulsion or the worst beating of all. Much more real, the domestic God in fact, was the Housemaster, who, much in the manner of a captain in the Nelsonian Navy, held the power of life or death over the pupils in his care.

Where did this system originate? The most common answer usually given is that it derived from the 'Dames' or women who ran what were in effect the lodging houses for Etonians. Yet the real drive to the boarding House was part economic, part social. Economically, when Edward Thring wanted to build up Uppingham School from being the poor relation in a dual grammar-school foundation with Oakham, one of the few ways open to him was to invite men to build boarding Houses at their own expense and run them as a business, in effect paying a licence fee to the school for the privilege. On many occasions this led to appallingly low standards of food and accommodation, since the Housemaster pocketed the fee the parents paid, and any money not spent on the pupils was profit for the Housemaster. It is rumoured that the last privately owned boarding House was not bought out by the school until the 1950s.

Socially, the creation of the boarding House was also a divide-and-rule policy adopted in part to counter the appalling misbehaviour and frequent mass riots that typified the eighteenth- and early-nineteenth-century schools. The early public school could act like Facebook, Twitter or other social media, and allow almost instant communication between a large number of pupils, and coordination of what they planned. It is no accident that most schools frowned on boys having contact with those in other houses.

Harold Nicolson summed up the social situation endured by many public-school boys:

> We were not allowed to consort with boys not in our own house; a house consisted of thirty boys, whom ten at least were too old and ten too young for friendship; and thus during those four years my training in human relationships was confined to the ten boys who happened to be more or less my contemporaries.[6]

At Uppingham I do not remember being expressly forbidden to talk to boys in other houses, and the boarding Houses were larger, containing fifty rather than thirty people. Yet the same was true, if only because the various boarding Houses were spread so far apart round the town of Uppingham that sheer distance made fraternisation impossible. Each House also had incredibly strong identity and was in effect its own little tribe, and it would have seemed most odd to want to join another tribe. I can remember boys who changed schools, but cannot remember anyone ever changing House.

One reason why the boarding House has not been afforded the importance it deserves was that the House system as we know it, a classic divide-and-rule technique, only really flourished in the Victorian and post-Victorian periods. Yet the most colourful and scandalous times in these schools were earlier than that, when the Etonian remembered his time in the infamous Long Chamber at Eton or the forty-strong long or old dormitory at Westminster.

An irony of the power of the Housemaster was that it was not until very late in the day that the Headmaster of a public school

---

6 Nicolson, *Some People*, p. 31.

was allowed to choose Housemasters: 'At Eton, where the lodging system had evolved haphazardly over many years, it was not until 1933 that the headmaster managed to attain any right over the selection of housemasters.'[7]

In some schools, where the money to create the houses in the first place had been provided by the Housemaster so that he could in effect run a private business, the last owner-Housemasters, as noted above, were not bought out by the school until after World War Two. It illustrates how much these all-controlling institutions were for much of their time out of the control of those supposedly leading the school.

If the Housemaster in the fully grown public school was God, then beneath him were the demigods of the House Prefects. Prefects, or senior boys at Eton, ran the House for the Housemaster, and the school for the Headmaster, from morn till night. The driving reason was economic. At Eton in 1809 the Headmaster had seven to nine 'beaks', or staff, to control 515 boys. Boys' controlling boys was a cheap alternative.

Up until the mid-1970s many schools still allowed House Prefects to beat pupils, a ritual shown in all its horror in the film *If*. If the system was savage, it could also be ludicrous. The ornithologist Peter Scott recounts one episode:

> I can quite remember late in my public school days having tea with a contemporary in his study. He had been made a house prefect, and I had not. As we began our tea a message was brought in to say that it was known I had not watched the match that day. As Duty Prefect it was his job to deal with the matter. 'Of

---

7   Hickson. The Poisoned Bowl, p. 45.

course', he said, 'I've got to give you four – that's the standard thing. Shall we get it over with or wait till we've finished tea?[8]

There was also a peculiar sense of the status of a Prefect being a reward for past suffering. One endured all the humiliations of being a junior pupil in a public school, and there at the end in the tiny world of the boarding House the victim became the master, lord of all he surveyed. It gave appalling power over the world in which they lived to those who were still relatively young boys, a power many were never able to replicate in adult life. One of my all-time heroes, the poet Charles Hamilton Sorley – killed in 1915 in World War One – took the decision to leave Marlborough earlier than he had to precisely because he was nervous about the impact all that power might have had on him:

> When one reaches the top of a public school, one has such unbounded opportunities of getting unbearably conceited that I don't see how anyone survives the change that must come when the tin god is swept off his little kingdom and becomes an unimportant mortal again. And besides I am sure it is far too enjoyable, and one is awfully tempted to pose all the time and be theatrical.[9]

Personally, I'm more scared by those who *did* manage to replicate the power they had in the Sixth Form of a public school in adult life. However, that power and status in part explain the

---

8 Ibid., p. 166.
9 Charles Hamilton Sorely (ed. W. R. Sorley), *The Letters of Charles Sorley*, p. 42.

nostalgia for those heady days felt by so many former public-school boys, and their roseate vision of their schooldays. When I chose – as much as anyone had a right to choose in those days – to leave my public school at the end of my fourth year, and so to relinquish the due reward for what I saw as four years of penal servitude, I remember how bitterly I felt the loss. Only in my dotage have I tended to think of myself as a pupil of Uppingham School. For most of my life I have seen myself as a product of Highfield House, which happened to be at Uppingham. Frankly, it could have been in any school, and it would have mattered as much to me. It was Highfield that dictated my quality of life. Would I have been a different person now if I'd attended a different House? It illustrated the awesome power those years had over me that I can honestly say yes.

There is a house a mile away from me with a large sign outside reading 'HIGHFIELD HOUSE'. Fifty years after I left Highfield, my heart gives a flutter every time I pass that sign. This particular sentence is being typed on an internal Chinese flight from Cheng Du to Beijing. I returned to working on the manuscript for this book after three weeks' absence. And what did I dream of last night? The evening meal at Highfield on the first day of my last Summer term there. I can no more rid my mind of the impact that House had on me that I can change my genes.

A friend of mine was a very successful prep.-school Headmaster. I was surprised when he announced that he was sending his son to Rugby, which was in one of those phases that schools pass through where it was seeming to be getting a bit casual about its Heads and 'losing' rather too many of them. When I raised an eyebrow at his choice of school, he replied, 'Ah! But he's going to the best House in Rugby.' The boy did very well.

Fagging

Fagging, or the system whereby junior boys acted as servants to senior boys, has generated as much comment as, if not more than, any other core feature of the English public school. From the outset it had its critics:

> I have my doubts upon allowing the system of *fagging*
> – it may inculcate subordination, on one side, but it
> encouraged tyranny, on the other; – it may, perhaps,
> curb the overweening spirit of the heir apparent to
> an an Earldom, when the son of the rich shop-keeper
> sends him upon a message; – it may, also, fill the child
> of a wholesale dealer with notions of equality, unfit
> for his future commerce; – and , as great boys fag the
> smaller, (both being free-born little men,) it seems that
> 'might overcomes right,' – which is the principle of the
> African Slave-Trade.[10]

On the other hand, it was an experience for many years shared by all public-school boys, often viewed with a sentimental affection seemingly at odds with the facts, as in a Harrow school song by S. W. Gore (later a Wimbledon champion and first-class cricketer):

Jerry

Jerry, a poor little fag,
Carrying kettle and tray,
Finding his energy flag

---

10   George Colman the Younger (b. 1762), *Random Records*, 1830, quoted Craig, *Oxford Book of Schooldays*, p. 153.

> Let them all fall on the way.
> On him his monitor dropped –
> 'Pick up the pieces at once!
> Off to my room to be "whopped",
> Jerry, you duffer and dunce.'
> Heigho! Heigho!
> 'Jerry, you duffer and dunce.'

A postwar female writer, writing on how a woman might understand the public-school boy, in the 1980s, wrote about fagging:

> Fagging started . . . in that mournful period when rich ignorant yobs joined the poor intellectual snobs at School. The basic principle was survival of the fittest, physically rather than mentally. In other words, the big thick boys beat weedy brainy boys to the other side of eternity and back, and therefore proved that might may not be right, but it's unwise to say so if you're a seven stone weakling . . . Thuggery, they said, in about four time as many words, was a good thing. It was a useful illustration of how a society governs itself and therefore was a top-hole preparation for life in the Big Bad World, though that they knew about that beats me.[11]

For years English public-school boys have laughed at stupid Americans who confuse the public-school practice of fagging with 'faggots'. I've never been sure whose side the joke lay on.

---

11   Irvine, *Girls' Guide*, pp. 71–80.

Prefects had junior boys act as 'fags' to them, meaning they were, in effect, servants, making their fag master's bed, cleaning his study and running errands for him. In many schools, the senior boy had only to yell '*Fag!*' at the end of the corridor for all the junior boys to come running. The last one got the job. In my school, as in many, there was a rigid hierarchy. One was in effect a fag for one's first year, then eligible for fag duties only if commanded to do them by a School Prefect as distinct from a House Prefect, and then promoted to the dizzy heights of a 'three-year non-fag', whereby positively no one could command you to do fagging duties. I have to say, my memory is of receiving nothing but kindness from my fag masters, and being deeply grateful for the money I was paid for the appallingly inept service I rendered. I could never make my own bed, never mind someone else's. But, then again, I was a far-from-beautiful child.

I was lucky. One former pupil of Westminster described his fagging as being 'as hard and as barbarous as the treatment of the negroes in Virginia'.[12] The following extract from a boy at Westminster in 1820 is typical of the descriptions that have given fagging its image:

> Every fourth day I have things to do for the Third Election [senior boys] – to clean their (ten) candlesticks, to get candles for them, to put them on their desks. I make their ten beds, which takes a great while, for I must do all my Master's things just the same. I have to brush clothes for ten fellows, fill eight pitchers, and clean eight basins, to wash up their (ten) sets of tea things

---

12 Chandos, *Boys Together*, p. 87.

when they have tea or coffee . . . and do sometimes a
few jobs for them . . . We have no supper.[13]

Reactions to fagging are as varied as the people involved.
Occasionally it can become hilarious, particularly in one thirteen-
year-old's recollection in the 1960s of services surely above and
beyond the call of duty: 'Once I have even been fagged to write a
love letter to my fagmaster's ex girlfriend. I was told to make it as
disgusting and revolting as I could.'[14]

The fagging system was often attributed to the ruling classes
needing to know what it was like to be a servant, and needing to
learn how to handle servants. It was a good way to justify a system
that in effect provided servants for free, and rewarding senior boys
for running the school. More than anything else, it gave to certain
people power over other people, a power they and the schools
fought bitterly hard to retain. Several attempts to abolish fagging
in the nineteenth century met with failure.

Rather oddly, it does not seem to be personal tyranny or
sexual exploitation that dominates the memoirs of former fags.
One thing that does seem to have been hated was 'cricket fagging',
whereby, in effect, the junior boy was condemned to fielding
duties only – in effect, fetching and carrying the ball – and not
allowed to bat or to bowl. There was also a crude form of natural
justice. It was generally considered bad form to order the fag
to assist in a criminal activity, such as theft. The problem came
when boy culture deemed an act OK while beak culture deemed
it worth a flogging if the culprit was caught. Buying alcohol for a
senior boy was one example. Somewhere in the middle was the
Westminster tradition of choosing a fag of equal size and weight

---

13 Carleton, Westminster School, p. 51.
14 Lambert, Hothouse Society, p. 65.

to take on in single combat any 'barbarian' or 'ski' (local youth) who dared trespass on college turf. Presumably, victory bought as much honour as defeat brought shame.

Fagging was not all bad. When it worked well, it gave the junior boy a protector against bullying, and many a fag was grateful to exchange the cold of his living quarters for the warmth of his Master's fire, even if the price of that warmth was holding the toasting fork in front of the fire. The scholar John Chandos believed the abolition of fagging at one school led to an increase in bullying:

> When John Russell abolished fagging at Charterhouse, bullying at once increased, and the atrocities committed in private schools without praefectorial or fagging discipline were vicious and uncontrolled to a degree unknown in public schools where the authority of senior boys prevailed.[15]

Hmm. Really? As an insider, both boy and teacher, I personally doubt it was the abolition of fagging that resulted in an increase in bullying. It may have given rise to an increase in *reported* bullying, but, if there was a real increase, it's more likely to be because no alternative system was put in place to replicate what little control fagging used to offer. Fagging may have stopped some bullying by offering the child a protector, but it made it easier for the child to be indentured to a persecutor.

The truth about fagging is probably both simple, and pragmatic. For much of the existence of the public school, families who could afford to send their children to public schools

---

15   Chandos, *Boys Together*, p. 104.

could, by definition, afford servants – and would have found life quite impossible without them. We forget now the status afforded to the ruling classes, and the status they demanded for themselves. In the museum of the University of Kazan, situated two hours' flight east from Moscow and the albeit temporary *alma mater* of both Tolstoy and Lenin (both left before taking their degrees, for very different reasons), a resplendent uniform hangs in a case. Is it the uniform of a noble? No. It is rather the uniform of the servant employed to open the doors to nobleman-students, as nobility were not allowed and did not expect to open doors for themselves.

Different country, different culture – of course. But our egalitarian, democratic and Western culture over the course of the twentieth and twenty-first centuries has forgotten rule by the autocratic power of the nobility. We call them now the upper classes, or perhaps even the Establishment. Earlier – and perhaps more honest and accurate – ages called them the Ruling Classes. In any event, they held sway in and over the public schools, until well after World War Two. They demanded, needed and expected servants. Where, in public schools, servants as such were in short supply, the substitute was easy, to hand and cheap: the fag, or junior boy. In effect, the fagging system was born because ruling-class boys were born and brought up to a system of autocracy, and had no other way of providing themselves with the freedom from mundane tasks they had been brought up to believe their rank demanded and merited. When lesser nobles inherited the public schools the system was too much fun and too useful to discard, and small boys were kept on to serve and to service senior boys. After all, who willingly gives up power?

Casual cruelty

My Dear Dear Mother,

 If you don't let me come home, I die – I am all over ink, and my fine clothes have been spoilt – I have been tost in a blanket, and seen a ghost.

 I remain, my dear dear Mother,

 Your dutiful and most unhappy son,

 Freddy

 PS Remember me to my Father.[16]

So wrote Frederick Reynolds as a new boy at Westminster in the 1800s, in a pathetic letter that in pre-Internet days did the equivalent of going viral. He didn't come home, and he didn't die, by the way. He was not alone. Public schools for many years defined themselves by their cruelty – casual, yet carefully planned – to new boys:

Readiness to offer a friendly welcome to strangers is one of the marks of a civilised community. The traditional welcome to new boys at [public] school has long been to punch their heads, jeer at them, or, at the best, ignore them altogether.[17]

Punching heads was a relatively minor form of welcome at many schools. Variations include branding a boy with an anchor mark on his arm (Marlborough), tossing in a blanket, roasting in front of a fire and the ubiquitous being made to stand on a table, sing a song and drink a mug of saltwater.

16 Carleton, *Westminster School*, p. 30, and many other published sources.
17 Lamb, *The Happiest Days*, p. 13.

In medieval times, casual cruelty was a stock ingredient of education, not just a public-school education. In 1373 the Bishop of Norwich banned teaching in the numerous churches of King's Lynn, because the cries of the beaten pupils distracted worshippers.[18] Hundreds of years later, William Pitt the Elder declared he had, 'hardly known a boy whose spirit had not been broken at Eton'.[19]

The frequency with which the cruelty and severity of life at a public school forced boys to run away, particularly in pre-Victorian days, was the apparent existence of a job for the 'Pursuivant of Runaways' at Eton around 1765, with no fewer than three assistants.[20] The great Victorian Headmaster Edward Thring cited the ability to endure pain as one of many reasons for sending a boy away to school, including it among, 'The learning to be responsible and independent, to bear pain, to drop rank, and wealth, and home luxury . . .'[21]

A frequently reported aspect of public-school life, certainly endemic until relatively late in the nineteenth century, was the prevalence of a culture of extreme physical violence, bullying and intimidation, even if one excludes the penchant for flogging and official corporal punishment. The particular expert in this field seems to have been Winchester, with Westminster a close second: 'But at Winchester (and Westminster) the cruelties were more formal, carefully though out, ritualistic . . . There is, indeed, an arguable case for calling Winchester, at its *worst*, the most sinister of the schools.'[22]

It was symptomatic that boys known as 'juniors' at other

---

18 Turner, *The Old Boys*, pp. 3–4.
19 Ibid., p. 61.
20 Percival, *Very Superior Men*, p. 20.
21 Parkin, *Thring*, Vol. 1, p. 196.
22 Ibid., p. 80.

schools were known as 'inferiors' at Westminster. The modern Wykehamist is a far gentler and kinder soul than his eighteenth- and nineteenth-century counterparts (or so I'm told), but a remarkable number of those I have met, worked with and known have given the impression that, in their hearts of hearts, they believe anyone who did not attend Winchester is an inferior. Etonians may think it, but are too polite to show it. All juniors at Winchester were subjected to the 'tin gloves' regime in the 1840s and for an unspecified period thereafter. In order to prepare them for their work as fags with the handles of hot coffee pots, frying pans and so on, they were forced to have their hands seared by a 'hot end' or burning brand of wood. Anthony Trollope is on record as having contemplated suicide at Winchester.

Roasting in front of the fire and being forced to sing as a new boy, with the forfeit of drinking a pint of filthy, salted water, are documented in *Tom Brown's Schooldays*, but are to be found in many schools. Blundell's School had a story of a boy who, strapped to a 'form' and roasted in front of the fire, died when the senior boys in charge were either summoned away or were distracted by events on the Green. Interestingly, it is a good story if one likes blood, but as far as I know has never been verified as having actually taken place. One variant of the story tells of junior boys who ignored the piteous calls of their fellow to move him from the fire, in case, when the seniors returned, they would be punished for their temerity by being made to take his place. We know the name of the boy who died in a fight at Eton, and (see below) the name of the boy scalped by being tossed in a blanket. I find it inconceivable that, if a public-school boy had been burned alive at school, his name would not have survived.

Tossing in a blanket, as vividly described in *Tom Brown's Schooldays*, was a common initiation rite in many schools, including Harrow. One Etonian, Rowland Williams, was scalped when someone let the cloth slip and his head brushed against an iron bedstead. Boys due to be tossed were 'pinched in' by all the others before the ordeal, and it was not a good tossing unless the victim touched the ceiling several times.

Apart from ritualised violence, there were frequent fights between boys, this being a universally recognised method of settling a dispute. There was usually a designated place chosen by the pupils for such contests to take place, and woe betide any 'beak' or master who tried to interfere. Many of these fights were truly dreadful affairs, bare-knuckle boxing at its most unregulated, and pupils could bear lasting scars, and, in a number of documented cases, meet their death. A 'knock-down' did not mean the end of a fight, but merely the end of a round. Fights could go on for over two hours, and were largely a test of endurance. Contestants died as a result of these fights.

Yet this cruelty and overwhelming physical violence beg to be placed in context. The cruelties took place in an age when there were no painkillers, and when surgery, bone setting and tooth extraction were undertaken without anaesthetic. In ages when there was no cure for pain, the ability to endure it became a prime virtue, or perhaps even a necessity of life. This also helps explain the prevalence and acceptance of corporal punishment.

Illness was rampant, cures in short supply. Certainly some pupils died because of the physical injuries inflicted on them by their peers, but many more died of illness. Most public schools, when they could afford it, built often huge sanatoriums. The one at Haileybury was more like a civic hospital. We think of them as hospitals, but their more important role was that of isolation hospital, somewhere where the risk of infection for the whole school might be reduced. Nor did the risk stop at communicable diseases. Edward Thring had to evacuate Uppingham to Borth in Mid Wales before persuading the town authorities to construct a water supply into which local cesspits did not drain (more on this later). Washing and bathing facilities were primitive in the extreme, as were arrangements for the disposal of faeces. Ironically, one of the schools most criticised for the hygiene and health in 1861 was Epsom College, which had been founded by doctors as 'The Royal Medical College' in 1855. 'After a third outbreak of scarlatinsa there was a general inspection of the College to which an expert, Dr Aldis, was invited to submit a report. 'There are circumstances', wrote Dr Aldis, 'connected with the construction of the buildings which would favour the spreading of any epidemic.'[23] The height of luxury in Victorian times, many of which remained until the 1950s, was a channel of running water over which was poised a row of lidless lavatory bowls. A favourite trick was to make a paper boat out of newspaper, light it with a match and send the fireship downstream at the busiest time for the latrines in the morning. Success was judged by the number and volume of the shrieks and howls. Pain, suffering and violent death were the partners of all people until after World War One. I owe my own life to the fact that my father was one of the first people to undergo a trial for the new-fangled antibiotics, which for the first time brought numerous killer illnesses under some sort of control. Here again, the public schools were not an extreme version of a trend or tendency, but merely a reflection of it as it was evinced in wider society.

Living conditions at public schools were dire by our standards. In the early nineteenth century numbers of pupils would share the

---

23   Salmon, *Epsom College*, p.19.

same bed. At Eton, rough beds had a thin flock mattress expected to last eleven years, with three thin blankets, a sheet and woollen horse rug. A small 'standup' (no seat) desk had a work surface and tiny storage area. Heat in most comparable buildings, if provided at all, came from an open fireplace fiercely guarded by the biggest or oldest boys. Making a virtue out of necessity, boys used to pour buckets of water over the floor in the middle of the night so that there was a slide there for them next morning. The most common complaint in memoirs and letters, apart from perpetual hunger, is of the cold. But until recently even the houses of the wealthy did not have central heating, and open fires were the only available heat, sending most of their warmth up the chimney. The Spartans got there well before public schools. One of my initiations into the occasional horror of public-school life was being treated to a lecture by a truly dreadful Chairman of Governors at one of the public schools in which I taught. Warming his backside in front of a roaring fire, he announced, 'Decided not to put central heating in the Hall [his home]; worried it might spoil the wife.'

Spoil her what for? one wonders. His public school would have been proud of him.

Note the absence of 'I' in the quotation above. A classic symbol of public-school arrogance is the man who leaves 'I' out of his statements, because, as the most important person in the world, he believes it obvious that every statement refers to him.

It is easy to think that casual cruelty vanished from the public schools in the Victorian era. It did not, at least in boarding schools. The cruellest people in a school can be the pupils and, while the top layer of physical cruelty may have been suppressed, it lived on in bullying. Listen to a seventeen-year-old writing in the 1960s about people who offended against the pupil code:

Nothing would be said to him unless it was intended to remind him of what he had done. He would generally be treated like dirt, i.e. his bed would probably be dismantled into about a dozen pieces and distributed through the house, he might get his hair cut, or have various other unpleasantries done, such as dubbining his balls and squeezing toothpaste up his arse.[24]

I have never been able to look at a tube of toothpaste in the same way since I first read that extract. The incident described above is horrific enough, but it is physical. Time will heal the physical wounds, and lessen the pain of the memories. How different from the child in the Internet and social-media era, where things stay online for ever and the bullying can so easily be anonymous. The cruelty of the Internet era is the electronic message that says 'No one likes you', and the recipient does not know if the message is supported by one person only, or hundreds. I am reminded of the Jewish soldier in World War One who actually rather preferred life at the front to life in London's anti-Semitic East End. 'At least at the front,' he told me, 'the enemy wears a different uniform and you have a rifle to defend yourself.' The child subject to cyberbullying does not know who the enemy is, and has no rifle. We tend to recoil in horror, quite rightly, at the physical horrors inflicted on children in the past. When in the next millennium the body count is made for children who committed suicide in the 'old days' as a result of physical intimidation as compared with those who committed suicide in modern times because of the malign influence of the Internet, I wonder which will be the greater.

---

24 Lambert, *Hothouse Society*, p. 235.

Another very worrying comment from the 1960s is, 'If theres [*sic*] one thing that makes me puke its juniors who think that they have got basic human rights.'[25]

However, the worst form of bullying in the post-Clarendon schools was to make a child a pariah, the outsider in the group, to deny him popularity and friends. The most moving accounts of this, by the pupils themselves, are found in Royston Lambert's book *The Hothouse Society*.[26] We certainly had one such boy in my year in the boarding House at school, and, far too late in the day, I hope he will accept this, my apology. I have not made a big thing about it in this book because it is not something limited to public schools: just look at the seven-year-old at the state primary school who is the one in the class not invited to the party.

An illustration of the fact that public schools and public-school boys can take a perverse pride in physical suffering occurred to one of the first women to be employed as a teacher at a very traditional boys' boarding school at the end of the 1970s. She was walking back to her home across playing fields covered in snow when she came across a group of thirteen year-olds in rugby kit running backwards and forwards into a five-foot snow drift as what little light there was was rapidly fading. 'What on earth are you doing?' she asked in astonishment. The answer? 'Please, Miss, it does wonders for our thighs.' As Master in Charge of Visiting Speakers at Sedbergh, I well remember (and regret) being responsible for asking an Old Sedberghian who was an Arctic explorer back to talk to the school. The semi-maniac rant that ensued could be summarised as having as its theme, 'If you don't bleed while or after doing it, it's probably not worth doing.'

---

25 Ibid. p. 239.
26 See in particular pp. 280–5.

Sedbergh deserves a book in its own right on the worship of sport, at least for a period in its chequered history. The 'Wilson' or 'Ten-Mile Run' (it was actually longer) was a sporting highlight of the year, run at the end of the Easter term. Virtually the whole Sixth Form took part (it was 'voluntary', but . . .), and the run was a fearsome ordeal over the fells. The climax of the day was the 'Ten Mile Concert', held in Powell Hall, with the first half consisting of 'light music'. The second half was school songs, the most important being the 'Ten Mile Song'. The runners had to troop into the hall in the order in which they came in the race, and sing the song on stage. It was all a perfect Victorian throwback (I witnessed it between 1983 and 1987). It was said by a boy at another school in the 1960s, but the comment might equally have applied to 'The Ten': 'Someone should follow the race to pick up the dead bodies.'[27]

The irony of public schools is illustrated by the fact that many years on I'm working professionally with a boy who was in that audience, and who has turned out to be one of the gentlest, most civilised and doting fathers imaginable. Similarly, the boarding House at Haileybury run by a totally Philistine Housemaster produced a string of artists, actors and musicians. Opposites may attract, but they can also stimulate each other.

Yet there is another side to the casual cruelties of public-school life, namely the casual kindnesses. I have spent a lifetime reading about schools and education, and have a strong impression that writing on public schools follows the 'SMALL EARTHQUAKE IN CHILE – NOT MANY DEAD' syndrome. Old boys and commentators tend to focus on the extreme, the horrific and the bizarre. 'I was very happy at school' is not good copy, unless one is writing about

---

27   Ibid., p. 112.

Eton, which throughout its history has exercised a positively narcotic effect on its pupils.

Even in the worst days of the public schools there were moments of tenderness and beauty, most of which one feels have never been recorded in print. One tiny example comes from my own experience. In my second year at school a group of us could hardly help but notice that a new boy in the year below was standing in the shower blissfully unaware that he was in a state of sexual arousal. He should have been taunted and teased near to death, humiliated and scorned. What did we do? We went to one of the kinder Prefects, who was changing out of sports gear, and had a quiet word with him. Equally quietly, he whispered a few words into the ear of the boy in question, and ushered him out of the shower with the Prefect's towel draped around him. It was never mentioned again, by anyone. I don't think we were special, just that all humans have equal amounts of kindness to cruelty in them.

Another example came in my first headship. In one class of fourteen-year-old boys there was a seriously overweight, spotty and bespectacled boy, whom I shall call George, described cruelly by one remarkably non-PC teacher as 'an open invitation to bullying'. The PE teacher who took the class once a week was of the old school, and in the summer, before letting the boys see how many discuses they could cram down their shorts or how near they could come to nailing an innocent passer-by with a javelin, he would make the whole class run round the perimeter of the sports field. The last boy in was made to run round again, in solitary humiliation. For three weeks it was always George who had to trudge round the field again. Then, one week, a particular boy took pity on George, and he and a few mates drew straws to see who would come last for a few weeks. The first time the race was rigged, George had started off automatically to run round again, and had to be called back. By the end of the term, George was no longer coming last, but eighteenth or nineteenth out of twenty-four. But there were only four boys who drew straws, and they had stopped rigging the run weeks ago.

The place where you do find such stories is not in the official histories or academic accounts, but in novels or the profusion of thinly disguised autobiographies. *Goodbye, Mr. Chips* and *Lord Dismiss Us* are rarely seen as reliable academic treatises, but can help show the gentler side of public-school life.

Food

It is not only in the musical *Oliver!* that food matters so much to the urchins gathered around Fagin. Food, or rather the lack of it, runs as a continual complaint though most memoirs of public-school life. It has been suggested that the average Marlburian in the 1960s was some four inches taller than his counterpart in the 1870s.[28] One reason was the appalling quality of the food, and the lack of it. A weekly menu drawn up for Christ's Hospital in 1678 was little different from the food served well into the late nineteenth century.

Sunday	Noon: boiled beef and porridge, with 5 oz of bread
	Night: roast mutton (this was later withdrawn, as the Governors decided to provide instead breeches for the boys)

---

28   De Honey, *Tom Brown's Universe*, p. 216.

Monday	Noon: water gruel with currants
	Night: cheese
Tuesday	Noon: boiled beef
	Night: cheese
Wednesday	Noon: milk porridge, bread and butter
	Night: pudding pies, without bread
Thursday	Noon: boiled beef
	Night: cheese.
Friday	Noon: milk porridge, bread and butter
	Night: pudding pies without bread
Saturday	Noon: milk porridge, bread and butter
	Night: cheese

The above, of course, gives no guide as to either quantity or quality, which certainly the consumers described as very little and very bad.

Many boys were dependent on their own money to achieve even a basic diet. The lack of attention paid to food was partly as a result of the greed of those who ran schools, but also part of the casual-cruelty ethos that saw a major part of a school's role to 'toughen up' a boy. This, incidentally, is satirised brilliantly in the shape of the outstanding Molesworth, the unlikely hero of Geoffrey Willans's *Down with Skool!*.

An account of Samuel Taylor Coleridge's education at Christ's Hospital gives pole position to: 'The food was repellent, and there was not much of it; vegetables were entirely absent.'[29]

The emphasis placed on food by contemporaries means that no account of the English public school could be complete without reference to food, or rather the lack of it. In the pre-Victorian

---

29 Marples, *Romantics at School*, p. 54.

public school, food as provided by the school was simply in very short supply. The wealthier the pupils, the more their ability to buy in supplies. In the Victorian and post-Victorian schools, the food was still often awful, but the reasons for this were more complicated. There was a belief that:

> If boys at school are fed upon inflammatory food they are apt to lose control of themselves and have fits of irritability, leading very often to moral vice. Whereas, those fed upon a cooler diet of cereals and vegetables run far less risk of these storms of super-abundant vitality.[30]

There was also the fact that, in the privately owned boarding House, the less money spent on food, the greater the Housemaster's profit margin. There is also the fact that institutional cooking is a skill mastered by only the few. Dickens's *Oliver Twist* had said it years earlier.

In an ironic twist, I was put at risk for asking for less. I must in all fairness state that such memories as there are of my rebellion at public school differ widely. My memory is of a bizarre Matron with an obsession with our bowel movements, a topic that I continue to believe should remain private until compromised by medical emergency. Anyway, it was house lunch, and we were being fed prunes for the umpteenth time. I very politely refused my helping (I hate prunes) and, before I knew it, was being told that I was leading a hunger strike. It really hadn't been my intention. I was in deep trouble, and my father (horror of horrors) was summoned down from Sheffield, I thought to take me away. He, I think, was

---

30 Hickson, *The Poisoned Bowl*, p. 40.

more amused by the business than horrified, and talked me out of trouble, never once in his life referring to the incident again despite the turmoil it must have caused him.

Much later there was an even more forceful comment on the quality of public-school food. As joint Housemasters, Jenny and I were offered the chance to order food at a discounted rate. With a young family to feed, we ordered a pack of beefburgers. Uniquely, our permanently ravenous three young sons turned them down. They went into the dog's bowl. I won't tell you what that dog, a Labrador, had eaten in the past, but it wouldn't touch the beefburgers. In desperation I threw them out into the garden. A week later I had to pick them up from where I had thrown them, untouched, and put them to their final rest in the dustbin. There at least they were taken away from us.

As with all things to do with the public schools, their history is peppered with farce, and stories about food are no exception. John Keate, a nineteenth-century Eton Headmaster, once intercepted a small boy bringing hot sausages back for his lords and masters. With nowhere to put the confiscated, greasy and still sizzling objects, Keate emptied them into a passing workingman's hat. The Governors at the newly founded Marlborough in the 1850s gave a £5 gratuity to a member of the domestic staff who invented a machine for cutting butter, which was expected to save considerable sums from the food bill. Marlborough had been founded as a cut-price public school for the sons of clergymen, but the Governors got their sums hopelessly wrong, and the butter-cutting machine failed to put the school in the black.

2

ALL BOYS TOGETHER: SEX AND THE PUBLIC SCHOOL

'Public schools are the nurseries of all vice and immorality' – Henry Fielding, *Joseph Andrews*[1]

'"There is no such thing as sex at College," the Master used to observe, "and if there is I knock it hard on the head"' F. B. Malin, Master of Wellington College, 1920s[2]

Whatever else it may have been defined as, the 'manliness' so worshipped by public schools for so long sought to promulgate a vision of the male that both denied any sexuality and saw femininity in terms of weakness. In the late 1880s the Housemaster of Haileybury's Melville House felt so strongly about the latter that he banished the pink stripes worn on his boys' caps in favour of Empire Scarlet.[3]

---

1   This is frequently cited as Fielding's own view. He was an Old Etonian. In fact Fielding puts the words into the mouth of a disgruntled tutor who has lost a wealthy pupil to Eton.

2   Worsley, *Flanelled Fool*, p. 123.

3   Hickson, *The Poisoned Bowl*, p. 145.

The sexual history of the English public school would often be funny if it were not at the same time tragic, and it goes back a long way. Nicholas Udall was a Headmaster of Eton in the mid-sixteenth century, and notorious for appalling sexual behaviour with Etonians. In an extraordinary saga that beggars belief, two boys accused of theft appear to have threatened to expose their Headmaster's sexual misdoings. It ended up with the Privy Council no less, and in Udall's case the then-standard sentence of death for buggery was commuted to imprisonment. It seems to have done Udall little harm. On his release he went on to become Headmaster of Westminster. Funny? I suppose. But I wonder how amusing it seemed at the time for Udall's victims. The story of Udall has another facet, which illustrates what has been one of the major fascinations of the public school for me: its habit of veering so fast between farce and tragedy that sometimes one is hard pushed to know which is which. Udall's biographer presents an interesting argument for believing that Udall's crime was actually 'burglary' rather than 'buggery', the confusion arising because of the handwriting of an overworked clerk. Tragedy that a man might have stood as a sex offender for five hundred years because someone's writing was obscure? Or Farce? Udall may have been a bugger or he may have been a burglar, but there seems no doubt he was a brutal beast. Thomas Tusser was a pupil of his, and left this memorial:

> From Paul's I went, to Eton sent,
> To learn straightways the Latin phrase,
> Where fifty-three stripes given to me
> At once I had;
> For fault but small, or not at all,
> It came to pass, thus beat I was;

See, Udall see, the mercy of thee
To me, poor lad.[4]

Udall had friends in high places, which was probably why he got the job at Eton in the first place. When after seven years as Master of Eton he found himself in the Marshalsea Prison, those friends soon secured his release, and he wrote one of the most unconvincing job applications in history in a vain attempt to get his job back: 'Accept this mine honest change from vice to virtue, from prodigality to frugal living, from negligence of teaching to assiduity, from play to study, from lightness to gravity.'[5]

As if . . .

There is a problem for any historian trying to tell the history of sexuality in public schools, in that successive Headmasters felt obliged to warn their charges of the dreadful consequences of *any* sexual activity without ever actually mentioning sex in any shape, size or form. One account of the situation reads, 'On the one hand, ashen-faced headmasters issued cryptic warnings and zealous housemasters prowled dormitory corridors. On the other, schoolboys remained stubbornly indifferent to the staff's obsession with homosexuality as a moral issue.'[6]

Or there is this recollection:

The Headmaster, Dr Warre, addressed us. It was in Upper School. The occasion was, for us, tremendous. There he stood, waiting, this great square man, with a broad silk band round his middle, gazing at a high window, and chewing the inside of his cheek, as was

---

4 Holder, *Anthology of School*, p. 153.
5 Lamb, *The Happiest Days*, p. 125.
6 Hickson, *The Poisoned Bowl*, p. 15.

his habit. He looked all justice and authority. 'Come up here, boys, don't be afraid.' An enormous voice rumbled from the depths of him. And then he spoke to us, paternally, dropping his final G's, moving his strong lips as one does to a lip-reader, now in a vibrant bass, now in a sudden tenor. He spoke of our responsibility as Etonians; he was encouraging and kind. Then, out of the blue, came an astonishing admonition. He told us to beware of 'filth', to avoid even talking 'filth'. I was completely baffled. I knew a great deal about filth, after that summer among the footpaths and bushes of Valois. But here, at Eton? Could he be telling us to look where we trod, because of the occasional dog-mess on the pavements?[7]

Some commentators believe that much of the machinery of the Victorian public school and after was dictated by fear of sex – the divide-and-rule house system, small, single-age dormitories, phased bedtimes, uniform, Chapel seating and so on. Oundle's Headmaster, Rev. T. C. Fry (1883–4), produced a daunting list of house rules designed to stop homosexual behaviour:

1. No study door shall on any pretence be locked.

2. No non-study boy shall visit a study; and in a house where there are junior studies, no junior study boy shall visit a senior study, except when sent for by the senior prefect of the house.

---

7   L. E. Jones, *A Victorian Boyhood*, 1955, quoted in Craig, *The Oxford Book of Schooldays*, p. 196.

3. No boy except a prefect shall leave his study or work room during evening work without leave from a master or from the prefect in charge.

4. A boy from one house shall not be allowed to visit a boy in another house without distinct leave given on each occasion by the housemaster. Prefects may visit prefects.

5. No boy is allowed to go to any dormitory but his own on any pretence whatever, except on duty authorised by his housemaster.

6. During prayers in dormitory, after the gas is out, silence shall be observed in every dormitory: before gas is out, and in the morning, talking must be quiet, and general order strictly kept.[8]

It is worth pointing out that one of the most scholarly books on the late Victorian public school believes that the real fear they felt was not of homosexuality, but of masturbation.[9] 'Masturbational insanity' was a quasi-medical theory (granting that much medicine was 'quasi' in the eighteenth century) that came over from Europe and became rooted in the UK in the 1830s. Masturbation was linked to brain disease, 'hysteria, asthma, epilepsy, melancholia, dyspepsia, mania, suicide, dementia'.[10] Signs of the evil at work were dark rings under the eyes and general loss of energy, leading inevitably to an early grave. There is no doubt that Victorian

---

8   Hickson, *The Poisoned Bowl*, p. 166.
9   De Honey, *Tom Brown's Universe*.
10   Ibid., p. 169.

Heads did wage war on masturbation, but there is sufficient documentation to suggest that it was a war against two enemies, neither of whom could be named in plain language.

The reaction to any overt homosexuality could verge on the hysterical. Just one example was in 1892, when Brighton College closed a boarding House and expelled eleven pupils in an attempt to cut out the cancer of homosexuality. As pupils at Uppingham in the 1960s, we all knew who were the semiprofessional gays among the boys, and which House they were in. It was quite exciting when the most notorious was discovered and given the sack. We knew nothing about the whys and wherefores of the business, but did note that the prettiest 'little boy' (the term used at Uppingham in my time to refer to what was most commonly known as a 'tart') was allowed to stay on. I was woefully ignorant and naïve, but I remember wondering if the 'little boy' had been beaten as his punishment for being 'queer', and thinking even then that, if this had been his punishment, there were levels of irony in it. I had no doubt that to be a 'queer' was a horrendous and sackable offence.

The attitude towards homosexuality, or indeed any deemed lack of 'manliness', if not the severity of the actions, continued for many years. When I taught at Haileybury in the 1970s there was one housemaster who took exception to one of the reprobate and motley crowd of 'arty' boys who infested our private accommodation. Coward (not his real name) was chubby and, it has to be said, tended to mincing when he walked. The housemaster spotted him mincing from one building to another across the vast width of Haileybury's quadrangle, and roared at the top of his voice, '*Coward! Stop mincing!*'

'Mincing?' the boy replied. He was always most polite. 'Of course, sir. I'll stop immediately,' he said, and minced off. Subsequently he had the misfortune to be taught Religious Studies once a week by this same Housemaster. The boy made a special trip into Hertford to buy the cheapest and must offensively sweet-pungent scent Woolworth's had for sale, and soaked the paper on which he wrote his weekly Religious Studies essay in it religiously every week.

What is not in doubt is that until the 1970s public schools were boys-only, and as such did not only breed an adolescent form of sexuality, but indeed offered little alternative. The reason why public schools were male-dominated until the end of the Victorian period is obvious enough: society itself was male-dominated, and here, as everywhere, public schools reflected society. The grammar and other schools founded from the sixteenth century onwards existed to give their pupils the smattering of Latin grammar to qualify them to enter the Church, or a very small range of other careers. These jobs were simply not available to women. When these schools expanded to meet a growing demand for education, particularly in the nineteenth century, both universities and the world of work were more or less exclusively male preserves.

Women's work was to get married and have children, and you did not need a school to learn how to do that (though quite a lot of boys who graduated from all-boys public schools in the late-nineteenth and twentieth centuries needed more help than they got regarding the process). Here, as in so many instances, the public schools simply acted as a mirror to nature.

Male sexuality is a frighteningly powerful force, and there seems little doubt that in the absence of women it was exercised with full force on younger boys in particular. To the modern reader, many memoirs of former pupils show all the symptoms of an abused child. Sydney Smith is just one example. Outwardly, he was a successful pupil at Winchester, whose old boys are known as 'Wykehamists' after the name of the college's founder. He became

Captain of School, and was deemed bright, and successful. Yet he clearly hated the memory of his time at school, and was having nightmares about it long into adulthood. As editor of *The Edinburgh Review*, he wrote a number of articles actively hostile to the public-school system. He described public school in terms of 'premature debauchery that only prevents men from being corrupted by the world by corrupting them before they enter the world . . . abuse, neglect and vice . . .'[11]

Smith was neither the first nor the last to point out that public school saw a boy start as a slave and turn into a tyrant. Given the absence of adult supervision – as we shall see later, the schools were in effect run by the pupils – the public schools expressed in real life what William Golding's *Lord of the Flies* expressed in fiction. Eton Collegers slept and lived together in Long Chamber, all ninety of them, without adult supervision from evening until morning, and it seems to have been more than a match for any fiction in its violence and grotesquery. It bore strange fruit in that a product of the Long Chamber was Edward Thring, who went on to establish Uppingham with one of his main precepts being that every boy should have a study. Ironically, this led on occasion to problems of loneliness. The study door no one knocks at is the equivalent of the 'You have no messages' on the mobile phone.

In any event, we shall never know from the mouths of those who suffered what the precise nature of the 'debaucheries' they had inflicted on them were. It is likely that they were less dominated by single-sex predators than today's fervid imaginations might concede. Heterosexual sex was not hard to purchase in eighteenth- and nineteenth-century England, particularly for the sons of the ruling classes with disposable income. It was the cloistered,

---

11 Chandos, *Boys Together*, p. 37.

monastic and inward-looking masculinity of the Victorian and Edwardian public schools that provoked the homoeroticism of these schools. Yet, as late as 1986, an author was categorising the different nature of different schools by the heterosexual behaviour of their alumni, seeing a Harrovian in terms if someone who was prone to 'the quick seduction of their best friend's sixteen-year-old daughter in the back of a taxi'.[12]

I use the word 'homoeroticism' because what took root in these schools was not conventional homosexuality, whereby the male feels only sexual desire for the fellow male. Rather, it was displaced heterosexuality, whereby sexual desire for the female on the part of the male was temporarily replaced, in the absence of any females, by the nearest thing: pretty, prepubescent boys. 'Fooling around' with other boys might result in expulsion if caught out by the authorities, but the same would happen if heterosexual activity was suspected, and the punitive response to both homo- and heterosexual activity was not so much gender-specific as part of the fear of sexuality of all types felt by the public schools. Perhaps, like the Church, it was the fear of an essentially authoritarian institution that distrusts a passion so strong that it cannot either suppress or divert it to its own ends.

What many outsiders who have become obsessed with sexuality in the public schools have failed to acknowledge, or perhaps even recognise, was that a temporary deviation into same-sex relationships was an accepted part of English public-school culture. It is summed up by Simon Raven:

'I don't mind you playing with a few little boy's pricks,' Lumley's pater said, 'we've all been up to that at your age and bloody nice too; but I won't have you passing yourself off as a twenty-four carat Nancy Boy . . . just you start wagging your arse in front of the recruiting board and I'll put a pair of Purdey's up it.'[13]

For those who did not go to public school, Purdey's are the most fabulous shotguns available to man or woman, though usually thought of as more suitable for the slaughter of innocent grouse or pheasant, rather than 'Nancy Boys'.

Well, yes, there we are – or, rather, there we used to be. One problem with this apparent acceptance of schoolboy homosexuality is that it belittles the social impact of being 'found out':

> It must be remembered . . . that at the time of which I write, their wages (if found out) was social death. For expulsion from a public school was generally attributed to sexual depravity and any boy so disgraced would find universities and professions barred to him unless, like one of Conrad's anti-heroes, he was prepared to expiate his guilt by service in some remote fever-ridden outpost of Empire.[14]

Yet there are widely differing accounts of the severity with which schoolboy homosexuality was greeted by wider society. Sexual attraction to younger boys was what we would now call a phase, and one that society expected its young men to grow out of. It is summed up by a boy writing in a boarding school in the mid-1960s:

---

13 Ibid., p. 97.
14 Hickson, *The Poisoned Bowl*, p. 52.

God will there be any of the pretty boys outside; if I look at the pretty boys I always blush. Am I queer? I ask myself this 1,000 times; I don't think so; I mean the thought of actually buggering a little boy is repulsive to me but they're just a substitute, something pretty to look at when there are no girls around.[15]

A variation on the same theme is recounted by Jonathan Gathorne-Hardy, who on meeting with an Old Haileyburian saw the old man's eyes light up at the Elysian memory[16] of unlimited sex at school. Hardy asked if the boys encouraged sex:

'Oh yes, dear me, yes,' the plump face glowed, the eyes darted; 'there was a great deal of sex, a *great* deal. I had an enormous amount – but I wish I'd had more . . . Make you a bugger – certainly not. I don't think so. The most active person I knew became a tremendous womaniser.'[17]

However, the obsession with homosexuality was something the Victorians brought to the view of a public-school education. Prior to the Clarendon Commission times it was not homosexuality or young men chasing after straight sex that was an issue with the public-school classes. While it was not encouraged, it was accepted as part of nature's way that young men would seek to have their way with girls. The fear was not of sexuality itself, but rather that the boy would make an unsuitable marriage. Though never to my

---

15   Royston Lambert, *Hothouse Society*, p. 12.
16   'Elysium' was the name of the elite dining club for boys that existed for many years at Haileybury.
17   Gathorne-Hardy, *Public School Phenomenon*, pp. 163–4.

knowledge written down, a lasting theory as to why the great and the not-so-great boarding schools took their pupils at age thirteen was that this was the time when the young master set out to bed the housemaids. It would fit in with the thoroughly pragmatic attitude to sex adopted by the pre-Victorians: a pregnant maid would have to be dismissed, and good servants were hard to come by. A poem written in 1781 by someone who had clearly received a good public-school education in the classics suggests nothing in the way of homoeroticism:

AMO, AMAS

Amo, amas, I love a lass,
As a cedar, tall and slender,
Sweet Cowslip's grace is her nominative case,
And she's of the feminine gender.

Rorum, corum, sunt divorum,
Harum, scarum, divo!
Rag-tag, merry derry, periwig and hat-band,
Hic, hoc, horum genetivo.

Can I decline a nymph divine,
Whose voice as a flute is *dulcis*?
Her *oculis* bright, her *manus* white,
And soft, when I *tacto*, her pulse is.

Rorum, corum . . . etc.

> O how *bella* my *puella*,
> I'll kiss *saecula saeculorum*,
> If I've luck, Sir, she's my *uxor!*
> *O dies benedictorum!*
>
> *Rorum, corum* . . . etc.
>
> John O'Keefe

However, in Victorian times, war was declared on any expression of sexuality, in any shape, size or form, whether graced by Latin or not. One writer summarises this as 'counter- codpiece' activity.[18] The drive to repress sexuality hardly countenanced women, simply because women, and particularly young and attractive women, were a rare commodity indeed in the all-boy school. Homosexuality was Antichrist, but so was masturbation. I was amused to read in one authoritative source,

> As the [nineteenth] century advanced schoolmasters and preachers became 'obsessed with impurity'. Even Montagu Butler . . . issued an order, soon after becoming Headmaster of Harrow, that all boys' pockets must be sewn up. It had to be rescinded owing to the indignation and ridicule it aroused . . .[19]

Really? In my time at public school between 1962 and 1966 the indignation and ridicule had clearly not reached Rutland. We had to have our pockets sewn up, and they were regularly checked to ensure compliance. The penalty for each unsewn pocket was what

---

18 Chandos, *Boys Together*, p. 338.
19 Ibid., p. 338.

was then the vast sum of half a crown, or 2s 6d (12.5p in 'new' money). We all knew that the reason was to stop us playing 'pocket billiards'. Only a few years earlier, none of the house lavatories had had doors on them. This was widely known as being a means to stop homosexual activity and masturbation. Even when doors were provided, it was an urban myth that prefects looked under the doors to make sure there was only one pair of shoes in the cubicle. The masses will revolt against persecution, and one of the subtle ways we showed our dissent was that when we changed into our Combined Cadet Force (or 'Corps') uniform, but before we donned at the last minute the heavy and desperately uncomfortable Corps boots, we would solemnly place them on the floor of the lavatory cubicle, toes forward, pointing the same way as our feet.

The ban on anything that might provoke sexual arousal made the Victorian covering of piano legs seem mild in comparison. John Percival, former teacher at Rugby and Headmaster of Clifton, 'insisted that boys playing football should wear trousers down to and tightened at the calf lest they should become inflamed at the sight of one another's knees.'[20]

In a counter to this, when I joined Sedbergh School as Second Master in 1983, I was solemnly informed that the reason a former Head had insisted all boys wear shorts (a decision rescinded only in very living memory when I joined) was that the most powerful anti-aphrodisiac on earth was the sight of a male adolescent's knees. The world awaits the academic study that will decide the outcome either way.

All of this raises the issue of sexuality, and homosexuality, in teachers. As referred to later, C. J. Vaughan, inspirational

---

20   Gathorne-Hardy, *The Public School Phenomenon*, p. 75.

Headmaster of Harrow from 1844 to 1859, lost his job and all preferment because of dalliance with pupils, and also referred to later – and earlier – is the infamous Udall of Eton, jailed for sodomy. There were numerous Heads deemed to be gay, including the charismatic Roxburgh of Stowe.

'Yet caution needs to be exercised. Possession of a particular brand of sexuality does not mean that the person concerned will inflict his (or her) sexual proclivities on pupils, any more than it implies a straight doctor will always make a predatory beeline for opposite-gender patients. Very few public-school Heads ever got into at least any public trouble over their personal sexuality.

The same is true of the staff soldiers in the ranks. In many respects the public schools were for many years designed for the teacher as a single man. Haileybury, where I taught for eleven years, had what I then believed to be an extreme form of this in its 'Common Room'. The term 'Common Room' is used in public schools to mean the staff room, but is actually the collective phrase for the whole teaching staff. In a throwback, 'Common Room' at Haileybury was the institution for the bachelor members of staff, who ate all their meals there, as well as being housed by the school, and had a formal dinner once a week, to which married staff had to be invited. Drink (sherry and gin) was served, or rather available to buy, every evening before supper and any teacher could partake of the privilege. Married men, particularly of the younger sort, were in the minority, and all hell was let loose when one of the first-ever female teachers at Haileybury was allowed to be on the staff photograph. At drinks in Common Room (this was in the 1970s) I was taken aside by a senior member of staff and reprimanded for not keeping my wife in order, and told that she had no business appearing on the school photo, where she was not wanted.

Later on, when I was a Housemaster (jointly with my wife, as it happened – it was a Sixth-Form Girls' boarding House), the Chairman of Common Room took me aside and told me off forcibly for referring to David Summerscale, the then Master of Haileybury, by his first name. My reply that he had directly requested us all to do so cut no ice. In many respects, the Haileybury Common Room was a conscious or unconscious attempt to base academic life on the collegiate structure of the Oxford or Cambridge College, which for most of their history had fed and accommodated single men as their teaching force. Indeed, for its first 50 years of existence, from 1862 to 1912, only three Housemasters had ever been married. One writer comments:

> . . . by 1967, the headmaster [pedantic author's note: actually known as 'The Master'] William Stewart (1963–75) was able to host a dinner party to celebrate the fact that for the first time in its history, Haileybury had not even one bachelor housemaster.[21]

That may have been so, but I taught at Haileybury from 1972 to 1984, and of the ten houses remember three of them being run by bachelors.

Visions of gay young men flocking to teach at public schools in order to immerse themselves in a vista of boyhood were unfounded in most schools, at least in my forty years. More often the opposite was true. Haileybury, and most public schools, had their own 'Sanatorium'. Small hospitals originally set up as isolation units for infectious illnesses. Two nurses were employed on a permanent basis, and, as one of the few sources of (usually)

---

21 Hickson, *The Poisoned Bowl*, p. 97.

unmarried women, were a magnet for the younger male staff. I remember as a young teacher being dragged unwillingly by one of the few young men on the staff to knock on the door of the 'San.' in order for him to eye up the new nurse. It was a short visit, as the huge oak door was opened by a stalwart lady in her fifties who looked as if she devoured several assistant masters every morning at breakfast.

Gathorne-Hardy summarises the situation when he writes, 'If a fair (but incalculable) proportion of public school masters were homosexual, on the whole they did not satisfy their inclination on their pupils.'[22]

This is an unfashionable theory at a time when the pendulum has swung from the assumption that child abuse did not exist to the belief that it exists everywhere. Yet in my experience Gathorne-Hardy is probably right. Increasingly, and quite rightly, we hear from those abused as children. Yet for many children, now and throughout history, we are in the 'SMALL EARTHQUAKE IN CHILE – NOT MANY DEAD' scenario. The vast majority of children not abused at school or elsewhere are not news and are not reported on or quoted. We hear only about the victims and the wounded. This is not to diminish the issue. It is to recognise that, if the words of a social worker friend are to be believed, a majority of child abuse occurs within families, as recorded in the Who's pop opera *Tommy*. We now know how many instances of abuse occurred under the umbrella of trust that was the Roman Catholic Church. It angers me, as a friend to public schools, that those organisations do at least have a record of removing employees guilty of child abuse, while the much greater institution of the Catholic Church has much less to boast about in this regard.

---

22 Gathorne-Hardy, *The Public School Phenomenon*, p. 164.

New young recruits desperate to break out of the monastic order of public schools became more and more common in the second half of the twentieth century. Sedbergh School in Cumbria is very isolated, its nearest station being Oxenholme, several miles away. Its Headmasters well into the 1970s used to interview for teaching posts in London, fearing the isolation would put off young staff, and perhaps even some of the older ones. In the late 1960s two young Masters were needed early on a Saturday evening for boarding House duties, but could not be found. They had gone to Oxenholme station, not to catch a train but just to stand on the bridge to reassure themselves that the trains to London were still running.

Yet it is a sad fact that boys' boarding schools in particular were a magnet for paedophiles, and it needed only one active such person to bring a whole school into disrepute and do huge damage to young minds. Royston Lambert's *The Hothouse Society* is a collection of writings from boys and girls at boarding schools. Some of the more graphic writing features a deviant housemaster: 'Mr Tomkins is a homo. He takes little First yr skunks into his room and fiddles about WITH THEIR balls';[23] and, 'When I was trying on a uniform, this bum bandit pressed his tool right up against me. Uggh! Get this homo banned.'[24]

Lambert surveyed sixty-six schools. In only four of them was there sustained protest about a member of staff, leading Lambert to write:

> Sexual deviation on the part of the staff however produces a less tolerant reaction. It seems to violate what children regard as acceptable. It is probable that

---

23 Lambert, *Hothouse Society*, p. 272.
24 Ibid., p. 273.

such situations are rare; in fact, the readiness of boys to comment suggests such activity does not remain undiscovered long.[25]

This conclusion seems to run counter to contemporary opinion, which sees child molesters as being everywhere. I suspect the truth lies somewhere in the middle. There were schools where appalling things were done by staff, with the intensity of what happened in those schools obscuring the relative innocence of many other, and perhaps even a majority of, schools. I find it remarkable given the understandable modern perceptions that in all my four years at Uppingham, with massively less protection than there is nowadays, not once did boy gossip report a bent member of staff.

One of the most hilarious aspects of public-school sexuality was the 'advice' given by staff to boys on matters sexual, usually warnings against masturbation or homosexuality. As already noted, an element of the absurd was inherent in any such talk by virtue of widespread reluctance to be specific about the nature of the dreadful evil that lurked within every pair of trousers. A second layer of the ridiculous was added by the fact that the speaker was often both acutely embarrassed and, one suspects, seriously lacking in knowledge of matters sexual himself. In my time at Haileybury the edict went out from the Master's Lodge that Housemasters should address their pupils on the facts of life. A senior Housemaster's version was to call the house together, slap the side of the newly acquired television in the pupil common room and say, 'I've been asked to tell you about . . . various things. I can sum it up by saying we don't want

---

25   Ibid, p. 272.

any of the nonsense you see happening on TV in this house.' He then left.

At the other extreme is the too-direct approach. I cannot trace the manual purportedly written by a Head that opened with the words, 'You may have noticed that you have something between your legs . . .' An Eton housemaster ignored a warning not to be too specific, and is reported as addressing his house while warming his backside in front of an open fire. He delivered lecture on the evils of 'boys putting their penises up other boys' bottoms', at which point the trousers of his CCF uniform caught fire.[26] The same writer records Dr Herbert James, Headmaster of Rugby, 1895–1910, telling boys. 'If you touch it, it will fall off.'[27]

If the Victorians spent most their times damning sex in public schools while raising the euphemism to an art form, modern commentators have gone to the other extreme. The historian faces on the one hand the fog generated by the Victorians, on the other hand the steam generated by later commentators. The truth? My sense, from forty years' work, reading and research into public schools, is that actual buggery was comparatively rare, and 'crushes' or intense relationships more commonly associated with girls' schools, were the norm: '… the smoke was suffocating but there was very little fire.'[28] At the same time, the intensity of the all-male atmosphere generated the climate for the most extraordinarily intense friendships, very similar to those I researched and read about among soldiers in World War One. These friendships – perhaps comradeship is a better word – often gave something soft, fragile and beautiful amid the harsh reality of school life:

---

26 Hickson, *The Poisoned Bowl*, p. 33.
27 Ibid, p. 35.
28 Hickson, *The Poisoned Bowl*, p. 203.

> If ever I tasted a disembodied transport on earth, it was
> in those friendships that I entertained at school, before
> I dreamt of any mature feeling . . . I loved my friend for
> his gentleness, his candour, his truth, his good repute,
> his freedom even from my own livelier manner, his
> calm and reasonable kindness . . . With the other boys
> I played antics, and rioted in fantastic jests; but in his
> society, or whenever I thought of him, I feel into a kind
> of Sabbath state of bliss; and I am sure I could have died
> for him.[29]

I comment in a later chapter that the emotional intensity of the all-male school friendship has another flowering in some of the lesser-known poetry of World War One.

If there was beauty, there was also savagery. A Bradfield old boy (1875–82) recalls:

> On another occasion I was saved again as by a miracle.
> The bigger boys were intent on raping me. I of course
> fought furiously with fists and toes. As they bound me,
> I used my nails and finally when they forced me on
> the floor, and I thought all was up, the chief devil's leg
> came within reach of my mouth. I was just able to raise
> my head and with all my strength I got his calf between
> my teeth, and I am sure he carried that scar until his
> death.[30]

One of the least attractive features of the public school is to claim success or the achievement of an enviable modernity long

---

29   Ibid., p. 119.
30   Ibid., p. 109.

before it reflects reality. Those who love public schools, or loved their time there, often succumb to an urge to write about what they *ought* to be like, as distinct from what they *are* like. A classic example comes from a book published in 1959, pontificating about how wonderful the attitude to sex is in the 'New Age' public school:

> . . . sex is now opened-up country, and is freely talked about without embarrassment between masters and boys . . . the situation in most Public Schools is thoroughly sound today and the whole thing sensibly and suitably handled in every way in which it arises . . .[31]

Really? Between 1962 and 1966 I would rather have died than talk about sex with a teacher at Uppingham, and probably have been put to death if I'd tried. I've known and liked my Housemaster for fifty-five years, and I *still* haven't mentioned the topic to him.

---

31 Snow, *Public Schoosl in the New Age*, p. 56.

3

WHITEWASH!: THE CLARENDON COMMISSION OF 1864, THE PUBLIC SCHOOLS ACT OF 1868 AND THE HEADMASTERS' CONFERENCE

In *Public Schools and Private Education*, Colin Shrosbree tells us,

> The Clarendon Commission . . . established the principle that secondary education was a privilege to be paid for . . . Secondary education was developed for established social groups who could afford to pay; elementary education was developed for people who could not bear the whole cost themselves.[1]

The Clarendon Commission was a Royal Commission established in 1861 to investigate the state of nine leading schools in England. It was in large measure complaints about almost every aspect of Eton – its management, its finances, its buildings and

---

1   Shrosbree, *Public Schools and Private Education*, p. 4.

above all the perceived licentiousness and unbridled anarchy that prevailed among its pupils – that provoked the inquiry. It took three years (until 1864) to produce its report, and a further four years for any legislation to be passed, in the form of the Public Schools Act of 1868.

In fact the Clarendon Commission was bedevilled, and eventually, emasculated, by politics. It came into being only because its prime directive was to investigate financial irregularities at Eton. This very specific aim rendered impotent the veritable army of old Etonians in the House of Commons and the House of Lords, who would otherwise have blocked any attempt to interfere with the school but dared not do so in case it made them appear in favour of corrupt finances. Its Chairman, Lord Clarendon, was a Liberal who was a pain in the neck to the Conservatives and others in his own party because of his views on foreign policy, and his chairing the Commission was seen as a way of keeping him quiet. There was serious advantage to the Liberal Party in chasing reform of the public schools, much as there is advantage for the modern Labour party:

> . . . it did not threaten party unity; it was supported by public opinion, and it attacked . . . an institution associated with Conservative tradition and Tory politics. In its financial dealings, Eton could not be defended without appearing to condone greed and mismanagement; here was an issue where the Liberals could not lose and the Conservatives could not win.[2]

Yet win they did. The schools themselves, and involved parties

2   Ibid., p. 48.

such as the Mercers' Company, played politics themselves to delay and disarm legislation.

The Commission saw and heard all that was wrong with the system, but excused much of it because it believed that the public schools had contributed much that was good to the English character: 'It is not easy to estimate the degree to which the English people are indebted to these schools for the qualities on which they pride themselves . . .'[3]

Did the Commission and the subsequent Public Schools Act seriously affect the schools? Certainly, the Victorian public school, a positive Stalinist state in comparison with the violent carnival of the earlier schools, started to come into being at roughly the same time at the Public Schools Act, but I suspect the Act merely marked the change in the climate of public opinion, rather than caused it. The basic truth about public schools is that they follow the bottom line. If they cannot persuade wealthy and influential people to pay good money to send their children there, they cease to exist.

By the 1870s, for whatever reason, parental taste and preferences had changed, not least of all because of the worship of Empire and the sense that what England needed to sustain the largest empire the world had seen was for its young people to be trained in a sense of service and duty, rather than self-willed riot and defiance of any authority except that of the pupils themselves.

If the Commission and the resulting Act of Parliament illustrated the truth that the public schools always followed rather than influenced public opinion, then they illustrated also a second lasting truth, which could be summarised as the suggestion that the Establishment should never be set to report on the Establishment. Members of Parliament may or may not have disapproved of

---

3   Clarendon Commission, quoted in May, *The Victorian Public School*, p. 27.

what the public schools had become, but their disapproval was one thing, sharing that disapproval with the unwashed masses another thing altogether.

The Commission's terms of reference were: 'To inquire into the nature and application of the Endowments, Funds and Revenue belonging to or received by the hereinafter mentioned Colleges, Schools and Foundations; and also to inquire into the administration and management of the said Colleges, Schools and Foundations'. The nine schools comprised seven boarding schools (Eton, Charterhouse, Harrow, Rugby, Shrewsbury, Westminster and Winchester), and two day schools (St Paul's and Merchant Taylors'). However, the 1868 Act concerned itself only with the seven boarding schools. Fairly late in the day, the Commission wrote to four new foundations, Cheltenham College, Marlborough, City of London School and Wellington. The drive for this was the outmoded curriculum followed by the Clarendon Nine, and particular interest in the introduction of 'modern studies' at Cheltenham and Marlborough and science at City of London.

To its credit, the Commission did give something of a picture of life in the great schools, but the emphasis on finance in the original terms of reference is telling. The majority of the schools destined to become known as public schools had started life with an endowment, in order to allow them to educate local children. By the 1860s many of these endowments had mysteriously vanished. Gonville & Caius College, Cambridge, never could satisfactorily explain to me what actually happened to the endowment left by Dr Stephen Perse to found the Cambridge Free Grammar School. The Perse School is no longer free. For some reason the money to found the annual extravaganza of The Perse Feast still exists.

Seven years of questioning failed to elicit from the Mercers'

Company if the John Colet Foundation still existed, and, if it did, who controlled it. It was certainly not the High Master or non-Mercer appointees to the governing body of Colet's school. The Clarendon Commission looked in detail at neither of these schools. The situation regarding St Paul's was potentially damaging to the Mercers' Company, but was never fully explored, not least of all because legal issues were cited as a reason why no conclusion could be reached. In essence, St Paul's was extremely wealthy, with the estate of its founder, Dean John Colet, enough to pay for the education of the 153 children named in Colet's founding deed. To put into perspective how vast a number that was, the neighbouring Latymer School was endowed for eight boys. Colet was from a Mercer family, and entrusted his school to the Mercers' Company on the grounds that he had found less corruption among men of business than among the Church or the universities. A member of the Commission, Grant Duff, was vocal on the issue of St Paul's.

> The evidence relating to St Paul's is peculiarly interesting
> . . . Its surplus revenue amounts to a very large sum, its
> accumulated capital is very great . . . Surely it should
> be made what Dean Colet evidently intended it to be
> . . . It is scarcely credible that Dean Colet . . . should
> have wished The Mercers' Company to have been
> beneficially interested in the surplus revenues of his
> property, and only obliged to maintain the school as a
> charge upon them.[4]

The Mercers' Company was heavily involved at the time in a legal dispute with Baron Rothschild over an exchange of property

---

4   Shrosbree, *Public Schools and Private Education*, p. 118.

that Rothschild argued was beneficial to the charity. The Mercers'
Company argued that it was not obliged to devote the whole of
the income from Colet's Foundation to St Paul's School, but
was obliged to maintain the school. In other words, the Mercers'
Company seems to have been arguing that it was not the *trustee*
of the estate, obliged to spend it only on St Paul's, but rather
the *owner*, with an obligation to keep up Colet's school but not
necessarily to devote the whole of the endowment to it.

The Mercers' Company won its case against Rothschild,
but the court declined to give a judgment on the owner/trustee
issue. A case brought by the Attorney General in 1870 ruled that
the Mercers' Company *was* the trustee, but the Mercers' had
successfully appealed to the Lords Select Committee to have the
school excluded from the Public Schools Bill of 1865, despite
the opposition of both Clarendon and the Prince of Wales. The
unplanned consequence of this 'victory' was that St Paul's came
under the jurisdiction of the socially far less respectable Endowed
Schools' Commission of 1869, and did not escape government
intervention. As late as 1868 A. S. Ayrton, reforming MP for
Tower Hamlets, asked why St Paul's and Merchant Taylors' were
left out of the Bill,

> . . . and bitterly criticised the Mercers' Company
> over their management of St Paul's School and their
> conduct over the reform of the school by Parliament.
> He criticised their extravagance, their secrecy and
> their disregard of Parliament, and accused them of
> deliberately instigating legal proceedings in Chancery
> in order to evade Parliamentary control.[5]

---

5   Ibid., 199–200.

The given reason why St Paul's was excluded from the legislation was that the issue of who owned what was *sub judice*. The ducking and weaving in response to the Clarendon Commission were not St Paul's finest hour, any more than they were for Eton. What is rarely mentioned in coverage of the Clarendon Commission and its aftermath is that St Paul's had a very different social mix from those of at least seven of the other nine 'great' schools:

> St Paul's . . . only received 109 boys who might conceivably have belonged to the upper classes during the early nineteenth century up to the accession of Queen Victoria, and even this tiny intake showed a pronounced falling off towards 1837.[6]

The Commission's findings, emasculated though they were, were influential in terms of curriculum and governance. If it could do nothing about the corruption of the past, it at least made it far more difficult for that same corruption to take place in the future.

My problem with the Clarendon Commission is one of comparison. As Chairman of HMC, I was summoned to appear before one of the first Parliamentary Committees examining the vexed question of charitable status for public schools. It is much vaunted that these committees can summon whomever they like. It is less vaunted that this means in effect they can summon completely the wrong people. As it was, they summoned me as Chairman of HMC, Jonathan Shepherd, the then Secretary of ISC (Independent Schools Council), and Dr (now Sir) Anthony Seldon, Master of Wellington College, because back then that was what you did. The Commission sent me on one of the biggest

6   Bamford, *The Rise of the Public Schools*, p. xii.

learning curves I have ever experienced. First, I learned that these committees are the last resting place of politicians who have either blown it or are going nowhere. It is therefore the only elephants' graveyard where the elephants are able to shout a message that will, at long last, get them back into the media. These committees are the last resort for MPs who have nowhere else to go.

They are also extraordinarily rude. Reacting offensively to witnesses is a speciality of any committee appointed by the House of Commons. They can be as hostile or negative as they wish. After all, they have a mandate, don't they? In all too many cases, a presupposition of guilt and blame prompts these politicians, meaning that they frequently do not place their witnesses on trial as much as interrogate those whom they have already in their minds found guilty.

The Clarendon Commission was very different. Reading through its records, one is continually struck by how unfailingly *polite* it was in all its dealings.

The manner in which the Commissioners proceeded about their business is interesting, in that to modern eyes it suggests how much the Commissioners probably did *not* know about the schools they reported on rather than how much they did. Their prime source of information was a questionnaire, which in some cases was not returned for nine months, but the point about such a questionnaire is that it was up to the school what answers it gave. There was no independent corroboration of the 'facts' the school provided. As both a cynic and a child of the 1960s, I would be as inclined to believe what public schools said about themselves as I would the men contacted by Kinsey and asked to say how many times they had sex.

The Commissioners, or some of them, did subsequently make visits to the schools, but for almost derisory amounts of time.

They spent three days at Rugby, two at Shrewsbury, Winchester and Harrow, but only one day at the London day schools and, remarkably, only one day at Eton, perhaps because two of the Commissioners, Lord Lyttelton and the Earl of Devon, were Etonians. There were six Commissioners in all. Lord Clarendon himself had never attended school. Edward Twistleton was born in Ceylon and is not recorded as attending any pubic school. Twistleton was the member probably responsible for encouraging the Commission to look, albeit rather perfunctorily, at variations on the classical curriculum. Henry Vaughan went to Rugby, and was a Professor of Modern History at Oxford. Bernard Mountague was the Chichele Professor in International Law at Oxford, and went to Sherborne. A hundred and thirty witnesses were interviewed, science gaining its only entry into the Commission by means of six Fellows of the Royal Society, two doctors, a Professor of Chemistry and a philologist. As noted above, they did take cursory notice of four newly founded schools – Marlborough, Wellington, Cheltenham and City of London – and noticed King's College School, Sandhurst and Woolwich, though interviewing none of the Heads of these. At least one commentator has claimed distinction for the nine Heads of the 'great schools' who were interviewed: Edward Balston (Eton), George Moberly (Winchester, described as 'pompous, dogmatic and pedantic'[7]), Charles Scott (Westminster), Richard Elwyn (Charterhouse), Herbert Kynaston (St Paul's), J. Hessey (Merchant Taylors'), Montagu Butler (Harrow), Frederick Temple (Rugby) and Benjamin Kennedy (Shrewsbury); '. . . the interviewed headmasters showed great variety and some were in their own ways outstanding.'[8]

But I question this. The Commissioners were too late for

7   Alicia Percival, *Very Superior Men*, p. 153.
8   Ibid., p. 139.

Arnold (Rugby) and too early for Thring (Uppingham). Keate (Eton) and Butler (Shrewsbury) were long gone, Sanderson (Oundle) not even a gleam in his parents' eyes. Temple was a future Archbishop, but is better known for that than his headship. All in all, the heads interviewed by the Commission were neither innovators nor educational theorists, but solid and dependable men of their type. The key to the quality of the Clarendon Commission is the relative ease with which the nine heads defeated the Commission's original intent to interview boys. The tendency of the Establishment to ignore the view on education of those who are its recipients – the pupils – has not gone away. In an Ofsted report into the teaching of the most able, written in the first decade of the twenty-first century, buried in an appendix is the pathetic plea of a child: 'If we're meant to be so clever, why don't they ask us what we think?'

The Clarendon Commission achieved some reforms, but in essence it was a fudge. A major cause of its being created in the first place was to investigate the 'convoluted and long-standing practices of dastardly ingenuity, through which the fellows at Eton had pocketed revenue that could have been put to better use if spent on educating the pupils.'[9]

What a pity we no longer use phrases such as 'dastardly ingenuity'. This focus on finance actually handicapped the Commission, in making it relate to one school rather than the generality. It left the Governors and Trustees who had in many cases swindled poor children out of their education largely untroubled. Though it set shockwaves through the system, it set up no regulatory body to ensure that corruption or mismanagement could recur. It did nothing to redress the fact that in the 1860s there

---

9   Turner, *The Old Boys*, p. 139.

was developing a system whereby the rich could buy an education but the poor remained ignorant. It did nothing at all for mass education in England, and may even have helped to establish in English culture the idea that secondary education had to be paid for, and only elementary education should be the responsibility of the state. It entrenched the class element in education.

Years later, when the Victorians decided to channel some of the vast wealth of the Industrial Revolution into a state education system, they did not staff their new schools from the universities, as did France and Germany (hence the German teacher being given the title in common talk of 'Professor'), but rather made teaching the way for the socially aspirational to convert their blue collar into a white one. Socially in England teachers in any school other than public schools have always been below the salt, or sometimes not seated at the table at all. It was the local vicar who was invited to fill the sudden empty space at dinner, not the local schoolmaster. Could the Clarendon Commission have changed this? Probably not. Its culpability is that it allowed itself to be unseated by a potent mixture of influence, politics, delaying tactics and appeals to the law.

The same cannot be said of the soon-to-follow Taunton Report. The Clarendon Commission has obscured what was in potential a far more dramatic and life-changing inquiry, the Taunton Commission. It was set up in 1864, to look at and report on *all* the endowed grammar schools in the UK, not just the 'Great Nine'. It found some extraordinary things, such as thirty-eight schools in Yorkshire and Durham with endowments but no pupils. It also described Sedbergh in Cumbria as merely 'cumbering the ground' on which it stood. The Taunton Commission represents the greatest missed opportunity in English education. Taken individually, the endowments for these schools may have been individually small, but in total provided a massive sum. No one has summed up the situation better than Jonathan Gathorne-Hardy:

> If all these endowments were put together and redistributed on a national scale, they could form the financial core of a great new system of secondary education. The Commission drew up detailed plans for this: the control to be central, via Parliament, a national exam [*sic*] system, regular inspection, a modern curriculum including science. But more than this, the system was to be for everyone, from every class: those too poor to pay would be educated free, those who could afford to pay would do so, augmenting the merged endowments. For a moment, the heart leaps. Supposing this had been done, just supposing those bastions of class and privilege, the new public schools, had been swept ruthlessly away into a national and classless system, and that proper secondary education for everyone had started to come thirty years before . . . it did – how different our country might have been.[10]

How different indeed! But of course it never happened. The proposals in the Endowed Schools Bill were never passed by Parliament. Some endowed-school-founded day schools linked to the Foundation, so that it appeared that they were fulfilling their obligation to educate local, poor children – Harrow founded the John Lyon School, Oundle the Laxton School – but others merely professed their willingness to take poor local children and

---

10 Gathorne-Hardy, *The Public School Phenomenon*, p. 98.

put in the small print that this was of course on the basis of their having an adequate knowledge of Latin. As late as 1940 a Provost of Eton (in effect the live-in Chairman of Governors) declared disingenuously that Eton was open to poor children; all they had to do was know Latin and Greek.[11] No problem, presumably, for the urchin living in Gasworks Row.

One lasting result of the Taunton Commission was the foundation of the Headmasters' Conference, or HMC, of which I was proud then, and still am, to have been elected Chairman.

The Headmasters' Conference

The Headmasters' Conference, known as 'HMC' to the *cognoscenti*, is the organisation that represents the 'top' public schools. It has 277 members, 59 international members and 12 affiliated UK state schools. I have used it in this book as my definition of what constitutes a public school. Its strapline is 'Leading Independent Schools', and, despite the existence of other organisations representing a variety of public schools, it probably does. Given that many of its schools are now coeducational, a considerable number have female Heads and that several girls' schools have joined it, it is now 'the Headmasters' and Headmistresses' Conference'. It is still a misleading title, and a much misunderstood organisation. Yes, it still has an annual conference, and, yes, those who attend it are still the Heads of England's most powerful public schools. Yet the conference after which it was named is only the tip of the iceberg. HMC always was, and still is, the most powerful combination of a trade union (which is actually its legal status) and a network and lobbying group.

---

11 Shrosbee, *Public Schools and Private Education*, p. 220.

HMC was the idea of John Mitchinson, Head of King's, Canterbury, who responded to the threat posed by the Taunton Commission by writing to Edward Thring, Head of Uppingham, in 1869, proposing a meeting of the endowed-school Heads whose schools and jobs were threatened by Taunton, to discuss the proposed legislation. It was an interesting manifestation of a basic and lasting truth about these schools that they truly come together only when someone threatens to close them down.

Thring was initially reluctant, believing that most of the other Heads would be a class beneath him. As it was, twenty-six Heads attended the first meeting, and Thring was pleasantly surprised enough by the experience to describe them as a 'very superior set of men'. Having had someone else think of the idea, take all the risks and push it through to fruition, Thring followed on in the subsequent pattern of many an HMC Head by talking and writing his way to taking all the credit. Though it is heresy to say so, the reason only twelve Heads came to the inaugural meeting at Uppingham in 1869 may have been that Heads tend to react away from Heads dedicated to self-aggrandisement just as the media love them to bits. But Thring was onto a winner. The Sherborne meeting in 1870 attracted thirty-five Heads, and there were fifty in 1871. The ultimate triumph came in 1874, when Eton and Harrow joined, and the rest is history.

'So the elders met, and so the tribes were unified into a nation.'[12]

I was elected by its members in 2004 to be Chairman of HMC, though it beats me how anyone could see it as a nation, never mind unified. I've great respect and no small amount of affection for it, but it makes herding cats look simple. It is an irony that

---

12 Gathorne-Hardy, *The Public School Phenomenon*, p. 99.

HMC members could cast their vote in favour of someone who was described after his first attendance at the Annual Conference as a 'dangerous maverick' (I think that's what I want inscribed on my headstone, if I ever merit one).

In my time as a member, from 1987 until now, HMC has changed dramatically. When I first slunk in as a very junior member, HMC was a gentlemen's club, though unlike the House of Lords not a very good one. It was dominated by a few grandees, Heads of 'major' schools. Dennis Silk, legendary Warden of Radley, held a drinks party at the start of the annual conference, which was rather like the shepherd's-pie party Jeffrey Archer used to hold before the Conservative Party Conference: an invitation to attend meant you were 'in', not being there meant you were 'out'. I was never invited. I used to come back from the annual conference terminally depressed. Like so many conferences, it was typified by people saying hello, shaking your hand and all the time looking over your shoulder to see if there was anyone more important behind you. It also managed to give the impression that somewhere else something terribly important was happening, but that you weren't at it.

I made both points in my speech at conference as Chairman, commenting that being Chairman appeared to make no difference to either manifestation, and added my serious criticism of HMC. There is a rank order of public schools, based often as much on their historical strength and influence as on their current achievement. Heads tended to be judged on the perceived ranking of their schools, rather than their personal qualities. Thus I received much respect as High Master of St Paul's and The Manchester Grammar School, but I could just as easily have been appointed Head of Dotheboys Hall or the school previously run by Jimmy Edwards.

People apply for headships when they've accumulated enough

experience or amassed enough career points, or the move is convenient for their children's education or their partners' careers. The headships that are available for them to apply for in any given year are random, depending on who is retiring that year, who has died or who has taken themselves out of the race by doing something disgraceful with Matron or whatever. A further random factor is added by the fact that Heads are chosen by Governing Bodies, often united by the fact that their only experience of running a school was that once upon a time they were a pupil at one.

'Random' is far too logical and reasonable a word to use of the process. There needs to be a new version of Gray's 'Elegy Written in a Country Churchyard' – perhaps Stephen's as yet unwritten 'Elegy on the Graveyard of a Minor Public School' – pointing out that many a person who could conceivably have led Eton to even greater heights of glory instead spent their days busting their gut to lure in the fee-paying pupil who would allow St Cake's to break even at the end of the year.

John Cleese's film *Clockwise* gives a brilliantly dramatic portrayal of HMC from the starting point of the fictional first-ever state school Head to be elected Chairman. It is an outstanding film, and lousy reality, bearing no relationship to what HMC is really like, but rather choosing to present it as people might think it ought to be. Actually, the reality is far less interesting. I once got into trouble for describing it as 250 overweight men in grey suits bragging about the size of their sports halls. It was, I now concede, grossly unfair.

It may indeed be true that in the late 1800s the tribes united and became a nation, but there is a strong argument that, like many an African or Arabian country 'unified' under colonial or other rule, it has reverted to tribalism, and so lost power. If it ever was a nation, it had one huge credit, and one huge demerit. The credit is that, unless parents are willing to pay huge sums out of taxed income to public schools, they cease to exist. This means that, in order to survive, public schools have to provide the education that parents want for their children, a commercial imperative absent from state schools. Personally, I trust parents to know what is best for their children far more than I trust politicians, pundits or 'educationalists'. We live in a world where the media are frequently hijacked by people who tell us what children need. I prefer to listen to those who state what they want for their children. The difference between the pundit and the parent? The parent loves their child. The pundit loves their career.

The demerit? Public schools are in the fiercest possible competition with themselves. When I was High Master of St Paul's I knew that, for the school to match its historical levels of academic success, I was in direct completion for the brightest and best pupils with Eton, Westminster, Winchester and King's College, Wimbledon. As it happened, I knew, liked and respected the Heads of three of those schools – the fourth I had simply never come across – which did not reduce the competition as such, but made it more gentlemanly. Nevertheless, Heads of public schools answer to their Governing Bodies for their success, not to HMC. If a public school has, say, a brilliant idea for the teaching of maths, its first instinct is not to share it with its competitors. Why should it do so? The result is that public schools have never been the hotbeds of innovation and experimentation that their independence from government should have allowed then to be. 'The rule about public schools is that they never initiate . . . they imitate, then intensify and finally entomb.'[13]

---

13 Ibid., p. 120.

This weakness – the failure to experiment or innovate – is also the downside of the dependence on parents. No one likes their child to be experimented on. The story of England's 'progressive' schools (those that delighted in experiment and the excitement of the new), such as Bedales, Dartington Hall, Abbotsholme and Summerhill, is and has been a topic for other books, but the fact is that, interesting though these schools are, they have never been accepted by the Establishment and their pupils have been singularly unsuccessful in achieving any eminence within that Establishment. Their founders might view their greatest success as being the fact that they have failed to provide pillars for a manipulative Establishment. The Establishment itself scorns such a view, and for hundreds of years has defined success as belonging to those who have played its games by its own rules, and come out on top. Prior to the Clarendon Commission the public schools were not places for learning anything new. Rather, they were the places for the children of those who held the social and economic power in England to learn and be confirmed in the rules of the game.

However, HMC has a further weakness so great that it amounts to a fatal flaw. It elects a new Chairman every year from Heads who are members. For this reason no individual can build up a sustained power base in the organisation (something members would hate) and, crucially, no Chairman ever become powerful enough to dare to tell schools what to do. The system may suit Heads who don't wish to be bossed around or contribute to a fellow Head's knighthood, but government and other power bases (including the media) hate it. No sooner do they become accustomed to dealing with someone than the person is gone, with the result that, by and large, government don't bother, and a potentially hugely powerful lobby is disempowered. The old Secondary Heads' Association, representing state school heads, had a general secretary who could shoot from the hip in response to any educational issue, and pick up the pieces afterwards if he offended any members. HMC is more likely to shoot the Chairman for being presumptuous.

A second weakness, crippling if not fatal, is that headship is a full-time job. I know at least one governing body of a top school that refused its Head permission to stand as Chair of HMC on the basis that the school could not spare him. Common sense and most management consultants would argue that the chairmanship of HMC ought to be a salaried post, full time and not combined with a headship and have a tenure of at least three years. Common sense has never ruled HMC.

A missed opportunity

The Clarendon Commission was an opportunity missed. It was also the classic example of 'great' institutions using the Establishment of which they were so crucial a part to divert, delay and discourage reform. Whether it realised it or not, the Clarendon Commission was outwitted by its potential victims. It took place at a crucial time in history, a cusp or watershed, which makes its failure even more regrettable. Prior to its time, the great Victorians or initiators of the Industrial Revolution – Stephenson, Brunel, Arkwright and the rest – had been able to fly to where they were by the seat of their pants, without the need for much in the way of a scientific, technical or mathematical education. They were a little like the Norman church builders, who had no knowledge of physics or the capacity of load-bearing walls, so just built them thick and heavy. You knew you'd got it wrong if it fell down.

But, increasingly after the 1860s, second-stage technology did require a basic knowledge of maths and science. Critics of that argument might seek to destroy it by citing the fact that Britain produced the first technological masterpiece of the twentieth century in the first all-big-gun battleship, HMS *Dreadnought*, in 1906. Yet *Dreadnought* achieved its fame and gave its name to a whole class of ship not because it brought in new technology. Other nations, notably the Italians and the Americans, had designed and were building similar ships. Rather, it won its place in history because Britain was simply able to build it more quickly than other nations, claiming to have done so in a year.

The Clarendon Commission could have sounded a clarion call to English education to rise to and respond to the times. Its recommendations as to curriculum and teaching are feeble beyond belief – and how different might that have been if its authors had sought to challenge rather than to perpetuate? A modern historian such as Correlli Barnett waxes poetic about the damage the reactionary and conservative public schools did to Britain in the modern world. I suspect he overstates the case, but there can be no doubt that their essentially backward-looking culture in its worship of dead languages and its general snootiness about maths and science did Britain a severe disservice.

Yet here again the sniping at public schools is all too easy. Yes, they were the dominant educational culture in the 1920s and 1930s, and they did discourage 'modern' subjects. Yet they were also part of the society that created the Spitfire, the Wellington bomber and the Mosquito; had far more sophisticated radar than the supposedly technologically savvy Germans; and was far ahead in the development of sonar, or ASDIC, as it was known in the war. It is worth remembering that Barnes Wallis went to Christ's Hospital, Winston Churchill went to Harrow and Alan Turing to Sherborne.

4

PLAY UP! PLAY UP! AND PLAY THE GAME: PUBLIC SCHOOLS AND THE WORSHIP OF SPORT

'Athleticism was one of the few new institutions of the late Victorian public school which was typical and universal.'[14]

Edward Thring, one of the most famous Victorian Head-masters, I was told as a child started his career at Uppingham by grabbing a cricket bat, hitting the ball for six and declaring, 'Now I am Headmaster!' It all depends on the quality of the ball he was required to hit, one might think (would you bowl out a Headmaster who had the power to beat you?) but apocryphal myths do not feed on facts. The important thing is not whether or not the incident happened, but the fact that it is told, revealing as it does the priorities of many Victorian public schools. Yet it is frequently forgotten that the 1850s and 1860s saw a marked growth in the worship of athleticism in the colleges of Oxford and Cambridge, marked by the purchase of playing fields and the

---

14   De Honey, *Tom Brown's Universe*, p. 117.

moving of the timing of dinner in hall from 3 o'clock to 5 o'clock or later, to allow for more daylight playing time. The public schools did not prompt this change. Where Oxbridge leads, public schools follow. Ironically, it was the flow of teachers *from* Oxbridge back into the public schools that gave the worship of team sport an even greater boost:

> The culmination of this tendency was the appointment of men on games ability alone, illustrated by the story told in *The Contemporary Review* in 1900 of a university blue [the full blue was first established for the boat race, then much extended in 1853–5] who on completing his century in the university cricket match received telegrams from five different headmasters with offers of posts.[15]

T. C. Worsley gives this account of his appointment to Wellington in the 1930s:

> It was purely on my athletic record that, after leaving Cambridge, I became an Assistant Master at a well-known public school. At my own school, Marlborough, I had been in the Cricket Eleven for three years, and in the Rugger Fifteen my last year. At Cambridge I had done pretty well all round at games and had kept well within the Old Boy network. That was the important thing for job-getting in those days. It more than counteracted a poor II_2 in Classics and an even poorer Third in English.[16]

---

15 Ibid., p. 113.
16 Worsley, *Flannelled Fool*, p. 11.

This resonated with me when I first read it, and I could not understand why. Then I remembered the succession of brain-dead Cambridge graduates, who had clearly collided head first with too many rugby posts, who had 'taught' me at Uppingham, and dried up for evermore any enthusiasm I might have had for the subjects they taught. I seem to remember that geography took more than its fair share of these less-than-incredible hulks. 'Bacchus [nickname] was "reading" geography, that curious "option" which the fanatical athletes used, to procure some sort of a degree – if only a pass degree – without their actually working for it.'[17]

The birth of athleticism as the equal to Christianity in public schools can be dated very specifically. In the early years of the public schools and right up to the Victorian period, sport, such as it was, was often seen as hooliganism by any other name. Boys of St Peter's, York, were caught playing football in the Minster, for which one Christopher Dobson was put in the stocks and given 'six yerkes with a birchen rod on the buttocks'.[18] In the 1850s and early 1860s, 'There were hardly enough spectators at the Eton–Harrow cricket match to form a continuous line round Lord's.'[19] Yet, in 1872 and 1873, 27,000 people paid a shilling each to watch the match.

The cricket team at Clifton who finally managed to beat their great rival Cheltenham in the 1880s, after three defeats and three draws, were met on their return by the whole school, more than six hundred of them. The horses were removed from the carriage, and a phalanx of boys drew the coach to its final destination (seriously injuring three boys, it has to be said, and nearly killing

---

17   Ibid., p. 42.
18   Rodgers, *Old Public Schools*, p. 14.
19   Ibid., p. 115.

the Headmaster). In this context it is also worth pointing out that Wellington's comment that Waterloo was won on the playing fields of Eton had nothing to do with organised games, which did not exist at the time. Rather, if he said anything at all, Wellington was referring to the mob-organised brawls, fights by any other name, that passed for sport and frequently resulted in serious injury and even death for the participants. In this area at least, *Tom Brown's Schooldays* gives an accurate account of the early version of team sports in the battle in which the plucky young 'un East is injured.

Physical courage and strength was the virtue most admired in the all-male construct of the public school. I say 'was', but this virus has proved very difficult to eradicate. It was certainly alive and well at Radley College in the mid-1970s, when a pupil wrote:

> Perhaps the one aspect of Radley that impressed me most was the extraordinary part that sport takes in the conversation of boys and dons [Radley slang for teachers] . . . From the third week in term it is difficult to find a table in Hall which is not talking about rugby in some way.[20]

As mentioned above, team sports, and primitive forms of rugby, were a relatively late creation, however, surfacing in time for a major mention in *Tom Brown's Schooldays* in 1857. The 'match' between School House and the rest of Rugby is by modern standards a chaotic bloodbath, as the Eton Wall Game remains to this day, albeit with more mud than blood. These particular instances give rise to myths aplenty. As I'm given to understand it

---

20 Heale, *School Quad*, p. 101.

by people who care about this sort of thing, it is almost certainly a fabrication that Thomas Webb picked up the ball and ran with it to found the modern game of rugby. As to the Eton Wall Game, I neither know nor care very much when a goal was last scored in that game. I do know that I had dinner once with an Old Etonian who clearly did care, and the date receded by ten years with every glass of wine he drank.

As the rules became more and more formalised towards the end of the nineteenth century, so team sport came to matter more and more in the ethos of a school. Worship of athleticism in young males is beautifully summed up by John Betjeman, describing Chapel at Marlborough in *Summoned By Bells*:

'The centre and the mainspring of your lives,
The inspiration for your work and sport,
The corporate life of this great public school
Spring from its glorious chapel. Day by day
You come to worship in its noble walks,
Hallowed by half a century of prayer.'
The Old Marlburian Bishop thundered on
When all I worshipped were the athletes, ranged
In the pews opposite.[21]

The athletes had ample time to establish their supremacy. The Clarendon Commission in 1864 found that the average Harrovian would spend fifteen hours a week playing cricket. As a latter-day Headmaster, I would see that as about the minimum amount of time my various admirable masters in charge of cricket would deem to be suitable for the sport. I love watching cricket.

---

21   Betjeman, *Summoned by Bells*, p. 67.

At the same time, I remember it as being an exam result killer (it takes up so much *time* in the summer term), and being told by a glum admissions tutor at Cambridge in my first year of headship, 'There are only two things that make me think a bright boy will end up with a third-class degree. The first is if he plays cricket; the second is if he acts.' There was no danger of the Victorian public school encouraging its boy to act. Indeed, the instructions to the architects of Haileybury's 'Big School', or school hall, were to make it as unsuitable for drama as possible. They succeeded: I directed three plays there. If you want a measure of how much public schools have changed, you only have to compare those days with the modern Haileybury, whose pride and joy is the Alan Ayckbourn Theatre.

Worship of the sportsman is found in almost every public-school memoir or semiautobiographical novel. Here is Alec Waugh writing in *The Loom of* Youth, the book that got him removed from the list of Sherborne old boys:

> The only thing he realised was that for those who wore a blue and gold ribbon ['colours' for rugby] laws ceased to exist. It was apparently rather advantageous to get into the Fifteen. He had not looked on athletics in that light before. Obviously his preparatory school had failed singularly to keep level with the times. He had always been told by the masters there that games were only important for training the body. But at Fernhurst [Waugh's thinly disguised Sherborne] they seemed the one thing that mattered. To the athlete all things are forgiven. There was clearly a lot to learn.[22]

---

22   Waugh, *The Loom of Youth*, p. 21.

This worship of sport was not something that died after the end of World War Two. Here is a pupil writing in the mid-1960s:

> A place on the rugger XV is more important than a place in the National Youth Orchestra. Sport is taken very seriously and it is wise to show keenness and enthusiasm in all sports. Apathy in games brands one as being a wet for a long time here.[23]

At roughly the same time I remember as a pupil at Uppingham that the whole school was ordered to turn out to cheer on (or not) the First XV on a Saturday afternoon.

But it's there also in *Death of a Salesman* by the American Arthur Miller. Willy Loman's son, Biff, rules the roost at high school, the greatest desire of Bernard, the wimpish son of Willy's neighbour, being to carry Biff's boots to the big match. In adult life, the wimpish Bernard calls in to see his father on his way to address the Supreme Court, while in adult life Biff has become a washed-out thief and ex-con.

There were tremendous advantages to the management in the cult of sport. It was not only that: as a writer in 1901 commented, 'It is the opinion of competent judges that the more athletics flourish in our public schools, the less vice will be found in them.'[24]

A driver behind the worship of sport was the belief that to exhaust a boy physically was to exhaust him sexually: 'By the late Victorian period a consensus prevailed that the two easiest ways to keep a boy's mind free of temptation was to toughen him up physically . . .';[25] and, 'One reason for the tremendous emphasis

---

23 Royston Lambert, *Hothouse Society*, p. 105.
24 Hickson, *The Poisoned Bowl*, p. 38.
25 Ibid., p. 37.

on "healthy" games . . . has been the master's desire to leave no room for anything else. "My prophylactic against certain unclean microbes was to send the boys to bed dead tired," the headmaster of the United Services College admitted to his most distinguished old boy.'[26]

It was also thought that sport provided a topic for conversation that would supersede sex. That's certainly the impression given in the Billy Bunter stories.

Of course sport was seen as an antidote to sex, but it was more than this. It diverted aggression, revolt and rebellion among adolescents into socially acceptable pastimes – and who is going to say that is a bad thing in an age in which gang violence dominates so many inner cities?

My introduction to the power of sport and athleticism was four years spent as Second Master at Sedbergh School in Cumbria. Sedbergh sits in one of the harsher areas of Cumbria, where the hills are not softened by water as in nearby Lakeland. The school sits in the shadow of Winder, a hill that defies its actual height by seeming to lower over the town and the school. In my time there in the early 1980s Sedbergh was renowned for rugby. I sometimes felt on entering the Chapel that, if someone had put rugby posts on the altar in place of the Cross, no one would have noticed. The Victorian songs still sung at the school epitomised the Victorian public school's devotion to sport. The refrain of one song was, 'Scorn defeat and laugh at pain'. I felt it could have been summarised by saying that if you didn't bleed at the end of it, it probably wasn't doing you much good.

Alongside the vision of manly strength favoured by many at the school back then, there were a vein of Old Boys who

---

26 Lamb, *The Happiest Days*, p. 45.

manifested what in my experience has often been the flipside of an overdevotion to sporting achievement, namely a strong fear and distrust of women. I say this simply because in my experience the schoolmasters and the schools most devoted to sport were those who showed the greatest fear and distrust of women. My wife was one of the first women to teach at Sedbergh, and the first to teach science. At the end of her first year, when for the first time in history the female-taught Fourth Form chemistry, Set 2, beat the male-taught Fourth Form chemistry, Set 1, in the end-of-year exams, the only way a male teacher could find to compliment her was to say, 'Well done, Jenny! You know, you teach just like a man!' I remember cringing at one old boys' dinner when the simpering wife of an old boy, bearing a striking resemblance to Olive Oyl in the *Popeye* cartoons, leaned over to me and confided in all seriousness, 'I think it's wonderful if boys and girls haven't mingled before marriage. The sense of mystery!' Times have moved on indeed, and Sedbergh is now coeducational. What my recollections reveal is the extraordinary speed of change in public schools, when they decide they need to change.

The Victorian public schools were terrified of sexuality, whereas for the most part their predecessors simply let their pupils get on with it, as with most things. It is no accident that the worship of sport coincides with the rise of the Victorian public school. Sport was an outlet for male aggression, a way of enforcing tribal loyalties, but also a counter-aphrodisiac. It is almost impossible to quote anything that proves this, simply because the Victorians and their successors were far too embarrassed to talk about sex, the nearest they came being thundering condemnations of 'vile practices' from the pulpit. Yet, as a schoolboy at Uppingham in 1964, I remember being warned in all seriousness, with the rest of the team, not to masturbate before a crucial House match.

Sport filled almost every afternoon, and even on Sundays we were kicked out of the House for a walk, or played fives because there was nothing else to do. We understood this was to ensure that, come the evening and night, we were too tired to engage in evil thoughts or 'hanky-panky'. From memory, I believe it was singularly unsuccessful.

Just as the worship of sport was essentially antithetical to a civilised view of women, so it dealt a death blow to the worship or even cultivation of the intellect. This is beautifully summarised in *Tom Brown's Schooldays*, which in common with most fictional accounts of public schools (and, for that matter, *The Lord of the Rings*) treats sexuality by completely ignoring its existence. 'Pater' Brooke is the House Captain of School House, and a hero figure: 'plain, strong and straight, like his play'.[27] After a famous victory over the Rest of the School, Brooke announces to the adoring throng, '"I know I'd sooner win two School house matches running than get the Balliol scholarship any day" – (frantic cheers).'[28]

One of the many unintentional ironies in *Tom Brown's Schooldays* is the fact that this demigod proceeds to deliver a lecture on the evils of bullying, after which Tom, a new boy, is tossed in a blanket.

Greater experts than myself can comment on whether or not the male brain is hard-wired to worship sport as well as sex. What I would vouch for is that when a lot of males are gathered together, required to live supposedly chastely in semi-monastic communities largely separated from the company of women, a number of things happen, with the worship of sporting prowess being one of them. Just look at those sepia photographs of Victorian or turn-of-the-century public-school teams – the

27 Hughes, *Tom Brown's Schooldays*, p. 114.
28 Ibid., p. 115

insouciance, the arrogance. They were masters of all they surveyed, demigods.

It is also fair to say that what these schoolboys learned on the playing fields probably stood them in better stead if they proceeded to work in or for the Empire, or the armed forces.

Sport became inextricably entwined with the standing of a public school. Its fixture lists defined the type of school it was. In 1866 Westminster delivered a slap to the upstart Shrewsbury:

> The Captain of the Westminster Eleven is sorry to disappoint Shrewsbury, but Westminster plays no schools except Public Schools, and the general feeling in the school quite coincides with that of the Committee of the Public Schools Club, who issue this list of Public Schools – Charterhouse, Eton, Harrow, Rugby, Westminster and Winchester.[29]

The fact that these things change is shown by Westminster's having rejected Charterhouse in 1818. Rather later, the American Ivy League of universities was to be arrived at by much the same means, as in who played whom at sport.

The sadness of this is that sport needs to play a crucial part in modern education, and the excessive devotion to it of the public schools has done it no favours. The seven-year-old who is goalie for the Third XI learns a lot about resilience and coping with failure when they droop home having nine goals slotted past them. Teamwork and risk management are vital skills for an adult, as are commitment and dedication, and these are all skills that can be learned easily from sporting activity. This is one area

---

29 Ogilvie, *The English Public School*, p. 168.

where the modern public schools deserve credit. I can't remember how many of the most successful Rugby XVs in recent memory at St Paul's in my time as High Master went on to win places at Oxford or Cambridge, but it was a lot; so much for the legacy of young Brooke, proving you could win Cock House *and* get a top scholarship to Baliol.

The other thing about public-school sport was its encouragement of the amateur. Winning was a jolly good thing, but one had to do it without being seen to try too hard. It was the cult of the 'gentleman versus player'; it was dreadfully working-class to be paid for playing sport, and, in some vague, undefined way, unfair.

I have a personal gripe against the public-school addiction to team sports, which is not merely that I was no good at them, but the memory I mentioned earlier of being taught a variety of subjects by brain-dead Oxbridge graduates who had clearly been hired because of their Oxford rugby blue rather than their intellect. Academic snobbery? You didn't have to sit through forty minutes of their reading from the textbook about glaciers.

The victim of the obsession with games was academic endeavour. It affected feeder schools as much as senior schools. Leonard Woolf was at St Paul's from 1893 to 1899. Of his prep. school, Arlington House, and of St Paul's until he met a certain teacher he wrote, '... it is a remarkable fact that until the age of sixteen, when at St Paul's I got into A.M.Cook's form, none of my teachers ... ever suggested to me that it was possible to read a work of literature or other serious book for pleasure'[30]

There were and always have been inspirational teachers at St Paul's. It is also true that the boy who was reasonable at games

---

30   Woolf, *Sowing – An Autobiography of the Years 1880–1904*, p. 66

could get by with being an intellectual as well, as again was shown at Arlington House: 'I was sufficiently good at games to make intelligence and hard work pass as an eccentricity instead of being chastised as vice or personal nastiness.'[31]

And it is true that boys who were not good at team sports could boost their self-esteem and the regard they were held in by their peers by involvement in non-team sports. Cross-country running and fives provided such an opportunity, as in a small number of other schools did fencing and sailing.

However, the idea that the public schools were the cause of the English becoming a mass of Philistines is completely unfounded. In one tiny area alone prior to 1914 – poetry – they managed not to do any visible harm to Siegfried Sassoon, Robert Graves, Rupert Brooke, Edmund Blunden, James Elroy Flecker and Edward Thomas. Marlborough helped to develop Charles Hamilton Sorley, one of the most brilliant poets and minds killed in the war. There is no evidence that English artists were inferior to their European or other counterparts. Byron was sufficiently proud of having played for Harrow in the first Eton-versus-Harrow cricket match that long after the event he was prepared to exaggerate his score in that match.[32] What is probably true is that the public schools had a dire effect on the study of science and maths, taking these as subjects to be respected out of the culture of the English ruling class. A number of Heads genuinely thought maths and science were lacking as subjects because they had no ability to *humanise* the learner. They appeared to overlook the fact that at the time most children had the classics flogged into them, hardly the best way of humanising a person.

The glass has been fogged by the fact that *middle-class* English

---

31   Ibid., p. 69
32   Marples, *Romantics at School*, p. 132.

culture, which affected the public schools but was not the same as it, chose as its most popular literary heroes such figures as feature in John Buchan novels, or Bulldog Drummond. These get out of problems by one mighty leap of their body, not their brain.

There was a further dimension to the Victorian worship of sport. It was believed that not just battles were won on the playing fields, but whole Empires won through the features inculcated in boys by team sport. These virtues included team leadership, courage, fortitude, determination, resilience and organisational skills. The idea that sport prepared young boys to be the stars of the future is shown at its most offensive in Sir Henry Newbolt's poem 'Vitaï Lampada' ('The Close' is the cricket field at Clifton, the 'ribbon'd coat' the colours awarded to top boy players):

> There's a breathless hush in The Close tonight –
> Ten to make and the match to win –
> A bumping pitch and a blinding light,
> An hour to play and the last man in.
> And it's not for the sake of a ribbon'd coat,
> Or the selfish hope of a season's fame,
> But his Captain's hand on his shoulder smote –
> 'Play up! Play up! And play the game!'

> The sand of the desert is sodden red, –
> Red with the wreck of a square that broke; –
> The Gatling's jammed and the Colonel dead,
> 'And the regiment blind with dust and smoke.
> 'The river of death has brimmed his banks,
> And England's far, and Honour a name,
> But the voice of a schoolboy rallies the ranks:
> 'Play up! Play up! And play the game!'

Newbolt's poem takes pride in seeing Zulus, natives or whatever as mere players in a game of sport, and indeed assumes that killing people is itself a game. Every professional soldier I've met believes that any jumped-up little squirt telling soldiers to play up, play up and play the game in the middle of a ferocious battle would be more than likely to be shot by his own men, never mind killed by the enemy.

But hold on. It is rather too easy to mock the Victorian public-school boy dashing around with his knees covered disposing of natives as if a colonial war were little more than a qualifier for the World Cup, where lives rather than goals were the measure of success. Sport *is* healthy for young people, and we of all generations, who are producing a generation of obese children whose main exercise is to move their thumbs on the controls of an Xbox, can hardly afford to feel superior to our predecessors. It doesn't stop there. The child whose team has lost 9–0 learns resilience, and in our world, which increasingly tries to overprotect children, the ability to cope with failure is an essential skill for a successful life. Those trying to counter gang culture have found involvement in team sport a superb method of redirecting aggression into a socially acceptable channel.

I could bang on at length, but need not do so. Sport is a good thing for young people to do, with massive physical and mental positives for those who take part, and the public schools have flown that particular flag through times when no child was allowed to lose a race in case it rendered them permanently damaged. Throughout their history, public schools have failed to rise to challenges, most notably the challenge to teach maths and science, but at other times this conservatism has provided an antidote to the occasional madness of fashion in education. This does not apply only to the usefulness of team sports in educating a child: public schools have stubbornly hung onto a sense of the importance of art, drama and music. They actually invented the concept of a child's paying back some of the debt he or she owes to the wider community, in the form of Community Service and, back in history, the Boys' Club movement. For all its sins, Uppingham was sending me as a young boy in the 1960s into the seedier end of the town to talk to a lonely old lady who, far from feeling patronised, said, genuinely, I believe, 'You're a lifesaver.'

Perhaps even more importantly, public schools clung to the tradition of separate academic subjects and resisted the dreadful move to lumping the arts together into a bland and beige amorphous mass called 'humanities'. In effect, the public schools at times have acted like the spectator who called out the truth on the Emperor's New Clothes, acting like a layer of acid thrown on the trendy, the fad and the latest fashion. They have not always discriminated in the hurling of that acid, but their capacity to get it right and to get it wrong in equal measure is, for me, part of their fascination.

The public schools at times defy categorisation. How else do you explain that, despite their reputation as capitals of corporal punishment, more boys were caned in one term during my teaching practice in a state school in 1971 than in my whole four years at Uppingham? The Manchester Grammar School was sending boys to camps in the Lake District (absolutely brilliant events, which thrive and prosper to the present day) when outdoor pursuits to most MPs meant fox hunting. This injection of a variety of genes into the educational system is a major reason for keeping the public schools. They have frequently appeared to be out of tune with 'modern' times. As anyone who looks at a 1970s tower block can confirm, modern times do not always have the answer for the future. The English public school has frequently adhered to traditions that are outdated or simply reprehensible, and been condemned for so doing. At other times, it has preserved proven good practice, and preserved it against the assault of the trendy and fashionable. At times I've found myself comparing it to a zoo, an institution in itself increasingly under attack. Public schools have acted to preserve endangered educational species, albeit in an environment that many find artificial and untenable, that might otherwise face extinction.

5

MUSCULAR CHRISTIANITY: PUBLIC SCHOOLS AND THE WORSHIP OF CHRISTIANITY

'Sermons preached in public school chapels could be a
powerful agent of social control.'[1]

Outwardly there is little or no correlation between religious belief and athleticism, as suggested in the phrase 'muscular Christianity'. One of the more perfect statements of what it was came from Dr Potts, Head of Fettes between 1870 and 1889: 'I should like my boys, and all boys, and all men, to be ever mindful in the hottest scrimmage and at the most exciting period of the game, that they are not only football players but also Christian gentlemen.'[2]

I was reminded of this phrase while watching the hottest scrimmage at a most exciting period in a game between the England rugby team and Australia, and imagining myself as the coach addressing the team at half-time to be mindful that they were not

1   May, *The Victorian Public School*, p. 6.
2   De Honey, *Tom Brown's Universe*, p. 228.

only rugby players, but Christian gentlemen. I don't think, as far as half-time talks go, that it will win us the World Cup.

What is noteworthy about the Victorian public school in particular is that contemporary praise of the public schools (and, in the latter years of Victoria, virtually all the coverage given the schools was praise) did not laud them for producing Christians, or for producing gentlemen, but for producing the combination – the 'Christian gentleman'. It was as if one could not be a gentleman without being a Christian, and only gentlemen were real Christians.

Just as does the link with sport and athleticism, the link with religion lies deep within the DNA of the public-school system. It was how they controlled their pupils, how they gave a moral dimension to their existence and a central part of how they defined their product. The influence came from the top. Many of those who founded the schools that became public schools were churchmen. Colet, who founded St Paul's School, was Dean of St Paul's. Hugh Oldham, who founded Manchester Grammar School, was Bishop of Exeter. William of Wykeham founded Winchester to train boys for the Church, and early pupils had to wear the tonsure, or monk's haircut. When Thomas Arnold fired up those who cared with his sanctimonious Christian hypocrisy, he was not a revolutionary, but a revivalist. Public schools may have been a seminaries for the Anglican church in that many of their pupils and indeed their staff went on to high positions in the Church, but the reverse is also true. Most of the Heads and many of the teachers who formed the public schools were ordained clergymen.

Buried deep in the catalogue of the Cambridge University Library, and not, I imagine, the most borrowed book in its collection, is a work by Arthur C. Champneys, grandly titled *A Soldier in Christ's Army – An Explanation of Confirmation and the*

Catechism for Public School Boys.[3] The title alone tells you a great deal about public schools and religion. Public schools understood armies – after all, in their hierarchies and their quest for unthinking obedience they were quite like an army themselves – and there was something deeply satisfying to them in thinking that their boys were an army that would take good old European Christianity out to the barbaric natives of the world, bash them over the head and worse with it and perhaps even subjugate them through it. Christianity in general gave public schools their morality, or at least allowed them to pretend it did. They were pretty Godless places, so they needed some moral purpose, or at least a mechanism to pretend to the outside world that they had one. I quote elsewhere the comment that, before Arnold, Rugby was a bear pit, and during his time it was a bear pit in which the boys compulsorily attended Sunday Chapel.

To my mind the public schools are at their most hypocritical when it comes to their adoption of a very localised and naïve interpretation of Christianity. When the Normans conquered England, they put up two buildings to dominate London's skyline. One was the Tower of London, to proclaim their mastery over their subjects' bodies. The other was the first St Paul's Cathedral, burned down in 1666, to proclaim their mastery over their subjects' souls. So it was with the public schools. Christian worship was the Establishment, and the Establishment was Christian worship. If the birch or the ash rod was the symbol of the school's dominance over the bodies of their pupils, so Chapel was the symbol of the school's dominance over their souls. And it was as a pretty boiled-down, simplified and simplistic version of Christianity that they used to exercise that dominance.

I find it extraordinary now to recollect that, when I was a new boy

---

3   For those who can't wait to buy it, it was published in London by George Bell & Sons in 1900.

at a public school in 1962, I was required to attend two services every Sunday, a Matins and an Evensong. When I was confirmed in the faith (note *when*, rather than *if* – it simply did not occur to me as even a vague possibility that I might opt out) that rose to three, though admittedly early-morning communion was not compulsory. I also find it extraordinary that in the hundreds of thousands of words I have read for this book that have been written by public-school boys, I cannot think of one from any age that castigates, criticises or challenges compulsory Christianity. There are plenty of complaints about Headmasters 'prosing' (lecturing) pupils about wrongdoings in Chapel, or the terrible risks of a certain physical indulgence so horrific it could not be named even in a forty-minute address. Incidentally, I've yet to meet anyone of my generation who was actually told it made you blind. The reason why these diatribes were delivered in Chapel is prosaic and simple. In many schools for many years the Chapel was the only building capable of housing the whole school, or a large part of it. Pupils often *used* Chapel as the forum for rebellion by not turning up, hissing or booing unpopular speakers and undertaking singing strikes. Yet all these were not protests about enforced religion, as such, but merely used the opportunities the ritual of forced religion allowed.

To be personal again, the tradition of using Chapel as an expression of rebellion against the Establishment was alive and well when my brother's eldest boy went to a leading public school in the mid-1970s. He proudly boasts that he sat through only one full Chapel service in all his five years in school. At that first service, as a new boy, he realised that one could slip into a seat towards the furthest aisle behind the prefects, have one's name taken as present and slip out again, with no one the wiser. To my eternal regret I never latched onto this at Uppingham. Instead I chose to smoke cigarettes, as the only way I could break the rules with a reasonable chance of not being caught. I remember the delicious sense of risk to this day, and the strange taste in the mouth of nicotine and Trebor mints, preferred over Polos because they had a stronger kick.

Of course, part of this is the recurrent theme of this book, that the public schools simply reflected the society – or that portion of the society – that they served. For most of the time that the public schools served the Establishment, Christianity was central to the existence of that Establishment, and as automatic as breathing. In the sense that it could serve Lord and Master and Servant at the same time, Christianity was the ideal belief-set for the public schools. It preached obedience, turning the other cheek and acceptance of the civil authority, acceptance in fact of much that was wrong, including the oppression, intimidation and violence of Roman rule. At the same time, its principal hero and leader was an underdog, clearly a member of that very same oppressed minority. As a friend of mine at school commented, 'No wonder this lot like Jesus!' – 'This lot' was the ruling powers in the school – 'He didn't hang Pontius Pilate from a lamppost. He let him crucify him.' I often wonder what happened to that boy. I hope he became a Bishop, as I became a Headmaster.

Yet it is important to remember that, vital though Christianity was to the Establishment, it is not always possible for the Establishment to force its will upon the people. Part of the fanaticism of Arnold and Woodard is down to the fact that Christianity was arguably in decline in the nineteenth century, as the cosy world of the village – in which the squire and local employers would know exactly who was and who was not at church on Sunday – was replaced by the teeming millions of the big industrial cities. The Victorians made a massive effort to overcome the impact of a growing population, the move to cities and the Industrial Revolution, not least by launching a massive church-building programme. Many of the new towns, cities and suburbs had no place of worship. Despite this significant financial contribution, and the success of Methodism in appealing to the new working classes, the Industrial Revolution in effect saw Christianity, and in particular Anglicanism, lose its grip over English culture and society.

Yet, even where that faith was being beaten into pupils, it provoked no great evangelical revival. The number of public-school boys entering the Church fell significantly between 1830 and 1880.[4] The problem, of course, was that institutionalised Christianity did not instil faith in pupils, but merely compliance while it was necessary. The mere fact that authority supported Christianity resulted in a certain attitude to it from the boys, summed up by the remarkably accurate Alec Waugh:

> As is the case with most boys, Confirmation had little effect on Gordon. He was not an atheist; he accepted Christianity in much the same way that he accepted the Conservative Party. All the best people believed in it, so it was bound to be all right; but at the same time, it had not the slightest influence over his actions. If he had any religion at the time, it was House football.[5]

Another novel that caused a great stir by appearing to criticise public schools, *The Harrovians* by Arnold Lunn, has in it, 'It is easy to exaggerate the harm caused by confirmation. The average boy . . . soon relapses into cheerful paganism.'[6]

---

4   See Appendix F of Gathorne-Hardy, *The Public School Phenomenon*.
5   Waugh, *The Loom of Youth*, p. 88.
6   Lunn, *The Harrovians*, p. 141.

An eighteen-year-old boy in the 1960s speaks for many when he writes,

> We have one compulsory house prayers and one voluntary one a week. The voluntary one gets about 5 people (there are 45 people in the house). The 'religious' situation here is rather amusing: about 80% of the school get confirmed and after about 18 months 80% of them prefer to be agnostic and don't go to communion. It just shows how badly religion affects the boys here. It is taken as rather a bore, and we are supposed to be a religious, royal and ancient foundation.[7]

It has to be admitted that for some boys (presumably the five who went to voluntary house prayers) public-school Christianity was a comfort, an inspiration and a true faith. I can't remember that it bothered me at school, but, as a teacher at Haileybury, I remember its worrying me that so many pupils were attracted to the voluntary early-morning communions held by a man I greatly admired, the Rev. Alan Steward. It seemed to me rather too easy for these lovely young people from comfortable and loving homes to accept a religion of peace, harmony and love. I was brought up in a middle-class house in the centre of a Sheffield council estate, and even that experience taught me that not everyone lived a middle-class life. Throughout the ages, Christianity – in which, perhaps strangely, I am still a believer – has been used by the ruling classes as a means of subjugation. What better way than a creed that argues turning the other cheek, and the reward for endurance is not in this life but the next? I did and do fear it is an

---

7   Lambert, *Hothouse Society*, pp. 100–1.

easy option for those who think the world is typified by Mayfair or Saffron Walden, rather than Rwanda.

A major reason for the rejection of school Christianity was association with the control the schools sought to impose on a person's life: 'Many pupils resent the dogmatic, narrow and above all compulsory aspect of religion in an institution which, in so many other respects, sets out to inculcate criticism, discrimination, breadth of view, self-direction and freedom of choice. This contradiction causes anger.'[8]

Another reason was simpler: the Chaplains and the services they ran were frequently rubbish: 'The final cause of the discontent with religion is the nature of the services . . . the content is monotonous . . . or cold and remote, something lacking spontaneity or giving no opportunity of participation to the pupils themselves.'[9]

Christianity was akin to the CCF (see below). It was there. You had to do it. You no more thought about it than you thought about how to walk. One of the many features that make children prone to abuse is their ability to accept whatever is happening to them as normal. Christianity happened to you at public school and you accepted it as normal.

Yet there is, or was, another element, in the acceptance of Christianity on the parts of the pupils. First, life at an old-style boarding school was a permanent battle, for survival, for the Holy Grail of popularity, for success. Queen Elizabeth did not demand a window into men's souls. The boy at a public school had his windows thrown open to the ruthless and revealing gaze of hundreds of other boys, many of them sniffing for the scent of fear. For totally nonreligious reasons, the precious hour in Chapel could be the only time, apart from sleep, when one was left alone with oneself and

8   Ibid., p. 102.
9   Ibid. p. 103

actually had time to think, instead of merely concentrating on how to survive. On a car journey recently one of my grandchildren asked if I had seen something out of the side window. I had to bite back the reply, in murderous traffic, that I could either drive the car or look out of the side window, but I couldn't do both. So it was in the frequently cold and cheerless Chapel. For a brief period, one had the time to look round one's own mind. Instead of doing the driving, you could sit back and relax. John Betjeman says exactly this about his largely unhappy experience as a pupil at Marlborough, in his poetic autobiography, *Summoned By Bells*:

> 'Give me a God whom I can touch and see.
> The bishop was more right than he could know,
> For safe in G. F. Bodley's greens and browns,
> Safe in the surge of undogmatic hymns,
> The Chapel *was* the centre of my life –
> The only place where I could be alone.'[10]

A second reason for the power of Chapel was the King James Bible and Book of Common Prayer. To me as a wrinkled and ghastly old adult, only Shakespeare matches the power of its language. To a thirteen-year-old, the rolling, sonorous words were unwittingly powerful and potent. To write the truth is to come dangerously close to sounding like the occasional old boy of a public school who in his dotage loses all self-respect and collapses totally into sentimental drivel about his schooldays, forgetting the manifold and various assaults on his human rights that he was subjected to, in order to wallow in a perfect world that almost certainly never actually existed. Yet the truth is that I shall remember until I die

---

10   Betjeman, *Summoned By Bells*, p. 67.

sitting on a Sunday evening in the Uppingham Chapel seeing the sun stream in though the stained-glass windows and singing the Nunc Dimittis: 'Lord, now lettest thou thy servant depart in peace ...' I am angry and resentful to admit that those and similar words seared their way into my soul. You get something of the flavour of it when Tom Brown goes weak at the knees in the face, or mouth, of a stirring sermon from the Doctor. But I don't think it was just the Doctor. Sit in the Chapel at Eton or Lancing now, and see, hear and feel what I mean. Or go to the Remembrance Day service at Haileybury. Adolescence is one of the most intense periods of a person's life. Put five hundred or a thousand young men together in one place, and it can be to intensity what five hundred or a thousand magnifying glasses would be to the sun.

The link between public schools and Christianity is one that goes right back to the creation of these schools. When Christianity came to England, it came in the twin form of Latin and sung services. Thus every cathedral or monastery found life easier if it had attached to it a school to provide a supply of Latinists and singers, and in many respects these early schools existed to educate future recruits into the Church, Thus, '. . . they were not just associated with the Church; the identification was far closer. They were almost a part of the Church.'[11]

Many of these Church schools later became the great and not-so-great public schools. King's, Canterbury, is a well-known example. St Paul's School did not move from its site in St Paul's Cathedral until relatively late in the nineteenth century, in 1884. Its stunning Waterhouse building – a veritable Harry Potter edifice – had to be abandoned in the 1960s, in my personal opinion as the result of misgovernance, when it was decided by local government to run the tail-end of the new M4 motorway

---

11 Gathorne-Hardy, *The Public School Phenomenon*, p. 22.

through the site. I have met at least one Old Pauline who claims to have mounted a sit-in protest against the demolition of the original Waterhouse building. If only the trustees had bought the extra land available in 1884 in what for snobbish reasons was called 'West Kensington', but which was actually the far less socially acceptable Hammersmith.

Yet there is another side of the coin. In the mid-1930s The Manchester Grammar School moved from its ancient site bang in the centre of Manchester next to the Cathedral. The area surrounding the original school was described as 'unsalubrious' (a classic understatement), and an Old Mancunian who moved out in his last year described seeing the windows cleaned at 9 a.m. in his classroom at the old school with a layer of soot covering them by 10 a.m. Conversely, he described his first morning in the new school when a teacher opened windows at either end of the new classroom and the boys watched with wonder as a bumble bee flew in one window and out the other.

Did the move from the Cathedral precincts affect both The Manchester Grammar School and St Paul's? Most definitely yes. The present situation in these schools and many like them would make Thomas Arnold turn in his grave. When I first became a Head in 1987, I gave a Christian assembly, complete with hymn and prayers, every morning. Twenty-four years later, Christian assemblies were a choice from a menu that included Jewish and Muslim assemblies.

St Paul's has an annual service in commemoration of its founder, John Colet, who was Dean of St Paul's. It is a magnificent event, always held in front of a packed house, at St Paul's Cathedral. Manchester Grammar has a similar annual service in Manchester Cathedral. Both services were unashamedly Christian, and, when I became High Master of St Paul's, it seemed to me that a depressing number of boys were refusing to attend, on 'conscientious' grounds. In fact, for most of the boys concerned, it was not about religion at all: they had none. It was a way of cocking a snook at authority and the Establishment, with highly articulate and intelligent Paulines delighting in challenging the school to force a young man to attend an event seen as celebrating one particular religion. You could see them rubbing their hands in glee at the forthcoming argument.

One of the few things I've learned over the years is that the best way to win a fight is to refuse to give one to those desperate for it. I remember one particular young man who had announced loudly to his peers that he would refuse to attend the service as a conscientious objector. He was a member of one of London's most talented, creative and artistic dynasties. You could see his eyes light up every time I came near him, desperately hoping that at the least the High Master would question him about his decision, at best berate him and demand his attendance. What I did instead was chat to him about everything except John Colet Day, and give an assembly with a simple message. I said that I didn't think going to the John Colet service was to pretend submission or allegiance to Christianity. The reason we went to a Christian service was that our founder had been a committed Christian, and to remember him in any other format would simply have been disrespectful. We weren't showing our respect for or belief in one particular faith by going to that service: we were simply saying thank you to the man who made our school and the boys' education possible, and showing respect for his beliefs, not subjugation to them.

I still don't know whether or not the boy who so wanted to be a martyr attended or not, because to have asked would have been to gratify adolescent rebellion. I knew all about adolescent rebellion. I'd been there and done that. It left me with the belief that the best thing to do with adolescent rebellion was to leave it to think itself through, not pour petrol on it. What I do know is that the number of boys refusing to attend plummeted dramatically. I don't suppose it had anything do with the fact that, instead of letting those who refused to attend go home, we insisted they stay at school during the service and do school work.

I took great comfort in the fact that so many Paulines and Mancunians chose to attend a service in a religion with which they were otherwise unfamiliar. I took even more comfort from a Jewish boy I appointed as Captain of School. It suddenly struck me that this young man, from an orthodox Jewish family, would as Captain of School be required by tradition to give a reading from the Bible (New Testament) to two thousand people packed into an Anglican service in St Paul's Cathedral. I asked him if it was a problem. No, he replied, he didn't think so. He'd have a word with his Rabbi. In the event, he read the lesson brilliantly. Afterwards, I asked him if the Rabbi had been OK with the whole business. 'Oh, no!' he said in a tone of mock alarm, and smote his forehead. 'Do you know, I completely forgot to ask him!' Personally, I think the world could do with a few more pragmatists and fewer religious zealots, and one of the more remarkable transformations undertaken by public schools has been their transition from fundamentalist Christian institutions to genuine multifaith communities.

When we think about the unlimited ambition of the Victorians, we often think about the almost unbelievable amount of money they put into sewers – or, to be factually correct, sewerage systems. There was an educational equivalent to Thomas Crapper and Joseph Bazalgette, who designed London's sewers. He was called Canon Nathaniel Woodard (1811–91). His plan was to divide England up into geographical areas, and have three Christian public schools for each area, aimed at the growing middle classes.

As a parish priest in poverty-stricken areas, Woodard confessed to being horrified by the sheer ignorance of the middle classes, in some case far greater than that of poor people educated in the parochial schools. When he died Woodard had managed 'only' eleven schools, but those schools were a tremendous tribute to his drive, energy and sense of mission.

Just as the drive to capture the Victorian middle classes for Christianity was a reflection of current culture, so was the social imperative behind the plan: the schools in each region were to have three tiers – top, middle and bottom, similar to the Victorian division of railway travel into first-, second- and third-class fares – with the fees from the top going to subsidise those at the bottom. Just as he had tried to play to Victorian social apartheid, so he fell victim to it. His 'top-tier' school, Lancing – with its inspirationally designed and situated Chapel that outdoes many a cathedral – attracted some gentry, but his bottom tier was deemed to be largely occupied by 'tradesmen'. As a consequence for many years Woodard schools were not seen as proper public schools, and were lacking in 'tone'.

My problem with Woodard is that I can't persuade myself that what he did he did primarily for the glory of God but rather that he did it for the glory of Nathaniel Woodard. Woodard was the classic missionary, convinced he had God on his side and was therefore possessed of the power to bring to life what perhaps might just have been God's will, but was certainly the will of Nathanial Woodard. To me he has always seemed sanctimonious, and a slave to conformity of the worst type: everyone had to conform to what he deemed the right way.

Public schools tended to build Chapels before they built Assembly Halls. The result was that Chapel was frequently the only place where the whole school gathered together. As is suggested in another chapter, this gathering was the ideal breeding ground for riot and dissent. As someone who on a regular basis for ten years faced a thousand thirteen-to-eighteen-year-old Mancunians virtually on his own in Assembly, I can testify to the terror of such occasions, and the sense of a fermenting brew that could explode at any time. But the Chapel was also the breeding ground for another perceived evil. As late as 1936 the Rev. Canon Edward Bonhote, Master of Haileybury, spent the then vast sum of £15,000 on rotating the pews in Haileybury's splendidly domed Chapel so that boys could not direct lascivious glances at junior boys opposite them.

The Rev. John Royds was a most unlikely Headmaster of Uppingham. I believe he had been a missionary, and certainly, when he was appointed, the Common Room saw him as the rank outsider, and christened him in those politically incorrect days 'the black man from Africa'. He was, of course, thoroughly Caucasian. It is to him that I owe my career in teaching, in that he gave me my first job. I remember his first sermon at the service for new boys, which ranked him in its eccentricity and total misjudgement of his congregation alongside the greatest Victorian Headmasters. He always used to wear a gown three sizes bigger and longer than his wiry frame merited. He swept up the aisle like the prequel to Darth Vader, ascended the pulpit and fixed the trembling new boys with his beady eyes. Yes, they really were beady.

'I'd like you to think about Death,' he said. And went on to remind the assembled new boys that, in between their saying goodbye to their parents and now, there could have been an accident on the A1. It wasn't a triumph of reassurance, and for the first time in my life evinced in me a strong desire to be very un-English and hug young boys, most of whom were in tears. I didn't, of course. Nowadays there's legislation that would lock you up if you did. Back then, commonsense told you it'd ruin a boy's street cred. At the same time, I knew what Royds was trying to say, though he never said it as such. You never know how much of life you've got left. So what you are now may be how you are remembered for ever. So behave now in the manner you want to be remembered for ever.

And the moral of the story, the extraordinary thing? Those boys respected and accepted John Royds, as did I. Why? Because he was what he was and made no pretence of it, because we all knew he cared passionately, albeit without being given the ability to express it and because he never sought to pretend to anyone that he was other than who he was. We are in danger of assuming that force of personality alone dictates successful headship. Wrong. It is the force that drives the personality that counts. Arnold succeeded in part because he genuinely believed he had God On His Side. It is not the cause to which Heads attach themselves that their pupils sense most strongly: it is their lack of hypocrisy.

I cannot let this chapter go without a word about the public-school sermon. A symbol of the drivel offered to boys from generation to generation is contained in the story of Charles Old Goodford (1812–84), who was appointed Provost of Eton in 1862. He usually preached for well over an hour, and a very long hour it was indeed for the congregation. It was the practice at the time for the preacher to finish his sermon and link it up with the next part of the service with the words, 'And now', giving rise to a verse in the *Etonian* of 1875:

> At the magic words 'And now',
> Runs a tremor through the hall.
> Joy awakens on every brow,
> Sleep is cast away from all.

Goodford inadvertently used the words, 'And now' is his sermon after a mere ten minutes, whereupon the congregation gratefully leaped to their feet for the hymn, and, faced with the Herculean task of getting them to sit down, Goodford gave up both the effort and the remaining sixty minutes of his sermon.

We tend to concentrate on the preacher/Headmaster, and many Victorian Headmasters (including Arnold) preached inspirational sermons. But for an actual public-school boy the sermon was usually a weekly ordeal delivered by a guest speaker. I sometimes wonder if God really cares about communicating his creed, because surely if he did he would have struck down many of those I have heard give sermons in public-school chapels. I'm hard pushed to remember one good one, man and boy. I can remember enough bad ones. Sedbergh was plagued by its reputation as a rugby school, which meant that many well-meaning visitors would preach 'the rugby sermon', as we came to know it. The boys could spot it coming miles away, and simply switched off. Life was a game of rugby, gaining salvation was scoring a try, and winning the game getting to Heaven. For some reason, Jesus was always a scrum-half. I'm not surprised, having met too many prop forwards.

As for me, and indeed most of the boys, we couldn't believe life was that simple, and I always felt like the player who had been sent off. Mind you, my competence at the game can be judged by the story of my last appearance on a rugby field. Back in the bad old days teachers could play rugby against pupils, albeit the staff side was trusted to play only the Colts team, as to play any better team would be to risk a defeat so tragic as to lose the staff all their credibility. My only hope was to tackle ferociously the smallest member of the opposition at the earliest opportunity, preferably, but not essentially, when he held the ball, in the most public manner possible, this giving the impression that I was violence unleashed (as distinct from a cowardly wreck), in the hope that the opposition might give me a wide berth. Unfortunately, an extremely large former Oxford Blue on my side had the same idea, and we met head first from opposite sides at considerable speed around the shins of some poor boy or other. I remember waking up several feet from the point of impact, and thereafter persuaded myself I was actually playing for the opposite side. That no one appeared to notice says it all.

I was mightily reassured about my feelings towards the Sedbergh Rugby Sermon when I read Arnold Lunn's hilarious account of the sermon preached by an Old Harrovian Bishop well over a hundred years ago. One of his reluctant congregation comments, "'They seem to think we're a lot of stupid yokels who can only be kept awake by cricket shop. Besides, he made such a horrid mess of his remarks.'Member his cover point, who was 'mighty slippy between the sticks?'"[12]

I occasionally dream about Sedbergh, and in one of those dreams I was for some reason doing the rounds of a watchman at midnight on New Year's Eve. Analyse that one, someone, but just don't let me know the conclusion. Anyway, in my dream I noticed a flickering light in the Chapel, and there at the lectern was a skeletal figure recognisable as the man who was Chaplain for most of the four years I worked at the school, reading out his sermon by the dim and wavering light of a torch. I won't mention his name, as he is the gentlest and kindest of men and still alive. He was the first and the last preacher I heard in Sedbergh Chapel, and I honestly think it was the same running sermon over the whole of the four years. It had no beginning and no end. It was

---

12   Lunn, *The Harrovians*, p. 97.

about 'love' – that I do remember. And there was a lot in it about a book written by a quite extraordinary man, but we never quite learned the title of the book or the name of the author. But the Book was Good, and Love was Good and people were Good, provided they received Love. I spent four years drafting in my almost-senseless mind the progression of this sermon surely to the inevitable message that the Love of God was the Best Love of All, superior even to beating Ampleforth at Rugby, but it never came, the needle being well and truly stuck in the groove.

Rubbish such as that clearly scarred my mind for me to be dreaming about it thirty years later. I wish I'd worked in Scottish schools, where one hopes the sermons were more akin to those I rather enjoyed in my youth. First, they had a temporal certainty: the good sermon lasted the length of time it took for a mint pandrop to dissolve in the mouth, and, if you got bored, you could always divert yourself with the effort needed not to crunch it prematurely. Second, they had theological certainty. Everyone was going to Hell, which was lovingly and grippingly described – except, of course, the congregation, which was always very reassuring and almost made it worthwhile going to the Kirk in the first place.

On the other hand there has been plenty of entertainment of the wrong sort in public-school Chapels over the years. R. S. Baxter, Warden of Winchester, was notorious for recycling sermons, but in his haste one day he grabbed in error a sermon from his days as a parish priest, whereupon the slightly bewildered boys heard themselves exhorted to bring their wives to Communion. Another short-sighted Head used to fill the time in which he was seeking to read his own handwriting with grunts, and the boys kept count in the hope he would break his record. Small animals such as squirrels, mice and rats have regularly been released in services, and fireworks set off. The best trick of all was to buy ten cheap alarm clocks and time a different one hidden round the Chapel to go off every six minutes. Letting rip a loud fart at a crucial moment in the service is another old favourite, hampered only by the technically demanding need for amplification if it is to have the maximum effect.

A variation of the rugby sermon was the annual sermon given at the school service for The Perse School. It was a much more low-key affair, held not in Manchester or St Paul's Cathedral but simply in a local church. The local vicar was a simple man and a brilliant parish priest who more than compensated for the size of his brain by the size of his heart, but he lost the boys completely by trying to preach an academic sermon.

If it's a commonly accepted truth that the worst thing that can happen to a woman at a party is if two people arrive in the same dress, so it's accepted that in public speaking one of the worst things is to tell the joke everyone had heard before. This doesn't appear to have reached sermons yet, and there are certain tales that I heard time after time after time in my career. Perhaps the most common was of the Headmaster who founded and built a new school. Building after building went up, but still he was not happy. Then, at long last, he built the Chapel. 'Ah!' he said. (Or 'Hooray!' Or 'Eureka!' Or even 'My God! It cost *that* much?!' Who actually cares?) 'Ah! Now I have a school!' In this sermon, one is allowed to replace 'Now I have a school!' with 'Now my school has a heart!' Even more daringly, 'Now my school's heart is beating!' As distinct, presumably, from the school beating the congregations?

As a victim of these sermons, one learned to dread the speaker who spoke in capitals. For some reason, the Chapel Sermon changed the pronunciation of 'the school' from lower case to 'The School' after the Chapel had been built.

And, yes, I have known staff open a book on the length of a

sermon, not infrequently in the case of sermons preached by me as their Headmaster. And, yes, there is a game of 'sermon cricket', the rules of which make the Eton Wall Game look simple, but which in essence sees the sermon as a game of cricket between two teams. In the red corner is the Word of God, while in the green corner is the ego of the preacher. The game consists of scoring references to such things as 'God', 'Jesus' or 'Faith' as distinct from references to 'Me' or 'I', or phrases such as 'I Remember . . .' or, 'In my experience . . .' I'm afraid the Word of God usually lost by an innings or more.

Occasionally, one sensed that the preacher was using material he (or, rarely, she) had used previously in a Speech Day or Prizegiving speech. In most cases this consisted of comments such as, 'It may surprise you to know that I never took Chapel seriously when I was at School.' Actually, it was no surprise at all to us, but if it was boring at least it was honest. The Speech Day variant was more challenging, particularly in its two most common forms. The first was some appalling old wrinkly who must against all the apparent odds have achieved a degree of success in his life to justify being invited to speak, who would leer through his spectacles at the assembled young things and say, 'It might surprise you to know I never won any prizes at school,' at which the assembled young, with the wisdom of youth, would look at the evidence before them and think, 'Well, actually . . . ' This second variant was mercifully in decline in my later years, as the supply of visiting speakers who had been cheerfully beaten to a pulp at their own schools started to decline. These old bores would state to pupils who would have enlisted the services of a barrister if someone raised as much as an eyebrow to them, never mind a cane, 'I was beaten at school and it never harmed me.' The evidence often suggested otherwise.

Chapels at public schools were the home of much cant and humbug, but can also provide moments of true pathos, as in the three separate panels commemorating the deaths of the three Lyon brothers in World War One. They provided moments of hilarity, as when my wife vowed she would *never* do Chapel flowers at Sedbergh but of course ended up doing them for Speech Day as the Second Master's wife. Unfortunately, she chose to use wild garlic flowers for the displays. There were no vampires in Chapel that Sunday, but rather a congregation who all emerged as if they had spent the night in a bad Spanish restaurant. At least it meant she was not asked to do them again.

Many contemporary Headmasters in their hearts of hearts understand that, in terms of how the majority of pupils see Christianity, little has changed since the Bradfield College boy who wrote in the mid-1970s,

> Up to a few months ago, religion at Bradfield was treated as an archaic, cumbersome and extraordinary tedious routine that had to be tolerated, if only for appearance's sake. It had long fallen beside the clinical scientific wayside, and no number of truly well-meaning Good Samaritans could heave it back on its feet. It then gradually came to be regarded rather as an animal that is well on the way towards extinction . . .[13]

It is interesting that I never heard this view expressed at any meeting of the Headmasters' Conference. In the manner of the Emperor's new clothes, we all know Christianity no longer drives

---

13 Heale, *School Quad*, p. 27.

public schools or is much of an influence in them, but we're either not allowed or not brave enough to say so.

The School Chaplain

Yet many schools still feel the need to have a School Chaplain. With some stirring and notable exceptions, including one of my best friends, I have always been nervous about School Chaplains, increasingly so as they have been left with less and less to do. Christ apparently finds work for idle hands just as does Satan. Somewhere in the old-fashioned cloud there must be an Honours Board of a different kind, listing Headmasters who have lost their jobs through the malevolent action of others. On such a board, the list of villains would be headed by Bursars, but Chaplains would come a close second. I remember meeting an ashen-faced Head one day, and being so concerned about his appearance that I offered to fetch him a glass of water. 'Thank you, but it won't be necessary. I'm just recovering from interviewing six candidates for the post of School Chaplain. I never realised before what levels of depravity the human soul could sink to.'

Interestingly, that Head subsequently lost his job when the Chaplain he did appoint (presumably the least depraved?) turned out to be a drunkard and what I shall euphemistically refer to as a threat to young people, and, when disciplined, turned the whole of the Common Room against the Head. I've also had to tell a Chairman of Governors that his School Chaplain (a different one) was making it impossible for any Head to run the school, and there simply wasn't room for both the Chaplain and a Head in that particular town.

I need another book to list all my recollections of Chaplains I Have Met. It would have to include the man who proudly boasted to a dinner party that he spanked his sixteen-year-old daughter when she came in late. I should so mention, far too late to do him any good, the Rev. Ifor Jones (or was it Evans?), who had the misfortune to be my first Form Master as a raw twelve-year-old at Uppingham. I had a crippling stammer at the time, and indeed for all my time at school. Ifor was outwardly a classic muscular Christian, a bulldozer of a man who to all intents and purposes had the sensitivity of a rhino's bottom. He taught us Latin, and his standard practice, hallowed of course by public-school tradition, was to make his pupils read out their attempts at translation. I stammered my way through my first attempt, and saw him looking at me with a strange gleam in his eye, which frankly terrified me. Thereafter, I was never again made to read out in class, though it was managed so sensitively that neither I nor my classmates realised it was intentional. How often do we realise too late in life the debt we owe to people we never found the time to thank?

Of course, for Chaplains in general it's an interesting notion that someone serving a religion dedicated to the poor and needy should choose to spend their professional life amid the children of some of the wealthiest and most privileged families in the UK. Perhaps surprisingly, in what I hope is a venom-filled paragraph above, I'm not sure this washes. Children from rich families can suffer from failures in upbringing as much as any others, and be in need of spiritual solace as well.

In the final count, the monolithic stress placed by the public schools on Christianity had little effect. It left some people such as myself with a battered faith, but drilled indifference into many more: 'Educational history shows that formal religion has rarely had the effect that its most zealous exponents are eager to claim for it.'[14]

---

14 Lamb, *The Happiest Days*, p. 217.

6

SPARE THE ROD: THE PUBLIC-SCHOOL LOVE AFFAIR WITH CORPORAL PUNISHMENT

The pre-Clarendon public schools are renowned for their willingness to flog their pupils apparently at every conceivable opportunity, to excess and sometimes to an apparent risk of life or death. Post-Clarendon, popular opinion sees flogging as more licensed, but no less prevalent.

I find the vision, at least in terms of the modern age, rather startling. I managed to survive the 1950s and the 1960s as a child without being beaten either at school or by my parents, despite the fact that, in the comics I devoured, Dennis the Menace and Roger the Dodger were lucky to survive an episode without receiving the slipper from their father, and the rather lovable Teacher in the 'Bash Street Kids' stories seemed surgically attached to his cane. Many years on, and as a sad old man occasionally coming across ancient editions of *The Beano*, I cannot but note that Teacher carries a cane, but rarely uses it in action. Teacher in *The Beano* is one of my all-time heroes, the man who long-sufferingly knew how to cope with the most disadvantaged class in history.

I suspect I was lucky in that corporal punishment was unfashionable in my time in senior school. Yet as late as the 1980s at Haileybury some Housemasters, and one in particular, frequently beat boys. Before my wife and I became Housemasters at Haileybury, our flat was something of a second home for the rebels in the school and the artistic fringe. One of my most awkward moments was answering the phone to find Bill Stewart, redoubtable Master of Haileybury, on the line.

'Do you have that boy —— with you at the moment?' he bellowed.

'Why . . . yes, Master, as it happens, we do.'

'Good. Then send him to me, please. I need to beat him.'

It was not the easiest message I've ever had to deliver. The 'boy' in question is now a distinguished photographer.

A different story was told at my prep school in the late 1950s and early 1960s. The slipper or gym shoe was widely used by teachers, with no nonsense about having to record punishments. The owner-Headmaster used to delight in caning boys, among other things making his victims take off their trousers and don a special pair of 'caning shorts', the reason given being in case the punishment harmed the boy's trousers. And we swallowed it, innocents that we were. Us boys, in our innocence, I can understand, but not my parents. Why did no one smell a rat?

One part of the explanation is the all-pervasive nature of corporal punishment, in different forms, for much of the history of the public schools. Soldiers and sailors were being flogged for long periods of their existence. The birch could be prescribed for young criminals as well as public-school boys. Midshipmen in the Royal Navy could be caned long into the twentieth century. The result is what to modern eyes and ears is a strange acceptance of legalised violence towards children. Oddly enough, a good example of this is the film *Bottoms Up*, starring Jimmy Edwards and released in 1960. The film was a spin-off from the popular TV series *Whack-O!*, starring Jimmy Edwards as the beer-drinking, horse-betting and cane-wielding Headmaster of Chislehurst College, a school 'for the sons of gentlefolk'. In that film 'whackings' are nothing extraordinary. Indeed, the pupils have a tacit acceptance of them. It's not that they are enjoyable or welcome, rather that they are just part of the weave of life as we know it. When the pupils rebel (wonderful image of Jimmy Edwards in a bomber jacket and beret, leading the assault on the pupils like a hugely inflated Field Marshal Montgomery) and their demands are met, 'whackings' are not even at the top of their list, and their demand is not for their abolition, but merely for fewer of them. One of the most hateful things about corporal punishment is the humiliation it can inflict on the victim. That humiliation is significantly lessened if such punishment is the rule rather than the exception, and so it was that, for many boys well into the first two-thirds of the twentieth century, corporal punishment was accepted as a fact of life, and sometimes its welts as a badge of honour.

This other side of the coin is also referred to by John Betjeman, whereby far from being shamed the boy who had been caned became a hero, taking pride in showing off his wounds, seeing them as marks of distinction. Betjeman is not the only figure to comment on this. The actor David Niven was a pupil at Stowe in its early years. In his autobiography he is faced with either expulsion or an extreme beating at the hands of the Headmaster. His wounds are admired by his Housemaster, and one struggles to think what would happen nowadays to a Housemaster who gazed at a boy's naked bottom:

> In the bathroom mirror, I inspected the damage. It was heavy to say the least. Suddenly, Major Haworth's [Niven's Housemaster] cheery voice made me turn, 'Pretty good shooting I'd call that . . . looks like a two-inch group.' He was his usual smiling, kindly self . . . When that sort of thing happened to me I used to sleep on my stomach and have my breakfast off the mantleshelf.[15]

Niven's autobiography shows clearly that he was capable of hating those who beat him, and nursing lifelong resentment – he actually returned to his prep. school to face out the persecutor of his youth, to find it uninhabited and semi-ruinous – but for J. F. Roxburgh, the founding Headmaster of Stowe School, he had an admiration verging on idolatry. This was despite the fact that the savage beating referred to above – twelve strokes of the cane – was inflicted on Niven by Roxburgh. One reason was that Niven was expecting to be expelled, for cheating in a public examination, and in that sense the beating was the lesser of two evils. More importantly, Niven respected Roxburgh. Time after time in reading recollections of punishment, it is clear that the times that leave the mental scars are when the boy has no respect for the person administering the beating, feels that it is unfair or senses the instigator is a sadist who takes pleasure in inflicting pain. In other words, what matters more than the beating is who administers it, and why.

---

15   David Niven, *The Moon's a Balloon*, pp. 53–4.

Niven's recollections give another insight into the cult of corporal punishment, similar to that noted by Betjeman and countless other less famous commentators. It turned miscreants into heroes, in schools where popularity was the be-all and end-all. In Niven's recollections, 'In the darkness, the whispers started – "How many did you get?" . . . "Did you blub?" . . . "What sort of cane is it?" "Promise to show us in the morning." All friendly whispers.'[16]

Another factor, surprisingly, that is evident in much contemporary writing, as well as in works such as *Wacko!* or Niven, is the apparent belief that the punishment they received was just, or fair enough. A former pupil of my prep. school served a life sentence for murder. We corresponded with each other over several years, including times when there had been serious riots in his prison of the moment. I will never forget his comment that in effect a prison can work only if the inmates cooperate in the running of it: there are simply too many prisoners, and too few guards. So it is with corporal punishment: the system would not have survived as long as it did without at least the tacit approval of the inmates.

Examples abound. One of the Billy Bunter stories features a young Master who eschews the cane in favour of modern teaching methods. He is given the bird by one boy in particular, and it is to the immense relief of the Remove that the Master remembers where his cane is and administers a sound thrashing. God is restored to his Heaven, and all is right with the world again. This, of course, illustrates more than anything else the inherent conservatism of boys, elevated almost to the status of a religion at Winchester in the nineteenth century, which states that whatever

---

16 Ibid., p. 54.

is there and old is by definition to be preferred to anything new or even different. Pupils at one school rebelled not at being beaten, but when the Head tried to abolish it in favour of 'sanctions'. Pupils felt that physical punishment was more 'gentlemanly' than the proposed alternative.

This is not to suggest that the whole thing was hunky-dory. I'm afraid I've met rather too many old men who've told me they were beaten like a gong at school and it 'did me no harm'. There were plenty of boys for whom a beating was a calculated risk: if you went off to the pub and were caught you knew what would happen. You did the sum regarding gain versus pain, and accepted the stakes. Yet I and thousands of others remember the Grandfather of The Manchester Grammar School, Ian Bailey, who served that school so brilliantly as boy and master. No one could have loved that school more than Ian, or given more to it, yet no one who heard him tell of the time he was (unjustly) given the cane can doubt that this lovely man received thereby a wound far more lasting than anything physical.

The stink of perversion and sexual gratification on the part of the beater could also turn what might otherwise have been a painful but routine event into something septic. Norman Hidden was for many years editor of a poetry magazine, and, as mentor to thousands of aspiring poets, proved himself an extraordinarily gentle, patient and kind man. Yet he carried a worm in his heart in the form of the perverted teacher, 'The Corpse', who had beaten him at school, as described in his semi-autobiography:

> The Corpse swished his cane. 'Filthy practices. Now undo your pyjamas. Let them drop.' . . . The boy untied the cord of his pink-and-white pyjamas.
>
> Obediently he bent over the brown arm of the

chair in the room's centre. He knew the procedure exactly: a slow, lingering and above all ceremonial experience. There would be a long pause between every swish of the cane. One had to wait interminably for it to happen . . . from the rear, light shuffling footsteps . . . one waited, all senses alert, for what might happen next. Corpse would hoveringly lift the end of the pyjama blouse and bend it back over the waist. He would step back sharply, cane quivering in his hand, contemplating his target, sniff-sniff – a sure sign of his mounting tension – short, hard, jabbing sniffs, and – whoosh! – his cane would burn a red smear like a flame-thrower across the buttocks.

As the pain shot along a thousand channels, flooding his nerve centres, Corpse would prowl away, catlike in his soft carpet slippers, to the statuette of the Virgin:

> Mary Mother, meek and mild
> Calm this sinful lustful child

Turning from his contemplation of the smooth glazed face of the Madonna he would swivel his velvet eyes back to the blurred smear across the boy's flesh.[17]

Norman Hidden bore a scar in his mind that long outlasted any physical mark, largely because of the stench of perversion in the evident enjoyment of the man who beat him. Yet even this was not a universal truth. John Maynard Keynes as a schoolboy wrote

---

17   Hidden, *Dr Kink & His Old Style Boarding School*, pp. 14–16

about being 'worked off' by a teacher: 'It gives him a great deal of pleasure and does not do me much harm.'[18]

Keynes was the exception. Being beaten because you deserved it was one thing. Being beaten because the person doing it enjoyed it was altogether different – unacceptable and potentially permanently damaging. There was an extraordinary veil of secrecy over the fact that some teachers clearly enjoyed beating, in both the mad, bad times and the Victorian and Edwardian eras – it truly was the sin with no name. It has not been reflected in the official histories of the School that the Founder of St Paul's School used to order boys to be held back from flogging until the good clergyman and mercer could attend to the business himself. A Victorian account commented,

> Colet, Dean of St Paul's, who, although he delighted in children, and was a good man, thought no discipline could be too severe in his school; and whenever he dined there, one or two boys were served up to be flogged by way of dessert.[19]

What is extraordinary to modern taste, as well as the stark denial of flogging as a perverted pleasure, is the comic-opera element that surrounded flogging in the pre-Victorian times, with mass floggings undertaken in public to huge accompanying hilarity and tumult. One author describes it thus: 'In the first three to four decades of the [nineteenth] century, flogging in the public schools was art of a conventional charade, ritual comedy, with the Headmaster, in the role of the fierce and irascible

18 Chandos, *All Boys Together*, p. 246.
19 Cooper, *Flagellation & The Flagellants*, p. 427.

Punchinello, struggling to subdue and chastise a multitude of Harlequins.'[20]

Pupils contributed with huge gusto and enthusiasm to the show. With pre-Victorian stiff upper lips, boys used to vie with each other as to how loud they could shriek under the rod, or imitate loud animal noises – sheep, cow, horse etc. – as each blow landed. One Etonian, a gymnast, played a trick on Keates's successor, Charles Hawtrey. He acquired from a local acrobat the skill of leaping into the air from a stationary position. Having gathered an audience for his next flogging, he leaped several feet at the first blow and was sent off to rest as his punisher thought he must have touched a nerve. In 1838, Old Etonian Lord Waterford led a successful midnight raid to steal the whipping block from the library.

If it is clear that flogging could give pleasure to the administrator, it is also clear that it could give pleasure to the recipient. Lord Waterford did not intend to retire the whipping block at Eton: it was put to its original purpose at his Lordship's seat (forgive the pun) at Curraghmore, at the dinner meetings of the Block Club.

Yet even in pre-Victorian times shame and scandal could be associated with men who had a predilection for beating or being beaten. No chapter on this sordid aspect of public-school history can afford to omit the story of Lieutenant-General Sir Eyre Coote, MP, who was discovered at Christ's Hospital with his trousers down in 1815, flogging boys and apparently being flogged by them:

> I . . . saw a gentleman uncovered as low as his knees
> from his breeches, was closing his trousers. I asked

---

20 Chandos, , *All Boys Togethe,r* p. 226.

him what he was doing there . . . 'I am doing no harm,
upon my honour. I was only flogging those boys . . .
do let me go, you don't know who I am, nor what I
am.' I said who you are I do not care, but what you are
I plainly see . . .'[21]

The equivalent to the Christ's Hospital Chairman of Governors
tried for a while to protest that, in paying the boys to flog and
be flogged by him, Coote had done nothing more than an act of
'unguarded folly'. The case came to court and he was acquitted,
but the Prince of Wales stripped him of his military rank. What
historians have never established is why Coote was humiliated in
this way, when one suspects so many got off scot-free. It is hard not
to think that, if the offence had taken place at Eton, Winchester,
Westminster or Harrow, the network would have managed a
successful cover-up. Christ's Hospital, a school for poor children,
carried no such clout. One can always hope that different action
was deemed worthwhile at Christ's Hospital because its children
did not have powerful parents to defend them.

The public spectacle and carnival atmosphere surrounding
flogging dissipated after the Clarendon Commission, which was
itself merely a symbol of an age of restraint and suppression.
Flogging remained, and in retreating behind closed doors became
darker and more diseased.

Perhaps inevitably, there are a number of urban myths around
the prevalence of beating. I was certainly told at Uppingham
that a former Headmaster, returning to his study after Assembly
and seeing a line of boys queuing up outside, beat them all as a
matter of course, only to find they were the Confirmation class.

---

21 Widely quoted, as in John Chandos, *Boys Together*, p. 236; Hickson, *The Poisoned Bowl*, p. 119.

This possibly apocryphal story is told of a number of schools, the most popular being Eton with John Keate as the Head. Another popular story is that certain boys had the skin on their backside so hardened and desensitised that a flogging evinced little more than a warming sensation. I am unaware of medical advice either way, and one hopes it would be difficult to find a child nowadays to confirm or deny the folk myth.

For the record, it was not Eton under Keate, nor even Winchester, Harrow or St Paul's (all noted in contemporary literature for the prevalence of flogging) that carried off the prize for being the worst in terms of ritualised violence to its pupils, but Christ's Hospital. Perhaps this was because, as a school that retained its status as a genuine charity, its pupils did not come from the same class of powerful families as in the more socially distinguished schools. Nothing very serious happened to those who indulged in excessive thrashing at Winchester, for instance, but where a case was proven family influence could at least produce some reaction, as when a prefect gave a pupil 150 strokes: 'The prefect in this instance was reprimanded by being deprived of his office; but this mild penalty was inflicted only because the victim's father was a man of sufficient consequence to make a fuss.'[22]

Public schools abandoned flogging when society in general abandoned corporal punishment, yet another example of the fact that throughout their history the public school has followed society rather than dictating or forming it.

---

22   Lamb, *The Happiest Days*, p. 185.

7

SOME CORNER OF A FOREIGN FIELD: PUBLIC SCHOOLS, EMPIRE AND WORLD WAR ONE

The public schools have frequently been seen as providing cannon fodder for the First and other world and local wars. The walls of many a public school Chapel confirm this impression, crammed as they are with memorials to old boys who died in the service of their country – poems such as Henry Newbolt's 'Vitae Lampada' (quoted earlier), or this by Newbolt:

CLIFTON S.A. WAR MEMORIAL

Clifton, remember these thy sons who fell
Fighting far over sea;
For they in a dark hour remembered well
Their warfare learnt of thee.

Such suggest the image of the public school as one great training ground for war.

We have all been soiled and polluted by the late-Victorian concept of manliness, which contained within it the concepts of 'pluck', patriotism and selfless sacrifice. Such a thing did not exist before the mid-nineteenth century:

> As for fighting for one's country – the boy who joined the army was a fool, probably a rogue. So far as the eighteenth and early nineteenth book went there is not a hint of that a boy is doing his country a service by going off with a recruiting sergeant; he has been gulled while sodden with drink, or he is a ne'er-do-well who has fallen foul of his employer, and when he limps back with a wooden leg years later it serves him right.[23]

All this changed when Arnold and his kin took over the public schools and their culture.

What is true is that the public schools are proud of their war dead. I taught for eleven years at Haileybury, which had amalgamated in the past with the Imperial Service College and had a particularly long list of such casualties. I remember showing parents round and arriving at the magnificent dining hall, erected as a memorial to those killed in World War One. I mentioned this to the parents, and the father asked me how many Haileyburians had lost their lives in that war. I told him, and he asked for the figures for all the other wars that had been fought since the school's foundation in 1862. I told him the rough figures as well as I knew them, and he pursed his lips and asked me how many pupils he thought had passed through the school in its history. That flummoxed me, but I made my best

---

23   Avery, *Childhood's Pattern*, p. 167.

guess and he closed his eyes for a few seconds, opening them to say, 'So what you're telling me is that mathematically if I send my child here there's a one in five chance he'll be shot?' I forget what my answer was.

There is a pervasive belief that the public schools acted as if they knew World War One was coming and prepared their boys for it: 'The class of 1914 had been prepared implicitly by the codes to which the schools subscribed, and explicitly, by the junior branch of the Officers' Training Corps, for the eventuality of war.'[24]

The schools have in part brought this false impression upon themselves by the cultivation of the 'OTC' or 'Officers' Training Corps', now seen in the schools as the 'CCF', or 'Combined Cadet Force'. Anyone who sees either the OTC or the CCF as inspiring a blind love for all things military has clearly never experienced either one of them. Jonathan Gathorne-Hardy comments, 'The overwhelming evidence is that up till 1900 the various Cadet Corps and Rifle Corps . . . were militarily completely ineffective, with little or no direct or serious connections with the Army. In particular, they met hostility from the games side; a fatal drawback.'[25]

Where he is wrong is in assuming that the Boer War and the run-in to World War One changed all that. In many respects the change that occurred mirrored the changing attitude to Christianity in public schools, in that a degree of militarism was taken into the culture of the schools by the Establishment and school leaders. There is no evidence that it percolated through to the boys, who in every extract I have read and in ten years as a CCF 'officer', saw the OTC and the CCF as something of a joke, albeit a fun one that allowed them to shoot the occasional gun, play at soldiers or do sailing and canoeing. In a dismal time at my

24 Parker, *The Old Lie*, pp. 17–18.
25 Gathorne-Hardy, *The Public School Phenomenon*, p. 196.

own school, one of the *most* dismal was being forced to attend the annual CCF camp.

At the other extreme, one of my abiding memories as a teacher is taking a group of fourteen-year-old boys to, I think, Chatham Naval dockyard. At the time it had an esplanade onto which was fitted an example of every type of naval gun fitted to ships in the Royal Navy. No 15-inch guns, of course, such as sit in barrel form only outside the Imperial War Museum, nor even the 6-inch guns found on HMS *Belfast*. But there was a twin 4.5-inch turret, and a profusion of Bofors and Oerlikon guns for the uninitiated, in effect very heavy machine guns with power assistance to raise and lower the barrel(s) and turn the mounting on which the gun sat.

When we arrived a large amount of practice ammunition had reached its sell-by date, and was about to be dumped at sea. In their wisdom, the authorities allowed the boys to shoot it all off. I shall never forget the sight of a diminutive fourteen-year-old in the driving seat of, I think, an Oerlikon gun, his finger on the trigger and his feet sending the mounting into a permanent dervish whirl, with his best mate loading ammunition into the feeder tray with the a dedication that might have won him a VC at Jutland.

Happy days! And, if it does not sound too silly for boys handling weapons of death, surprisingly innocent. I once got into deep trouble with ISC (the Independent Schools Council) when attending a presentation yet again proving how indispensable public schools were to the wealth of the nation. One point made was the contribution made to the defence of the country by the CCF, at which point I burst out laughing. If the defence of this country rested in any way on the contribution of the dear old CCF, then we had better start building whole rows of factories dedicated to the fabrication of white flags.

What commentators have failed to realise is that any incipient militarism in public schools ran counter to the cult of amateurism. It was that cult that saw the domination of the Gentlemen versus Players division for so long. It has been assumed that the number of public-school boys who went on to careers in the Army and Navy meant that to excel in the OTC or the CCF was not viewed as denying the status of gentleman, where the ultimate sin was being seen to work too hard at anything. Yet this was not so. Apart from anything else, a significant number of public-school boys destined for the Army or Navy left their public school early in order to attend 'crammers', or colleges that existed solely to prepare officer-candidates for the relevant examinations and tests. Furthermore, the actual experience provided by the OTC or CCF was so dreadfully amateur in most cases as to offer no hint of professional devotion to the armed forces.

Writing just before World War One, the poet Charles Hamilton Sorley described an OTC experience at Marlborough:

> The examination is divided into three parts – Company Drill, Tactical and Musketry . . . I entered with fear and trembling. Twenty questions I was asked, and I looked sheepish and said 'Don't know' to each one. Then he said, 'Is there anything you do know?' and I gave him the two pieces of knowledge I had come armed with – the weight of a rifle and episodes in the life of a bullet from the time it leaves the breech till it hits its man. Then I saluted really smartly, and the gentleman gave me sixty out of a hundred.[26]

---

26   Charles Hamilton Sorley (ed. W. R. Sorley), *The Letters of Charles Sorley* (Cambridge: Cambridge University Press), 1919, p. 42.

If it is a misconception that the public schools directly prepared their boys for war, what is true is that the public schools produced a person who was very useful when it came. This was summed up by R. C. Sherriff, author of the best play about World War One, *Journey's End*. Sherriff was humiliated when he initially sought to join up, as a grammar-school boy being rejected because he had not attended one of the 'recognised' public schools. He later came to understand this, writing,

> But the need was pressing. Officers had to be made quickly, with the least possible trouble. The Army command had to find some sort of yardstick, and naturally they turned to the public school. Most of the generals had been public school boys before they went to military academies. They knew from first-hand experience that a public school gave to its boys what had the ingredients of leadership. They had a good background. They came from good homes. At school they gained self-confidence, the beginnings of responsibility through being prefects over younger boys. Pride in their schools would easily translate into pride for a regiment. Above all, without conceit or snobbery, they were conscious of a personal superiority that placed on their shoulders an obligation towards those less privileged than themselves. All this, together with the ability to speak good English, carried the public schoolboy a considerable way towards the ideals that the generals aimed at for good officers . . . But these young men never turned into officers of the old traditional type. By hard experience they became leaders in a totally different way and, through their

patience and courage and endurance carried the Army
to victory after the generals had brought it to within a
hairsbreadth of defeat . . . Without raising the public
schoolboy officers onto a pedestal it can be said that
it was they who played the vital part in keeping the
men good-humoured and obedient in the face of their
interminable ill-treatment and well-nigh insufferable
ordeals.[27]

It is extremely unlikely that the Battle of Waterloo was won on
the playing fields of England. It is far more likely that the Great
War was won in the quadrangles of England's public schools. I
have spent much of my adult life trawling through memoirs of
World War One or letters written by 'ordinary' people. One of
the most extraordinary things to emerge from such reading is the
admiration felt by the common soldier for their public-school
officers. Two examples from many are:

At intervals the gun fired, time of flight, twenty-seven
seconds. I gave the Captain roughly where the shell
burst and damage, if any. My word, he didn't bat an
eyelid, another of these Public School boys.[28]

And:

He [the officer] was one of those trained in the big
public schools and the Royal Military College at
Camberley in those far-off days before the war, men
who thought they were indestructible, untouchable –

27 W. C. Sherriff, quoted in Panichas, *Promises of Greatness*, pp. 139 and 152.
28 MacDonald, *Voices*, p. 292.

and, by God, the way some of them acted we sometimes thought so too. Marvellous men they were, men one could follow.[29]

Much of what the public schools offered their boys in the way of training for being a volunteer officer came by the by: an ability to cope with hard living conditions; the sense of its being 'bad form' to moan or complain; familiarity with the all-male institution; and so on. There was another factor frequently missed out on by modern commentators for whom having servants is unthinkable. Any household that could afford to send its son to a public school would by definition have several servants. Those with servants soon realised that the servants knew virtually everything they did or said, and that someone who fell out with the servants did himself a great disservice and risked serious discomfort. There was a mutual respect across the class divide, seen, for example, in Bertie Wooster and Jeeves and in Lord Peter Wimsey's relationship with his servants in the novels of Dorothy L. Sayers. Such mutual respect transferred easily to the trenches. 'Real' gents knew how to treat the servants, which was why places in great households were so competed for. The worst employers were deemed to the nouveau *bourgeoisie*.

As mentioned earlier, the link between the public schools and the military has sometimes been confused by the fact that service in the armed forces was an acceptable career option for middle- and upper-class families, but in the case of the Army at least usually not the most intelligent sons. Many schools had an 'Army Side' for those destined for the armed services, but the route into a career as an officer was via a number of Colleges that

29   Bert Chaney, quoted in Moynihan, *People at War*, p. 118.

were combined into Sandhurst Royal Military Academy in 1947, or through the Britannia Royal Naval College. The best route into these was via the burgeoning number of Army 'crammers', or places providing specific instruction to enable candidates to pass the entry requirements. Thus the journey from public school to the army was likely to have one or two separate institutions between the public school and actual service in the Army. As only one example, very nearly all the most famous Royal Navy admirals of World War Two had had as their school not Eton, Harrow or Winchester, but the Royal Naval College HMS *Britannia*, two wooden-hulled old sailing ships moored together at Dartmouth.

The link between the public schools and the Empire is even more tenuous. The fact that Rudyard Kipling went to Imperial Service College (and left early) and that this school did specialise in Imperial service has had a disproportionate influence. Not only has Kipling been seen as the great literary spokesman for the British Empire, but he also wrote a public-school novel, *Stalky & Co.*, which in its day was very popular, though now neglected. The facts were different. In 1880, of the pupils who entered Harrow and Rugby, twenty-two were listed by occupation as 'overseas', the majority of those probably working on or for the Empire in one way or another. Yet forty went into the law, forty-seven into business and forty-one into the armed forces. Out of interest, nine went into the Church and a mere fourteen into 'Scholastics', which together with the nine for medicine illustrates that, whatever else the public schools might have been in 1880, they were not academic hothouses.[30]

The fact is that the public schools did not train their boys in military skills, or glorify the military nearly as much as they did

---

30 See Gathorne-Hardy, *The Public School Phenomenon*, p. 447.

athleticism or tried to do with Christianity. What they did do was turn out a boy whose skills set could be used to turn him into an officer. A veneer of respectability that they did not command among the boys was given them in the time of National Service and thereafter, where the teachers who were the officers for the CCF had at least seen service in the real armed forces. What did give the OTC and CCF credibility among boys was the existence of the annual Bisley shooting competition, the entry to which was inevitably via the CCF. But the credibility it gave derived from its being a competitive sport where one had a chance to biff Eton, Harrow or Wellington (always a good thing), rather than because it was a specifically military activity.

My view of all this is, of course, hopelessly influenced by my own experiences at school, though in fairness I did spend ten years thereafter as a joke of a Naval officer in the CCF. I was a founder member of the Naval Section of the CCF at Uppingham. In those days we wore proper Navy uniform, with white webbing, which we whitened up with the ubiquitous gym-shoe cleaner (if anyone young enough is condemned to read this book, I might explain that gym shoes were the primitive antecedent of trainers). That was great, until it rained one day, and we found out the hard way that gym-shoe cleaner ran in the wet. The contingent looked as if every seagull in the North Sea had dumped on them.

We were lined up one day by the side of the Eyebrook Reservoir – where we sailed old whalers rescued from scrapped battleships with a variety of rigs that would not have disgraced the Sea of Galilee – to be inspected by a visiting admiral. There is one simple universal rule that applies without exception to any visit to a CCF contingent by a senior officer. It is that the officer will always stop to talk to the recruit the school would least like him to meet. In this case he stopped opposite a seaman of very little brain, known to his fellow matelots as Baa Lamb, and barked at him, 'You there, Ordinary Seaman! How deep is this reservoir?'

Baa Lamb, who had difficulty remembering his own name, was reduced to confusion. He answered in his normal state of confusion, 'Er . . . don't know, sir.'

'Well,' snorted the Admiral, 'how do you propose to find out. Show initiative, boy!'

So Baa Lamb did. He jumped in. In fact, even with my limited memory of the young man in question, I suspect he probably fell in. In any event, after a few seconds, his tousled head broke the surface.

'Bloody deep, sir!' he had time to splutter before he sank beneath waves again. I remember his little round white sailors' hat bobbing prettily on the waves. The problem was Baa Lamb couldn't swim. You knew that about people, back in those days. Our officer, dressed in his woollen No. 5 uniform, had to dive in to rescue him. I believe Baa Lamb was soundly thrashed, not for jumping in, but for using a swear word in front of an officer.

But the best moment was when the whole contingent (that is to say, the whole school) mustered on the school playing field for Field Day to welcome the Inspecting Officer, who was due to arrive, wonder of wonders, by helicopter – a big thing back then. It was so important we'd actually had a rehearsal. We had a retired regimental sergeant-major to administer the CCF. I now can see that he was more or less permanently drunk. In my innocence as a young boy I just thought he had a speech defect that made him slur his words.

When the big day came he was well cut. Five hundred boys were milling around the field, more or less in range of where they were meant to parade in serried ranks. In the battle plan devised by the authorities for this ceremony, two platoons were meant to pair up with each other and stand to attention as one unit. In what was to prove a fatal misjudgement, they had allowed us to wander round a little, rather than stand easy in our positions. When the first rattle of the helicopter rotors was heard, the RSM climbed with some difficulty up onto the rostrum and bellowed his orders to the contingent. He had a voice so loud it could have stopped all the fighting at Anzio with one yell, but, in case this was not enough, he had been given a PA system that was so loud it had probably been looted by the Army from the Nuremberg parade ground. What he said was,

'*Contingent! Pair up in threes!*'

When the copter finally landed it was to see a writhing mass of khaki thoroughly enjoying all falling over themselves in an undisciplined muddy heap. Try pairing up in threes and you'll see what I mean. I never did learn to do it, but I did learn that, if you put enough sand down the barrel of a Lee-Enfield standard-issue rifle and fire it at your friend's bottom with a blank round it, leaves a satisfyingly large red mark.

In all fairness, I must add that the modern CCF, as far as I can see, is a very different animal that has stopped trying to pretend schoolboys or their teachers can ever be anything like real soldiers, sailors or airmen, and concentrates instead on outdoor pursuits and inculcating entirely bloodless skills of teamwork and leadership. It's entirely worthy – and perhaps just a little boring in comparison with what I experienced.

They did instil in many of their pupils a sense of service – and is that such a very bad thing? As I write this, I have just returned from trips to Russia and China, where I have interviewed many young people. OK, they were among the brightest and the best of their respective countries. Yet what struck me about these young people was the loyalty they felt to their country of origin, the pride they felt in it and their sense of service, their duty to pay back even a little of what they had received, from their parents, from their country and, yes, even their school. I wonder if I interviewed now some of the brightest and best young people in the UK they would express such a loyalty to their country, or to their school. Perhaps the public schools in history may have taken the sense of service too far, but perhaps also education in the UK now does not take it far enough.

As ever, public schools have been their own worst enemies when it comes to portraying their attitude to war, and the attitude shown by their pupils. Old Rugbeian Rupert Brooke (himself the son of a Rugby Housemaster) wrote the four famous patriotic sonnets that perhaps more than any other work have come to symbolise the welcome public-school boys gave to the prospect of dying for their country, as we see in 'The Soldier':

> If I should die, think only this of me:
> That there's some corner of a foreign field
> That is for ever England.

This was an attitude savaged by non-public-school boy Wilfred Owen in his poem about 'the old lie', 'Dulce et Decorum Est' (from a line by the Roman poet Horace, *Dulce et decorum est pro patria mori*' – 'It is sweet and seemly to die for one's country'). Yet the association with mindless patriotism is to oversimplify both Brooke's attitudes and those of many of his contemporaries. Never mind that Brooke's sonnets are classic adolescent self-glorification, in which the most important and repeated words are 'I' and 'me'. The sonnets are about Rupert Brooke more than they are about England. Never mind that Brooke was far more similar to Byron than to Tom Brown; here was a bisexual young man who was not only in a semipermanent state of nervous breakdown himself, but had a remarkable capacity to inflict nervous breakdowns on those closest to him.

A less well-known poem by Brooke refers to the war as 'swimmers into cleanness leaping'. Brooke did not welcome war as such. A hugely intelligent and unstable young man, Brooke was increasingly unable to unravel the complexities of his life. The war suddenly brought simplicity to that life, a clarity and simple target that allowed him to sideline doubt and uncertainty and devote himself to one lone dramatic cause that satisfied his yearning for extreme experience.

There were also a number of public-school boys who were killed in the war who made much of their love for their old school either before or in the process of dying. That pathetic and rather touching refrain that comes through many of these is the expression of the hope that they had not let the old school down. The schools themselves lost whole generations of boys, and, perfectly reasonably, were deeply moved by the loss of so many whom, in their own way, they had loved. What was actually a genuine expression of love for their pupils and regret at their loss, shown in writing, war memorials and memoirs, became joined and confused with love of warfare and unfeeling patriotism that actually the public schools did not have, at least in anything I have read.

Many poems of the time combined the sporting triumphs of the public school with the experience and sacrifice of war, illustrating if nothing else the widespread belief that public-school boys learned more on the playing field than they ever did in the classroom. One example that can stand for many is,

SOME CORNER OF A FOREIGN FIELD

IN MEMORIAM, J.H.H.

Last year, scarce one short season back,
They cheered your swift, triumphant pace,
And all along the Terrace[31] track
Acclaimed you winner of the race.

To-day they shout another's name,
O friend of mine so far away,
For you have played a greater game
For sterner stakes than I or they.

Yes, you the hardest race have run,
Where none might hope to cheer you on;
But now the agony is done
And all the doubts and fears are gone.

Brave heart, as often in old days,
You breast the tape before us all;
And down Death's unrelenting ways,
Your feet have passed beyond recall.

We have no place for wrath or tears
Where all around the thunders roll –
One friend the less for coming years,
One friend the more beyond the goal.

C. J. Ronald

---

31 The Terrace is the rugby pitch and running track in front of the imposing façade of
Haileybury College.

Personally, and often very unfashionably, I have found myself moved by poems such as these. I have never found that they glorify war, or even that they glorify sport. What they do reflect is the extent to which sport was bound up in the experience of so many public-school boys, while the other obsessions of the system, Chapel and Christianity, were the preserve of the adults, barely mentioned in the poetry of the boys themselves.

There are a great number of poems written by or about the public-school involvement in the Great War that rarely see the light of day. This is true about a lot of the poetry written about World War One. The story of why this was so is complicated. The cynicism and horror we associate now with World War One was, remarkably, not a feature in the comments of any of the many survivors of the conflict I was privileged to interview in the early 1970s as part of my PhD research. They were a very politically incorrect bunch. They were proud, as amateurs, to have defeated the most professional army in the world. Many of them believed that, if the politicians had handled with any degree of skill the victory they had won with their blood, sweat and tears, 5 million Jews might not have died. They neither rated nor read the poetry of Wilfred Owen or Siegfried Sassoon, and in particular detested Owen's poem 'The Dead-Beat' on the grounds that it made them look like losers. They kept in their knapsacks the poetry of 'Woodbine Willie', or the Rev. Studdert-Kennedy, Chaplain to the Forces. The intense bitterness we now associate with World War One was not created by the fighting soldiers who survived the conflict – and, despite the horrendous casualties, the great majority of solders who fought for Britain in that war did survive to tell the tale. That bitterness was created above all by the influenza pandemic that swept the world in 1918–19, and killed more people than the Great War

– estimates vary between 20 and 40 million people. A fifth of the world's people were affected. Of the US soldiers who died in Europe, half of then fell to the influenza virus. Unusually, it was most deadly to those aged between twenty and forty, the age of many of the surviving servicemen and their wives. Medical services, already stretched to breaking by the war, often simply could not cope.

It is difficult to imagine now the sense of bitterness and gross unfairness when those who had survived one of the bitterest wars of human history fell not to bullets or bombs but to a virus. What must it have felt like to have prayed for your husband or fiancé for the years of the war, welcomed him home, and then stood helplessly by when he died of influenza? What must it have felt like to have fought through that war, survived it all in the belief that you were fighting for your wife and family, and then come home from Hell to see your wife or fiancée die from a meaningless illness?

The combination of the flu pandemic and the Wall Street Crash and slump in the world economy produced a climate almost of despair among the literate classes in the late 1920s and 1930s. T. S. Eliot's great poem *The Waste Land* was published in 1922, and predicted as well as predated the economic and cultural depression of the 1920s. Gone were the joyous celebrations of nature so typical of prewar poetry, to be replaced by 'smells of steaks in passageways'. Gone also was the simplicity and sentimentality of much prewar poetry, to be replaced by ever-present dark irony and complexity of meaning.

In this climate even the searing pity of Owen's poetry was marked down as being too emotional – W. B. Yeats famously refused to include Owen in *The Oxford Book of Modern Verse* because his poetry was all 'blood, dirt and sucked sugar stick'.

Suddenly, to be accepted by the literary Establishment, poetry had to be ironic, tangled and complex. Owen, Sassoon, Rosenberg and the other 'war poets' were rehabilitated, perhaps because their poetry spoke to too many people for it to vanish, but literally thousands of rather good poems were left to rot in second-hand bookshops because they did not meet the irony test, or, Heaven forbid, were deemed sentimental. This was a pity as far as the public schools were concerned, because a number of those poems were written on or by public-school boys, and were neither sucked sugar stick nor mindless calls to patriotism.

The poem below is not great literature, but I find it worth reading. It is interesting if for no other reason than it hints at the theme of a far greater poem, Edward Thomas's 'As the Team's Head Brass', namely the unspeakable concept that, however big the catastrophe of World War One might have been, life does go on. The poem is also interesting because of its author. He was a teacher at Repton, and perhaps the only public-school teacher to play first-class cricket, in his case for Derbyshire. What a hero he must have been to his boys in the 1920s.

THE OLD HOUSEMASTER

'The blood ran red in these young brains and limbs,
Clear-eyed and laughing, lovers of the day,
They played their games, and worked, and sang their hymns,
Finished their course, and passed upon their way.
Now they have died, and nought remains of all
That spring of life in which they had their part,
But names half-carved, and portraits on the wall,
And memories of laughter in the heart.'

SOME CORNER OF A FOREIGN FIELD

So muses he upon his boyish dead,
Through the dumb night, while others in their prime,
His youthful England, slumber over head;
Then shuts the book upon his knee unread,
And lights his candle for the thousandth time,
And climbs along his creaky way to bed.

J. L. Crommelin-Brown[32]

Perhaps this poem gives a hint as to one of the little-heralded gifts of the public school to English education, namely the depth of the relationship between teacher and taught. By and large, Europe in general, and France and Germany in particular, saw the teacher as a lesser version of the university lecturer, someone who came in, delivered their lesson and left. I have recently had experience of Chinese and Russian students responding to teachers brought up in the UK state-school culture, and delighting in the personal care and attention they received from their ordinary classroom teacher. In our culture, the teacher is responsible for the whole child, not just the bit above his or her head. I suggest this is a direct influence from public schools and the boarding school in particular. As I approach seventy years of age I count myself lucky still to be talking to my public school Housemaster. I ceased to be a Housemaster myself in 1983, and have an appalling memory for names – yet so intense was the relationship with the pupils in my house that I have never failed even once to recognise and remember the name of any of my former pupils, even if it has been over thirty years since I last saw them. The public schools have given more than the cult of sport and a culture of superficial worship to English education.

---

32 Holder, *Anthology of School*, p. 124.

Empire

As well as providing the cannon fodder for World War One, public schools are frequently seen as the factories that produced the men who ran the British Empire. The impression is misleading: '. . . overseas service was unpopular in the highest circles . . .'[33]

Of 159 Harrow entrants in 1875, only 13 listed 'overseas' as their major occupation, or just over 8 per cent. Yet between 1880 and 1885 26 Sedberghians out of 106 (nearly a quarter) went overseas, while in 1905 at Clifton 15 leavers out of 28 (over half) went overseas.[34] What the figures show is, first, that the majority of those who went to serve the Empire were from relatively minor public schools, and that the figures varied hugely on a school-by-school basis. Haileybury, for example, had a particularly 'Imperial' tone. It was based on the old buildings of the East India Company, and as a result of amalgamation is still in some people's eyes 'Haileybury and Imperial Service College'. What has influenced the public perception is also that the most powerful figures in the administration of the Empire, the Viceroys, were dominated by public-school men. As for positions in the Indian Civil Service, in effect both an administration and a government, many of those who landed these top positions did so via a 'crammer' or specialist college, rather than entering directly from public school.

Many public-school boys did not expect to have to work at all, which is why they could be fed an employment-useless diet of classics. Of those who did need to earn a living, service in the Empire was merely one of many choices, including the professions, politics, academia, the church, the civil service and the armed forces, not to mention farming. Just as younger sons

---

33 Bamford, *The Rise of the Public Schools*, p. 216.
34 Ibid., p. 221.

rushed off on crusades in the Middle Ages, in hope of defeating *primogeniture* and gaining the land and hence the wealth denied them at home, so the Empire attracted some young men as Hobson's Choice. It is no accident that George MacDonald Fraser in his Flashman books had Tom Brown's fairly wild companion, East, doing heroic things in the far-flung reaches of the Empire.

The Empire was more than an employment opportunity. Like all frontiers, it was somewhere to send the wild bunch. The Empire was founded on greed and the lust for money. It was perpetuated for the same reason, providing among other things a captive market for the cheap textiles produced in the UK. Certain authorities even blame the public schools for losing us the Empire, not through the rot of homosexuality, but through lip service to Christian morality. For these people, the theory runs that, if Clive of India had met Gandhi in the early years, he would have had no hesitation in taking him round the back and putting a bullet through his head. It was only those educated in the spirit of Arnold who were soft and stupid enough to let people such as Gandhi live. What is true is that the cult of manliness favoured by the public schools was not bad training for work overseas:

> The doctrine of the stiff-upper-lip was no part of the public school code of the Arnoldian period. This gradually came in with the manliness cult of the 1870s and 1880s. For it would never have done for Empire builders and games players to exhibit their emotions.[35]

The public-school boy was actually seen as a liability in the 'white' regions of the Empire, as in Australia and Canada: 'In

---

35 Newsome, quoted in Bamford, *Rise of the Pubic Schools*, p. 58.

the new "white" regions the public-school man was unwanted, ridiculed, even rejected. This was common knowledge . . .'[36]

In contrast, when India gained its independence one of the few manifestations of colonial rule that were not thrown out were the boarding schools set up by the Raj on the British public-school model. Instead they were strengthened and enlarged, in the hope that a democratic entry into them could produce an elite to help run the country and replace the white-dominated civil servants.

The English public schools pre-1914 were not the home of brainless nitwits who flocked mindlessly like turkeys to their own slaughter. Rupert Brooke was a Fabian. Charles Hamilton Sorley planned a career as an elementary-school teacher after Oxford. The public-school boys joined up for the same reason as the rest of England: English culture in general in 1914. They believed in their country. They saw England as worth fighting for, and even worth dying for. As it happened, the public school had produced young men who were capable of being turned into officers relatively easily and – more important – relatively quickly. It was not what they were trained for. It was what they could become.

As for the Empire, that was simply the equivalent of the Crusades, the land where endless opportunities beckoned for the landless, the second or third sons, those without the brains or the application to suffer three years of more classics at Oxford or Cambridge. The public schools did not produce young men for the Empire. They educated young men, some of whom would inevitably gravitate to the Empire, in the way that the frontier has always attracted young men for whom the Old World offers no similar opportunities.

---

36   Bamford, p. 241.

8

BILLY BUNTER AND FRIENDS

The School years, with their echoes of *Stalky & Co*,
no less than *Eric, or Little by Little,* make merry
reading. In the late twenties and thirties it became
fashionable for youngish writers to turn and rend
the schools that had nurtured them. In tortured
sentences they explained how tedious was the OTC,
how trying the footer, how dreary the staff . . . by and
large the authors had all seen something nasty in the
boot-hole and were not going to forget it.[37]

M y intention in this chapter is not to give a regurgitated
account of some of the best-known fictional works written
about public schools, but rather to provide a shamelessly personal
list of those that I think deserve to be read today, or that, like

---

37   Arthur Marshall on *Tell England* by Ernest Raymond, quoted in *Girls Will Be Girls*, 1974,
quoted in Craig, *The Oxford Book of Schooldays*, p. 270.

a large concrete block in the middle of the motorway, simply cannot be ignored by anyone who wants to understand the English public school.

Neglected Classic 1: *Flannelled Fool*

Flannelled Fool by T. C. Worsley (1907–1997) is the autobiographical account of a naïve young man whose life at Marlborough in the late 1920s is totally dominated by cricket. Moving on to Cambridge, simply because it is there rather than because he has any interest in it or classics, he fails to make it either as a blue or as an academic. He was persuaded to take up a teaching post at Wellington in 1929, which was far more impressed by his cricket than he was. He almost by accident becomes the leader of the revolt against the appalling Old Guard at Wellington. The book is more than a telling description of the strangling conservatism of a 1930s public school. It is at one and the same time the story of a young man finally growing up, a young man coming to terms with his homosexuality and a young man living and coming to terms with the political and social turbulence of the 1930s.

The whole book is enlivened by the fact that by any standards Worsley's early life was dramatic and challenging. His father was the charismatic Dean of Llandaff Cathedral, holder of the Military Cross and the English long-jump record and a preacher who made old ladies weak at the knees. Unfortunately, it was not merely old ladies he was interested in, and he was a serial philanderer who, when about to be exposed and with his son at university, arrived down to breakfast one morning with two suitcases and told his family they would have to find somewhere else to live. He then vanished. Previously, a tear that never mended scored though

Worsley's brain when his younger brother, Ben, drowned on holiday. Worsley, who could not swim, was being dragged under by Ben's frantic hands scrabbling at him, and had pushed them away before somehow saving himself.

Worsley went with Stephen Spender to fight in the Spanish Civil War, and worked as a journalist and author, first for the *New Statesman* and then as theatre and television critic for the *Financial Times*. The book is fascinating on many fronts, and well worth reading regardless of any interest in public schools. To me, what it shows is that the public school could delay maturity and wisdom, but never destroy or stop them.

Neglected Classics 2: *The Lanchester Tradition*

The Lanchester Tradition was published in 1913. Its author, G. F. Bradby (1863–1947) was the son of the Master of Haileybury, and his life seems to follow a boringly predictable pattern: schooled at Rugby, on to Balliol College, Oxford (rugby blue), and the rest of his life spent as a teacher and Housemaster at his old school, Rugby. In fact he was far more interesting than that, and wrote poems, novels, literary criticism and hymns. He wrote opposing the Boer War, and one of his innovative books is *The Marquis's Eye* (1905), an early fantasy in which an innocent young Englishman receives an eye transplant from an overweening French aristocrat, and hilariously starts to see things as the Frenchman might see them.

The Lanchester Tradition may have been written in 1913, but, in common with most Heads I know, I have met and worked with every character described in its fictional Chiltern School. One of them at least is alive and worryingly well in a public school near you. Chiltern School labours the oppressive tradition of its 'second

Founder', Dr Abraham Lanchester, an amalgam of Thomas Arnold, Edward Thring and every traditional Headmaster you've ever heard of. Is it a book about schools? Or is it a book about 'change and institutional fear of change'?[38] It is certainly that, but it is also very, very funny.

I suppose it's no accident that my two neglected classics are both about fighting the Old Guard at public school. On a lesser and unfortunately nonfictional level it appears to have been part of my lot in life. Yet there is a further resonance for me in the story of *The Lanchester Tradition*. The Rev. John Royds was brought in as 'Headman' at Uppingham in 1965, one year after I joined. As an adult I subsequently came to both know and like him, but as boys all we knew (don't ask how we knew) was that he was a rank outsider (we were told he had been a missionary in Africa, though in fact he had been Head of a mission school in Addis Ababa) whose appointment had caused uproar among the staff. Royds arrived, saw that Uppingham was signally failing to adapt to the 1960s, and flung the brakes off. He stopped the decline in numbers, and saw them start to build up, but in all my four years as a pupil and my years as a teacher at Uppingham I never heard one good word said about him by a teacher. He was tolerated as far as I could see by his staff, no more and no less, while retaining the capacity to inspire awe in his pupils, not least of all the comedian, actor and writer Stephen Fry. Royds could have been a model for Mr Flaggon, the new Head of Chiltern. I would love to know if Royds ever faced a Common Room revolt, as did at least one other distinguished Head I knew, but I doubt the official history will tell me.

The Lanchester Tradition probably appeals more to those in the

---

38 Jacket blurb for the John Catt Educational reprint of the book.

trade than those outside of it. There is a gorgeous irony in that the major justification for dismissing the new Head is that he has broken with 'the Lanchester Tradition'. In fact, as we learn from the book, Dr Abraham Lanchester was a massive reformer and innovator. A delicious note to the book is found in the fact that Lanchester faced so many complaints from his teaching staff that he had inserted into the constitution the power for the Governors to reject a complaint before it came to an official hearing – precisely the loophole on which the new Head is allowed, almost by accident, to keep his job.

But this is not the least of the hidden gems in the book. There is the Bishop, a Governor. No cause is ever well and truly lost until the Bishop speaks in its favour, and he is in favour of dismissing the Head. Chowdler, the stupid, pigheaded and opinionated Housemaster who is the Head's main enemy, is a masterful portrait of the idiots who exercised power in public school for so long, and is the exact image of one Housemaster I had the misfortune to work with. One of his boys was hit in the crotch by an attempt to dropkick a goal in a rugby match. As the boy sank to his knees in agony he was heard to mutter (he didn't have much breath left) an expletive, and three days later, on his leaving the sanatorium, the man beat him for using an expletive on the field of play. Chowdler's sycophantic wife is another brilliant portrait, and reminds me of 'the wife' who insisted at all times, public and private, on referring in worshipping tones to her husband as 'Headmaster'.

The Lanchester Tradition can claim to be the most frequently rediscovered book in history. It is available nowadays only in reprints that claim it as a forgotten classic. It was almost certainly not forgotten by R. F. Delderfield, whose *To Serve Them All Our Days* was clearly inspired by it. Why is it not better known? Why was there no sequel to it, as was so clearly intended by the author? One reason is that it was published in 1913, and within a year the goings-on in a traditional public school appeared small beer in comparison with the massacre of a generation. I suspect a second reason was the integrity of the author. Lunn's *The Harrovian*, Waugh's *The Loom of Youth* and even *Eric, or Little by Little* were written with more than half an eye on their effect, their sales, their impact on the reputation of the author in the literary circles of London. I suspect Bradby simply wanted to write the truth. It doesn't guarantee immortality. But, if you ask me which of all the books in this chapter tells the most truth, it is *The Lanchester Tradition*.

Tom Brown's Schooldays

It is quite extraordinary that the title of a highly fictionalised and inaccurate novel about life in an English public school should have become a household phrase, that the book should still be in print and that it should be used as the centrepiece of a prominent article in *The Times* newspaper in 2016, in which wholly extravagant claims are made for the book:

> *Tom Brown's Schooldays* . . . gave birth to an entire genre of school fiction, from Billy Bunter to St Trinian's to Harry Potter; it helped popularise the sport of rugby. Theodore Roosevelt believed every boy should read the book; it spread the idea of 'muscular Christianity' worldwide, and created, in the school bully Flashman, one of the great antiheroes of literature. More than that, *Tom Brown's Schooldays* inspired the Olympics.[39]

---

39 Ben Macintyre, 'Modern Olympics began on the fields of Rugby', *Times*, 19 August 2016, p. 23.

Really? And presumably it solved global warming at the same time . . .

The book appeared in 1857, and was a smash hit then, and now. As with so many other books purporting to show life at a public school, it is a 'compound of romantic fiction and expurgated fact . . . The whole truth, "good" and "bad", of the unreformed public schools could not be told openly in an age which was, on certain subjects . . . an age of reticence.[40]

Tom Brown's Schooldays is intensely cringeworthy. It purports to tell the tale of a plucky young lad packed off to Rugby who becomes very naughty, but is rescued in the nick of time by the good Dr Arnold, who places a sickly and anaemic young man in his care. It contains serious bullying, about its only claim to reality. It is remarkable in that it tells the story of young men growing up without once mentioning sex, and the many public schools that have adopted it as their bible have ignored the fact that, a hundred years after it was written, Tom Brown would most likely have been expelled for 'taking up' the younger and disturbingly feminine boy handed over to him by Arnold. It contains much moralising, quite a lot of sport and absolutely no mention whatsoever of scholarship, maths or science. The book is not actually about Tom Brown at all, but about the saintly Dr Thomas Arnold, Headmaster of Rugby, written by one of the small coterie of boys who fell under his spell in their time at Rugby and was ruthlessly cultivated by him in the pursuit of his own myth. It is one of the earliest examples of a fanzine.

So what? It's a good story. Do you imagine Cinderella ever really happened like that? Yet one of the problems with public-

---

40 Chandos, , *All Boys Together* p. 45.

school fiction is that people have tended to believe what they read. The editors of the magazine that published the Billy Bunter stories received regular requests, written in all seriousness, to visit Greyfriars School. My advice to those who read *Tom Brown's Schooldays* is the same as my advice to those who go to see Shakespeare's *Richard III*: enjoy the play, but don't confuse it with historical reality. So with *Tom Brown's Schooldays*. Enjoy the book; just don't confuse it with reality.

Eric, or Little by Little

If *Tom Brown's Schooldays* is cringeworthy, another great classic of its time, *Eric, or Little by Little*, is positively nauseating, and might reasonably be retitled as *Eric, or Pass the Sickbag*. Written by the Rev. Canon Frederick William Farrar, Headmaster of Marlborough, in 1858, it tells the story of a decent young man who succumbs 'little by little' to a variety of the depravities available at boarding school, and sinks into moral turpitude. Eventually, he does something that even he is so ashamed of that he runs off to sea, hates it, returns to dry land and immediately sickens and dies. The author's preface to the 1889 edition (yes, it was still being reprinted thirty-one years after its first publication) forms the only example in my experience of an author's preface showing the reader why he or she should not read the book itself:

> The story of 'Eric' was written with but one single object
> – the vivid inculcation of inward purity and moral
> purpose, by the history of a boy who, in spite of the
> inherent nobleness of his disposition, falls into all folly
> and wickedness, until he has learnt to seek help from

above. I am deeply thankful to know – from testimony public and private, anonymous and acknowledged – that this object has, by God's blessing, been fulfilled.[41]

Farrar is one of those people who, as with those named in the Bob Dylan song, have no doubt that God was on their side. Farrar's sheer arrogance in stating that he has fulfilled his aim of creating inward purity and moral purpose – in everyone? – is breathtaking. The book can be seen as the 'Song of Experience' by the side of Thomas's Hughes's 'Song of Innocence', in that it shows what might have happened to Tom Brown had he not been turned by the Doctor. Personally, I can think of no one more likely to convert me to folly and wickedness than Dean Farrar. Of the hundreds of books I have read in the preparation of *this* book, the only one that has been a real ordeal and a trial to finish has been *Eric, or Little by Little*.

Stalky & Co.

Stalky & Co. by Rudyard Kipling appeared first in 1899. Perhaps because of its author, or perhaps because it is a flawed work, it is often more talked about than read nowadays. It is about the three inhabitants of Study 5, a trio of anarchic boys, Stalky, Beetle and M'Turk. They are at permanent war with the Housemasters King and Prout, and in awe of the Headmaster. The book was based on Kipling's own time at United Services College, a boarding school founded in 1874 at Westward Ho! near Bideford in Devon that was in effect a long-term preparation for the Army and a glorified crammer. It was always on shaky financial footings and

---

41   Farrar, *Eric, or Little by Little*, p. 1.

amalgamated first of all with the Imperial Services College (1906), which in turn amalgamated with Haileybury (1942).

One problem with the book is that Stalky, Beetle and M'Turk never grow up, and Kipling's grasp of a prefect and senior boy's life at a public school is limited – and it shows. A second problem is that there is no real narrative strand in the book, or character growth; it is simply a collection of episodes. A third is that the final chapter shows all three boys as officers and men, getting the better of the natives just as they got the better of their Housemasters, showing an acceptance of 'abolishing' natives unacceptable to post-Colonial sensitivities. Yet is in an interesting book. The three boys are classic underdogs who get the better of their foes by the use of their wits, and are occasionally hilarious anti-Establishment figures. Although it has an Arnoldian episode where the Chaplain seeks the help of the three boys to stop the bullying of a younger boy, there is a harsh reality in the effective solution undertaken by the boys, and a total lack of the sanctimonious religiosity of *Tom Brown's Schooldays*. It is a 'jolly japes' book, which in one sense precedes Billy Bunter and *The Magnet*, but it has an edge of darkness to it, and Stalky's clinical ability to manipulate the world around him and the people within it can be compelling. The best moment in the book for me is when an aunt sends the boys a copy of *Eric, or Little by Little*, which is treated with total derision. Here is one set of boys it clearly did not reform.

Billy Bunter

The fictional Billy Bunter is an iconic figure, and as with all icons means different things to different people: 'Bunter, the bilker that lurks in all of us, the con-artist, the social climber, the guzzler, the sycophant, the very spirit of crapula, Bunter buffoon and butt, toady, freeloader and screaming funk.'[42]

Bunter's readership included a large number – perhaps a majority – of boys who were not at public school themselves. To those who were, in the grip of the all-pervading demon of one's popularity, Bunter was a massive reassurance – the boy against whom it was impossible to be more unpopular, the scapegoat, the sacrificial lump of lard who carried all the fears every schoolboy and schoolgirl ever had about being excluded, unpopular, not 'one of the crowd'.

Bunter also has another feature of the likeable rogue in literature. He is utterly transparent. Shakespeare's Falstaff telegraphs who and what he is, so, if you fall into bed with him or lend him money it's no one's fault but your own. Even Milton's Lucifer is so honest in his dishonesty that he becomes admirable. In the television series devoted to Billy Bunter, he is summoned to Mr Quelch's study to receive a 'trunk call' from his father. Bunter, immediately on entering the study, denies he has stolen Croaker's oranges, thus immediately confirming that he has. No one ever has to accuse Bunter of anything: he does it himself. Instead of categorising him as a thief, it makes him pathetically vulnerable. He would, of course, be an impossible creation in our culture. He is a classic case of bullying, needs treatment for an eating disorder and is a victim.

Yet the real secret of Bunter's success, and the overwhelming popularity of the fictional word of Greyfriars School, was summed up by George Orwell:

> The year is 1910 – or 1940, but it is all the same. You are
> at Greyfriars, a rosy-cheeked boy of fourteen in posh

---

42   Raven, *Old School*. p. 5.

tailor-made clothes, sitting down to tea in your study on the Remove passage after an exciting game of football which was won by an odd goal in the last minute. There is a cosy fire in the study, and outside the wind is whistling. The ivy clusters thickly around the old grey stones. Lord Maweverer has just got another fiver and we are all sitting down to a tremendous tea of sausages, sardines, crumpets, potted meat, jam and doughnuts. After tea we shall sit round the study fire having a good laugh at Billy Bunter and discussing the team for next week's match against Rockwood. Everything is safe, solid and unquestionable. Everything will be the same for ever and ever.[43]

The Rebel Fringe 1: *The Harrovian*

Arnold Lunn's *The Harrovian*, published in 1914, has been overshadowed by Alec Waugh's *The Loom of Youth*, but deserves better. In its day the novel was a shocker. It is a beautifully written account of real life at Harrow. To modern taste there is very little in it that is explosive, but for the first time there was a book that questioned the reason for the tribal rules and customs so zealously guarded by the great public schools. It was accused of mocking the schools' devotion to sport, Christianity, 'house spirit' and the elevation of 'manliness' above culture or science. In fact it does no such thing. Instead it shows the healthy scepticism felt by normal schoolboys towards the tripe the Establishment fed them,

---

43 George Orwell in 1940, quoted in Walford, *Life In Public Schools*, p. 3.

'Yes,' said Manson, 'and then you have the ol' women in the hols who tell you how nice it is to be goin' back to footer – all boys love footer. Silly old ganders. Why do people think a small man likes bargin' into a big man? British grit, I suppose. The pluck that made our England what it is' – Manson was gathering steam – 'and then you have the blighters who come down and preach about the godly 'eritage – Pah! – and what a splendid privilege it is to be a Public School boy, and that we're having the time of our little lives. If I thought that I'd shoot myself. Hello, Cadby, had a decent hols?'[44]

The Harrovian was the first blast of the trumpet against the vision of public-school life peddled by Tom Brown's Schooldays. It is both honest and thoroughly cheerful, and in my opinion gives the best picture of the public-school boys who became men in the early 1900s.

The Rebel Fringe 2: *The Loom of Youth*

Alec Waugh's *The Loom of Youth* was a first, semiautobiographical novel published in 1917, and based on a thinly disguised Sherborne. It was in part inspired by Lunn's *The Harrovian*, and mentions it at some length. It is possible that it has achieved a greater fame than Lunn's book simply by Alec Waugh's being the elder brother of Evelyn Waugh. It would also cause a modern marketing agent to rub their hands in glee because its author was a recently left public-school boy who was serving with honour in World War One as an officer at a time when

---

44 Lunn, *The Harrovians*, p. 32.

very few good novels were being published, and all the rebels seemed to be hooked on poetry. *The Loom of Youth* is the classic example of the right novel, at the right time and by the right author. Unfortunately in literature, 'right' for its time does not automatically ensure a book is 'right' for later times.

The Loom of Youth is the story of one Gordon Carruthers, and his time at school, the end of which coincides with the first year of World War One. It was both scandalous enough to have Waugh thrown out of the Sherborne Old Boys' Society and to become a bestseller. It portrays public school as being dominated by the worship of athleticism, and shows just how little public-school boys believed in the Church, the Corps or telling the truth. It manages to make it quite clear that boys are having sex with each other (there is actually nobody else at Fernhurst to have it with) without ever explicitly saying so. It is at its best when it depicts with hilarious accuracy the sheer, mindless arrogance and superiority of the 'Blood'.

> The real blood is easily recognised. He strolls in [into the Tuck Shop] as if he had taken a mortgage on the place, swaggers into the inner room, puts down his book on the top table in the right-hand corner – only the bloods sit here – and demands a cup of tea and a macaroon. A special counter has been made by the bloods' table, so that the great men can order what they want without going back into the outer shop. No real blood ever makes a noise in the outer shop. When he is once inside the inner shop, however, he immediately lets everyone know it. If he sees anyone he knows, he bawls out:
>
> 'I say, have you prepared this stuff for Christy?'

The person asked never has.

'Nor have I. Rot, I call it.'

No blood is ever known to have prepared anything.

The big man then sits down. If a friend of his is anywhere about, he flings a lump of sugar at him. When he gets up he knocks over at least one chair. He then strolls out, observing the same magnificent dignity in the outer shop. No one can mistake him.[45]

It is a book I find it hard to warm to. Waugh's affection for his old school clouds its incisiveness, and characterisation of even the central character is clumsy. We are told quite a lot what to think about him, rather than let the reader form their own conclusions from what that reader hears the character say and sees him do. At regular intervals the reader is treated to a sententious paragraph or two, telling us what our conclusions after the previous paragraphs should be, in case we hadn't reached the right conclusions ourselves. Characterisation of staff is hopeless, and we know we are meant to admire 'The Chief' (Headmaster, and Housemaster of School House), but never really find out why. *The Loom of Youth* is a book written by a seventeen-and-a-half-year-old in six and a half weeks, and it shows. Its best critic is its author, writing in 1954:

I was in a nostalgic mood, but I was also in a rebellious mood. Intensely though I had enjoyed my four years at Sherborne, I had been in constant conflict with authority. That conflict, so it seemed to me, had in the main been caused by authority's inability or refusal

---

45   Waugh, *Loom of Youth*, Filiquarian edition, no date, p. 70.

to recognise the true nature of school life. The Public School system was venerated as a pillar of the British Empire, and out of their veneration had grown a myth of the ideal Public School boy – Kipling's Brushwood Boy. In no sense had I incarnated such a myth and it had been responsible, I felt, for half my troubles. I wanted to expose it. Those moods of nostalgia and rebellion fused finally in an imperious need to relive my schooldays on paper, to put it all down, term by term, exactly as it had been, to explain, interpret, justify my point of view.[46]

Waugh poses, but does not answer, one of the central questions about the English public school. It placed huge pressure on its pupils to conform – but did that pressure subdue them, or serve to bring out their individuality where it was in their bones? Waugh, a classic rebel and freethinker, faces the dilemma of so many like-minded old boys: did the repressive public school dim the flame of their rebelliousness, or serve to fan it to a heat and intensity that saw them through, with credit, their whole adult life? I have spent most of my life damning Uppingham for seeking to drive my rebelliousness out of me. I wonder now sometimes, in my twilight years, if it did not create it. And, though I now see that that same rebelliousness lost me many things, and cost me many more, I can also see that in many respects it was responsible for such success as I have enjoyed.

There is another worrying analogy here. Some of the bitterest enemies of grammar school in the UK were or are Labour MPs such as Gerald Kaufman and Roy Hattersley, themselves products

---

46 Ibid., p. 6.

of grammar schools. Do we learn from this, post-World War One at least, that what schools who really do influence their pupils have to fear most is the apparent urge of some of their most successful products to turn and bite the hand that fed them?

And is this just what I am doing in this book?

The Rebel Fringe 3: *If . . . and Bottoms Up!*

If . . . is renowned in the hidden world of public schools as the worst decision ever taken by a public school governing body, in allowing filming of the most vitriolic anti-pubic-school film ever at . . . a certain public school. It shows what is plausibly a 1950s public school in all its horror – prefect beatings, sexually frustrated housemasters' wives, and Che-Guevara-like rebel pupils, to the accompaniment of a trendy African mass. Brilliant stuff, even surviving the sudden move to black-and-white film when the money ran out, and the *serious* mistake of having the dead Chaplain pulled out in a drawer and reincarnated by the Headmaster. Someone must have thought it was a good idea at the time. *If . . .* is to public schools what *Oh, What a Lovely War!* is to World War One: a hard-left vision of what we ought to think.

Bottoms Up! could not be more different. In the Jimmy Edwards film spinoff from the TV series *Wacko!*, every vestige of political correctness is challenged in the truly appalling Chislehurst Academy for the Sons of Gentlefolk. Matrons are to be ogled, bottoms are to be whacked and no member of staff can spell 'curriculum', never mind teach it. Yet in the film the young boy-rebel Wendover – so called to allow for the command, 'Bend over, Wendover!' – leads a successful pupil rebellion against Jimmy Edwards's Headmaster. This is not capitalist versus worker, as in *If . . .*, but more owner versus trade union.

You Gotta Love 'Em 1: *Goodbye Mr. Chips*

Goodbye, Mr. Chips ought to be a dreadful book. It is the most hopelessly sentimental of all the books associated with public schools. Relatively short, it tells the story of a not-very-good teacher who comes to a not-very-good public school. The teacher falls in love with the school and the school, eventually, falls in love with him. He confounds expectation and the world by marrying a dashing young wife, who dies tragically in childbirth, and as a result Chips's emotional life, always wedded to the school, returns there with interest. He dies shortly after a new boy, summoned for tea, has left with the words, 'Goodbye, Mr Chips', and claims proudly that he, a man dying as a childless bachelor, has had thousands of children, namely the pupils of Brookfield School.

I love it.

Why do I love it? Possibly because I am a sentimental fool, and hope that as I am dying some former pupil will breathe softly into my wrinkled ear, 'Goodbye, Nobby!' (my nickname at Haileybury). Er . . . no. Don't think that's it. I love *Goodbye, Mr. Chips* because . . .

I'm sorry, but there is something extraordinarily special about the bond you forge with your pupils at a boarding school. Nowadays, much of that's been spoiled by the appalling revelations of predatory sexual behaviour on the parts of some teachers, but, honestly, for most of us most of the time it simply wasn't like that. You were *in loco parentis*, and you'd no more abuse that than most parents. You recognised the extraordinary privilege your job gave you in being present at the maturation of child into adult, and were both genuinely grateful for and terrified at the responsibility it gave you. Everyone remembers a good teacher is a modern mantra. An equal one that haunted my generation was 'Yes, but by God they remember a bad one too.' We loved our pupils. And – would you believe it? – we did so in an innocent way. *Goodbye, Mr. Chips* reassures me that that you can love young boys without wanting to molest them.

And the second reason I love this book? I was privileged to work alongside Mr Chips. He wasn't called that, of course. He was called Ian Bailey, and he was a boy at The Manchester Grammar School who fought throughout World War Two and came back to teach there, and was retained on the staff until he died, his job late in the day to show prospective parents and their children round the school. As a tour guide, Ian was the marketing manager's nightmare. I once met him with two sets of parents he had been given an hour and a half earlier. He had just reached 1745 in the history of The Manchester Grammar School. Yet both sets of parents subsequently signed up to that greatest of all schools. They didn't sign up to a vision of a school in 1745. They signed up to a school that had produced someone who believed passionately in that school, and believed passionately in its ability to mould young lives for the better.

In a lifetime of headship, the most difficult decision I have ever taken was not to go to Ian Bailey's funeral. The reason? It would have meant cancelling a meeting that might have led to a scheme that would have let poor children attend St Paul's School on free places. Of all people, I thought Ian was the one who would most have understood that true schoolteachers commit to the future of young people, not to memories of the past. As it was, I failed. That meeting did not produce the free places I had hoped for. I now bitterly regret not being at that funeral. Ian would have told me off, in his diffident but always kindly way. 'Nothing ventured, nothing gained!' he would have told me. Or so I hope.

Ian, or Mr-Chips-in-Real-Life, also had the capacity to be

totally infuriating, as did the fictional Mr Chips. As a man who had seen more than most come and go, he would without thinking refer to, 'the High Master of the day . . . ' or 'the forty-second High Master', the sense being clearly of, 'Forty, forty-one, forty two . . . Forty-three?' There was a good moral lesson for High Masters in Ian's thinking: High Masters come and go, but the school lives on.

Public schools owe much of the affection in which they are held by their former pupils to men who chose to devote their lives to a particular school and its pupils, men who did not so much love the pupils as love a school. It is sentimental and trite. That does not stop it being true.

You Gotta Love 'Em 2: *To Serve Them All Our Days*

To Serve Them All Our Days, by R. F. Delderfield, was published in 1972, and was the subject of an extremely successful and popular BBC dramatisation. Its plot was clearly inspired by *Goodbye, Mr. Chips*: rather unlikely young man joins minor public school, becomes good teacher, marries feisty young girl who dies tragically before her time. The difference is that Chips's delightful wife dies in childbirth, while Powlett-Jones's wife dies in a road accident, taking one of her twin girls with her to the grave. Both stories continue with the arrival of a new and clinically cold Headmaster, win their battle with him and go on to rule the roost. There is an ironic twist to *To Serve Them All Our Days*, where history repeats itself and Powlett-Jones, now Headmaster, interviews a damaged young man who has been bombed by Stukas in France, just as years earlier a war-damaged Powlett-Jones had been interviewed by Algie, the benign and understanding Head of the day.

There are some lovely moments in *To Serve Them All Our Days*, but I have to confess I find it overall irritating more than moving. One reason is pure grumpy old man. Delderfield continually refers to his hero serving three years in the trenches, as if it were continuous service in the front line. In fact, a major reason why there was no significant mutiny in the British Army during World War One was the rotation of troops, restricting time in the front line. Wilfred Owen spent less than a month in the front line.

Powlett-Jones also introduces the poetry of Siegfried Sassoon, Wilfred Owen and Isaac Rosenberg to his pupils. These became highly fashionable in the late 1960s, but none of the hundreds of survivors I interviewed in the 1970s had any time for Sassoon. They hated his poetry because it showed them as losers and victims. Rosenberg was 'discovered' only in the late 1960s, not least of all by the amazing poet and lecturer Geoffrey Hill, who taught me at Leeds.

One problem for me is that Powlett-Jones's main supporter on the governing body, the Brigadier, is an old boy who sounds at times worryingly like the father of Tom Brown in *Tom Brown's Schooldays*. Yet this is academic nit-picking. What I find more worrying about *To Serve Them All Our Days* is that it ignores the endemic snobbery of the 1920s public school. Powlett-Jones is the son of a Welsh miner. He is criticised by staff and pupils for his 'bolshie' political views, but never for being working-class. It is wholly unconvincing. Delderfield also skips over homosexuality, and seeks to create a public school in the 1920s and 1930s where beating is frowned upon. As if!

Finally, Delderfield produces two feisty women to squire his hero, including a pioneering would-be Labour MP, but appears satisfied when he procures for his own daughter at sixteen-plus the job of secretary at the school as the height of his and her ambitions. Delderfield takes a sweetened look at public schools in the 1920s and 1930s, and coats them over with an icing of what was becoming fashionable in the 1970s. *Goodbye, Mr. Chips* has the real feel of the 1920s and 1930s. *To Serve Them All Our Days* is the bowdlerised version.

9

MOST EXTRAORDINARY
MEN: HEADMASTERS

'Many Headmasters managed to be scholars and teachers,
as well as sadists.'[47]

There was no golden age for the English public school. Numbers varied dramatically from year to year, and one of the reasons Heads such as John Keate taught such huge classes was the fear that a new and expensive appointment to the staff in a good year might not be affordable in the next year. The key to the success of a school, at least in terms of pupil numbers, was the Head. Little has changed. As I write this I've just come from coffee with someone who has rejected their own and much-loved boarding school to send their son to another school. The reason? 'I liked the Head.'

Heads were crucial to a school's success, but we tend to forget that the concept of the Head as the person who controls, runs and

---

47   Marples, *Romantics at School*, p. 55.

directs the school is a relatively modern invention. *Tom Brown's Schooldays* does not use the world 'Headmaster'; Arnold is simply 'the Doctor'. Until Arnold's time, and even after it, the Head was 'the Master' – literally, the person appointed to teach the school, usually with the help of an usher or assistant. The term 'Second Master' is usually used now to mean Deputy Head. Initially, it was what it said on the tin – a Second Master to assists the Master to teach classes. So, when we look at early towering examples of brutal dictatorship, we are not looking at the equivalent of the modern conductor of a classical orchestra, but rather at the soloist conducting the orchestra from his or her seat at the piano – or, in the case of the Master, from his podium or lectern in the schoolroom.

As with so much in public schools, there is a spurious glamour nowadays attached to the Headmaster who still teaches in the classroom. More often than not, teaching a lesson is pure escapism for a Head, and does nothing for their performance of their real duties. Most Heads were once good teachers – it's hard to land a headship unless you are – but the skill set required to be a good classroom teacher is entirely different from that needed in a Head. A lesson is simple in comparison. It has a beginning, a middle and end; you know what it's there for and, unless you're a fool, you can judge pretty accurately whether it went well or not. It requires you to be knowledgeable about something you've actually studied or got a qualification in, and requires you to get children, who are naturally biddable, to do what you want, unlike your teachers, who are not. A good classroom teacher aspiring to be a Head is similar to the vicar who wants to be a Bishop: you can't get one without being good at the other. But they're totally different jobs.

When I became Headmaster of The Perse School, Cambridge, in 1987, I was the first Head since its foundation in 1515 not to have had a Cambridge degree. Draw what conclusion you like from the fact that my successor was a Cambridge graduate. The schools have tended to recruit exclusively from Oxbridge (in fairness, for many years there was nowhere else to go), sometimes even from the same college. From 1598 to 1764 every Headmaster of Westminster was a Christ Church, Oxford, man. Public schools also have a tendency to prefer their own, and Eton in particular, though there have been notable exceptions and they have stretched it to include Heads who had previously taught there. A real issue for public schools has been the narrow vision of those they have appointed to teach and to lead, symbolised by the well-trodden path of Eton followed by King's College, Cambridge, and then back to Eton to teach, or the round trip from Winchester to New College, Oxford, and then back to Winchester. The Clarendon Commission referred to this, and offered as a reason for the poor condition of the sector that it was not to the advantage of the schools 'to be officered exclusively by men brought up within its walls all imbued with its peculiar prejudices and opinions, and without experience of a system or any other method but its own.'[48]

Inbreeding has been endemic in public schools throughout their history. A variant of this not covered by the Clarendon Commission occurred when the schools were an integral part of a wider community that was itself inbred and resistant to new ideas. It might be thought that the presence of an external organisation in the governance of the schools would offset inbreeding, but sometimes it merely passed on the disputes of the overarching organisation to the school. One example in history is schools in cathedral closes, where sometimes the survival of the Head depended on his ability to navigate successfully through the

---

48 Clarendon Commission, Vol. 1, p. 32.

tangled politics of Dean and Chapter, religious belief and matters of theology. Another is the schools closely linked to Oxford or Cambridge. I became Headmaster of one such, The Perse School, Cambridge, or The Cambridge Free School as it was known. When Stephen Perse gave the management of his foundation to the University (or rather to a College) he was giving it to an institution that could be riven by internal dissent. Relationships between the Fellows at a Cambridge College have not in history always been amicable, and this could be passed on down the food chain. In the Civil War, the appointment of the Puritanical William Dell as Master of Gonville & Caius College inevitably saw the departure of a Royalist Headmaster. The Master of Gonville & Caius was automatically Chair of Governors at the Free School. The Usher, Crayford, temporarily took over the Headship, but the Governors appointed one George Griffiths over his head. Crayford violently assaulted Griffiths, the Headmaster, in front of the scholars, and followed it with, '. . . scandalous, opprobrious & reproachfull words . . . to wit, you are a striking knave: you come to steale away my due: I will take you a kicke on the britch & tred in your fette.'[49]

Winston Churchill, among others, has been cited as envious of the power wielded by a public-school Headmaster. The early 'Masters' of King's, Canterbury, were appointed by the Archbishop, and given by him the power to excommunicate.

Busby of Westminster famously explained to Charles II as he was walking alongside him that he did not take off his hat in the royal presence because 'if my boys supposed there was any greater in the realm than myself there would be at once an end to my authority.'[50] Busby had powerful friends, one of the reasons

49 Rodgers, *Old Public Schools*, p. 94.
50 Widely quoted, but see Rodgers, *Old Public Schools*, p. 28.

that allowed him to set a record by being Head of Westminster for fifty-seven years. He was the first of the great and truly grand Headmasters.

When Alexander Gill was High Master of St Paul's and a stone was thrown from the street into the school, Gill beat the supposed culprit, a titled gentleman (almost certainly innocent), who thereafter reportedly went out only to church and, even then, with an armed guard. Gill was also believed to have thrashed his grown-up, graduate son in public for a badly written letter to himself.

Though famous or infamous in the small world of their establishments, the majority of Headmasters of public schools have not been able to make a stir in the larger world outside the quadrangle. Exceptions are Lord James, formerly of The Manchester Grammar School, who was the founding Vice-Chancellor of the University of York, and Lord Pilkington, formerly of St Paul's School, who became chairman of the Broadcasting Complaints Commission. In previous years, of course, Heads might have expected to go on to a Bishopric – cue a mention for the Rev. Peter Hullah, one of the only modern HMC Heads to have managed this trick. If they did not have status in the wider world, what many Heads of public schools had was an excess of eccentricity.

> Braithwaite, the second Headmaster of Lancing, was for a lengthy period 'afflicted with some extraordinary form of indigestion which caused him suddenly to produce appalling belches . . . They were terrific, and absolutely uncontrollable. Even when he got his hand to his mouth in time, it was blown away in the explosion.[51]

---

51 Gathorne-Hardy, *The Public School Phenomenon*, p. 106.

Woodard schools seem to have had a *penchant* for eccentric Heads and staff:

> At frequent intervals the two staffs of Shoreham and Hurst [Hurstpierpoint, a Woodard school) used to meet together for a joint conference. The Rev. Frederick Mertens had no sense of taste or smell, and Pennell, one of the Hurst masters, was almost blind. Mertens was bending down low over his food to scrutinise it (his method of testing food owing to his defective sense of taste), and Pennell, simply seeing Mertens' clerical collar almost on the table, mistook it for the rim of his tea-cup, and proceeded to pour milk down Mertens' neck.[52]

The common vision of the public-school Headmaster, at least in history, is that he was a figure of immense power, at least within his own world. Some Headmasters certainly thought they had the right to extend that power. John Percival, the first Headmaster of Clifton, made it a rule that both parents of day boys were never to be away from home at the same time. Laughable? Perhaps. Unenforceable? Definitely. But possibly not so daft in an age of the latchkey kid. Of course, even the Victorian Heads, the size of whose sideburns should have been enough to intimidate anybody, often fell foul of parents. Vaughan of Harrow felt that *suttee* might not be such a bad idea after a number of disputes with widowed mothers, and Marlborough's Canon Bell is reported to have said, '. . . parents are the last people who ought to be allowed to have children.'[53]

Yet for much of their history the public schools have seen

---

52 Lamb, *The Happiest Days*, p. 116.
53 Quoted in de Honey, *Tom Brown's Universe*, pp. 149–50.

relative peace and harmony between Headmasters and parents. One reason for this is that throughout much of their history the Heads and the parents had both been imprinted from birth with the same class values. A second reason has been the tendency of parents, and particularly wealthy parents, to leave the upbringing of their children largely to the school. A variant of this was shown by my father, a product of the Scottish state system. He would no more have expected a parent to tell their son's Headmaster how to educate him than he would have expected one of his patients to tell the doctor how to treat him. He was wrong, of course. On the very rare occasions when he did intercede all that was revealed was how futile interference was. Sensing one of his sons was heading for disaster at A-level, he dutifully made the point to the Headmaster, whose reply was that nothing at all was wrong: the boy was Captain of the 2nd XV. Disaster duly struck. If I learned anything as a Head myself, it was that even the worst parent has an instinct for when their child is in real trouble, and, however much of a pain the parent may be and have been, any sensible school assumes as its baseline that the worried parent may be right. A variation was the number of old boys who treated their past Heads as one might expect a son to treat his father. 'It was said of E. H. Bradby, headmaster of Haileybury (1868–83) that none of his former Haileybury pupils ever took an important decision in life without consulting him.'[54]

John Keate

Keate is the only Headmaster in this list who predates the Clarendon Commission and the onset of Victorian morality.

---

54 Ibid., p. 158.

He was an extraordinary figure, a notorious figure who yet achieved cult status among his pupils, and a man who not only ruled Eton but managed for a period to become it.

Keate never doubted that he was in a permanent state of war with his pupils, but it was a war in which he frequently won both the respect and the affection of those pupils. After a rebellion, Keate managed to flog a hundred boys who had in effect denied his authority by having them seized by assistant masters in the depth of the night and brought to him for punishment. The next day he was cheered by his pupils, including many of those he had flogged:'. . . it was a sort of game: the boys playing not to get caught, the masters to catch. If the boys were outwitted in an ingenious way, they cheered.'[55]

There is an extraordinary link here between Keate and the popular 1950s TV series *Whacko!*, starring Jimmy Edwards. Here too the whole business between boys and masters is a game. Just as Keate's pupils knew what the consequences were, and accepted them if they disobeyed rules, so with *Whacko!*. The pupil Wendover – whose name must have been invented by the then young Barry Cryer, the scriptwriter, to allow for the line we saw earlier, 'Bend over, Wendover!' – deliberately traps his Headmaster's hand in a mousetrap as the Headmaster is searching a bag for contraband. Does he know that the price he will pay is a whacking? Of course he does. But, to put it in modern terms, Wendover has decided the cake is worth the candle. His street cred among his peer group has rocketed. Interestingly, Wendover later leads a hilarious rebellion, which he wins. In a later version of the same thing, the film *If . . .*, people have to die to make the same point. If *Whacko!* is innocence, then *If . . .* is experience. Public schools offer plenty of both.

---

55 Gathorne-Hardy, *The Public School Phenomenon*, p. 43.

If there is one thing that becomes clear from reading about the various Headmasters who made or broke public schools, it is that strength of character is the defining feature in successful Heads. Weakness or indecision on the part of a Head was the proverbial red flag to the young bulls in his charge who, if shown it, would trample all over him. That said, the same is probably true of the older bulls in Common Room, the teachers and Housemasters in particular. Has it changed? In one respect, yes. The pupils were the biggest threat to the Head in Keate's day. I remember seeking advice from a wizened and battle-hardened Head before my first headship. His advice was, 'When I started I thought my biggest problem would be the pupils, my second the parents and my third the staff. I now realise the exact reverse is true.'

Keate is an interesting phenomenon. The man was a beast at least in the public execution of his duties, and at times verged on the unhinged. Kept waiting by a boy he wished to flog, Keate was so furious that he seized the boy's brother (or his namesake: the record is unclear) and beat him instead. On another occasion a boy accused of a misdeed explained he had been somewhere else at the time. 'Then I'll flog you for that!' said Keate, and did.

Eton has a superb public-relations capacity, and it may be that influence which has been responsible for an increasing tendency to show Keate as actually quite lovable. It's true his pupils subscribed over £600 to buy him a leaving present, and cheered him 'heartily'. But, as one commentator has written, 'But schoolboys on such occasions, like B.B.C. audiences at variety shows, will applaud anybody regardless of merit; and a last-minute outburst of cheering does not make Dr Keate a good headmaster, let alone a great one.'[56]

---

56 Lamb, *The Happiest Days*, p. 132.

If we make Keate a great Headmaster we are making the criterion for greatness the number of young people a man can hurt.

Samuel Butler

Samuel Butler became Head of Shrewsbury School in 1798. He turned the school into one of the very best and most highly regarded in the country. He shares a feature with many of the most highly regarded Heads, then and now: 'Butler never seems to have succeeded in getting on with his Trustees (Governors) . . . they always seem to have obstructed him.'[57]

Edward Thring, discussed below, faced much the same problem. Governors and governance are the big untold story of the public schools. Many of the great Heads did their jobs despite their Governors, rather than with any help from them. Governance of public schools was often dire. Founders frequently placed the governance of their schools in one of three hands: the Church, Oxford or Cambridge, or the livery companies.

John Colet, who founded St Paul's School, was Dean of St Paul's and of all people might have been expected to place his school's future in the hands of the Church. Instead he chose to place it with a livery company, the Mercers', on the grounds that he had found less corruption in men of business. Even without the taint of corruption the fact is that endowments of schools have sometimes been proven difficult to trace. As for the Church, it was notoriously hungry for money. As we saw above with the Perse, the political and religious loyalties and clashed within the University could be inflicted upon a school, and its Headmasters

---

57 Percival, *Very Superior Men*, p. 87.

if they were of the 'wrong' faith or political persuasion. A further problem with the livery companies was that their ruling classes may have known how to be a mercer, grocer or fishmonger, but had no reason to know much about education or schools. The history of the schools governed by livery companies is peppered by requests for more money for new buildings in particular, and in some cases what started as a foundation supposedly paid for by endowment one suspects became a financial burden making a major call on a livery company's financial resources.

A further problem with a group or organisation taking charge of governance was that of their primary loyalty. A Fellow of a Cambridge College owes their primary loyalty to the College, not to the school they may be a nominated Governor of. In other words, the nominated Governor is likely to put who or whatever nominated them before the school they govern. Their power and their importance derives from the organisation that nominates them, not the organisation they are nominated to serve.

Yet, even where the Governors are not nominees of an apparent organisation, they are prone to problems. The Eton Governors belonged to no one but themselves, but the Clarendon Commission was formed in the first place because of worries about the then management of the College's finances. Governance of public schools was, and still is, one of the least transparent processes in England. I as a fee-paying parent have as much chance of accessing the minutes of my child's governing body's meeting as I do of accessing those of a cabinet meeting. As for the selection of governors, for many years it appeared to me as a mere teacher that Governors were chosen on the basis of who was thought to be a good chap at the golf club. I do believe those days are mostly gone, but the problem is that no governing body will knowingly appoint a Governor who will rock the boat. It is trendy to state that Governors are there to support *and challenge* the Head and senior leadership team. All too often the last thing the Governors will do is appoint someone to the board who will challenge them. The result? A list of Governors representing the good and the grand with a politically correct smattering of women and ethnic minorities.

And in case one is tempted to think that the unholy war between Head and Governors is a safe relic of the past, one only has to read the extraordinary diaries of John Rae, charismatic and utterly maverick Headmaster of Westminster from 1970 to 1986. Rae rescued Westminster, but his diaries show him continually having to cope with a governing body which he felt he could not rely on to give unquestioning support. Despite this, as with so many Heads, Rae made a brilliant fist of running his school.

As for Butler, with whom we started this diatribe, he had another problem to triumph over. In one of the bizarre accidents of governance that so afflicted public schools, Shrewsbury's Second Master was appointed not by the Headmaster, but by St John's College. They appointed John Jeudwine shortly after Butler was appointed, the problem being that Butler and Jeudwine simply did not get along. The situation was so bad that they did not speak to each other, but communicated by notes, mostly composed in the third person. This was to last for thirty-seven years. Butler's patience was stretched even further when a 'town party' developed in Shrewsbury: 'There was soon formed a Jeudwine party within the town which for some years pursued Mr Butler with a hostility that must have been singularly hard to bear without a loss of restraint.'[58]

Butler had just that ability to exercise restraint. A goodly number of Heads lacked that skill, and suffered accordingly.

---

58   Ibid., p. 81.

Butler was also an example of a feature mentioned at the start of this chapter that typified 'Heads' until well into the nineteenth century, namely that many were not Heads in our sense of the world at all:

> Samuel Butler . . . was in fact not a Headmaster at all in the modern sense of the term. He was essentially a teacher. The fame he brought to the school was due entirely to the fact that he was one of the greatest classical scholars of the day and had a genius for imparting scholarship to his pupils.[59]

The myth of Thomas Arnold and Rugby

Thomas Arnold rose to fame by doing what would have been deemed unthinkable by his predecessors in the days before the middle classes and moral crusading took over the public schools: an overwhelming belief that the job of the schoolmaster was to pry into the minds of his pupils, with a view to fostering 'proper' moral growth. Arnold was an autocratic and puritan moral crusader, much more in tune with the growth of revivalism in the low-church Anglicanism than with any educational tradition. For Arnold, everything came down to good or evil, with those two extremes entirely contained within the precepts of Christian teaching. He showed no real interest in academic matters or the curriculum (he abolished science classes in 1837), and even less in sport and games. If Hughes had not rescued him and made him into a saint in *Tom Brown's Schooldays* it is likely that history, had it remembered him at all, would have done so as an arrogant prig.

---

59 Lamb, *The Happiest Days*, p. 124.

Tom Brown's Schooldays was published in 1857 and had run to five editions and 11,000 copies that year. In 1862 the figures were 52 editions and 28,000 copies. However, there is an argument that the myth of Arnold was only extended by *Tom Brown's Schooldays*, and that it had its real origins in the hugely influential book *The Life and Correspondence of Thomas Arnold*, written by one of Arnold's anointed, A. P. Stanley, in two volumes in 1845.

Yet if Arnold was a prig, he was a highly successful prig. He built up the reputation of Rugby and its numbers, though there is a strong argument that Arnold's so-called 'reforms' were driven by economic rather than moral reasons: 'A perfectly tenable case can be made that the reforms carried out by Dr Arnold at Rugby in the 1820s and 1830s were panic reactions to falling numbers.'[60]

There is also a strong case for arguing that Arnold's achievements would have been impossible without the previous work of the largely forgotten Headmaster, Thomas James.

Arnold used the Chapel as his theatre and the pulpit as his stage, and avidly cultivated the myth of Thomas Arnold by seeking the widest publication of his sermons, essays and articles. In this sense he was a very modern figure, sensing the mood of the moment and pandering to it by every means at his disposal. How much difference he actually made has been a matter of bitter debate. My own view is that expressed by Kathryn Chadwick: 'Before Arnold, public schools were bearpits. After Arnold they were still bearpits, but with the bears required to put in compulsory attendance at Chapel.'[61]

In another sense Arnold was also a very modern figure. There were no league tables of academic performance in Arnold's day, but he pre-empted the modern practice by booting out students

---

60 Gathorne-Hardy, *The Public School Phenomenon*, p. 28.
61 Quoted in May, *The Victorian Public School*, p. 25.

who did not reach a given academic standard set by him within a given time. Chandos quotes him as saying, 'The first, second and third duty of a schoolmaster is to get rid of unpromising pupils.'[62] Really? And there am I thinking it was to turn the unpromising student into one of promise. Arnold was a thoroughly modern man: get rid of any pupil who won't help you, the Head, in your career. After all, education isn't about young people: it's about me. Sadly, the spirit of Arnold lives on.

Arnold did not actually like his pupils, seeing boyhood as a state of sin.[63] He was better at PR than he was at management. There is evidence that very little actually changed at Rugby in Arnold's time, and he was totally dependent on the quality of his Sixth Form to impose order on his school. Chandos quotes a very telling comment from a pupil after Arnold had decided to attend a Founder's Day dinner in 1835, when only nine other people turned up. 'I know for certain that more than a hundred would have attended if it had pleased the autocrat to have remained at home.'[64] The 'autocrat' concentrated nearly all his attention on his Sixth Form, or rather those who became his acolytes in the Sixth Form. Those allowed into that *coterie* worshipped him. Those on the outside had no time for him, any more than he for them.

Yet the use of the word 'autocrat' is interesting, and a further illustration of what we already know, namely that the successful Headmaster often made his reputation and his school despite his Governors, not because of them. Arnold fought fiercely to be independent of his Governors, and in all the books written about him the last mention of his Governors is usually the report that

---

62 Chandos, , *All Boys Together,* p. 251.

63 De Honey, *Tom Brown's Universe,* p. 23.

64 Chandos, , *All Boys Together,* p. 256.

they appointed him in the first place. The autocrat may have offended boys used to self-rule and bitterly resentful of any adult interference in their lives, but he was also good at fighting off the baleful influence of those theoretically over him in authority for whom school management was at best a hobby, and at worst a source for lining their own pockets.

A former senior figure at Eton for many years usually showed the extraordinary loyalty Etonians show to their school. It is as if anyone who did not go to Eton is by definition so far beneath the salt as to have no right to criticise it, or hear criticism of it. In my long acquaintance with that figure, only once did he say anything even vaguely critical of Etonians. It was in relationship to the Old Etonian Prime Minister David Cameron, and was to the effect that he had shown one of the defining features of an Old Etonian, namely a preference for working within a small group or cabal, rather than winning over the masses. Cameron certainly commanded the fiercest possible loyalty from his inner Cabinet, but never really carried the mass of Tory backbenchers with him. Sadly, he may go down in history as the man who failed to persuade working-class England to remain in the European Union. Cameron was also roundly criticised for honouring a large number of his former aides and advisers in his resignation list. A feature of Eton? Or a pattern Thomas Arnold would have felt entirely at home with? I suspect Eton does not have a monopoly of working through small groups, and failing to convince the masses. It summarises Thomas Arnold, and in my experience many public-school boys.

Arnold was subject to intemperate rages, and prone to over-hasty action, from expelling a boy before hearing his version of events (and refusing to speak to his parents), to beating an ailing young boy with eighteen strokes (and hospitalising him) when it later turned out he had been telling the truth.

What Arnold did do was assemble around himself a coterie of adoring Sixth Formers, though it is notable that remarkably few of the pupils at Rugby in Arnold's time achieved any notable distinction in later life. It was on these acolytes that Arnold left his mark, and they repaid him by recording that mark in what they wrote. Yet,

> Dr Arnold unquestionably made a deep impression on those boys who were brought into close communication with himself, but I cannot find that his influence survived longer than that of any subsequent headmaster.[65]

Nearly twenty of Arnold's staff at Rugby went on to headships in other established schools. The real proof of the pudding in terms of Arnold's actual influence on the public schools was that his ideas and his former staff were largely ignored when it came to the spate of new schools founded in the latter half of the nineteenth century, schools such as Marlborough, Haileybury, Rossall and Cheltenham. Nor did Arnold feature largely in the formation of the Woodard Schools, which were driven by Anglo-Catholicism and an obsession with the moral state of the middle classes. Arnold's influence was seen far more in the County Schools, the first one founded in 1858 by the Rev. J. L. Brereton. In its time very influential Trinity College, Cambridge, gifted it the land to found a school on Hills Road, now occupied by Homerton College. It has now sunk without trace, its only visible memorials being Framlingham College, Barnard Castle School and Cranleigh School, which reinvented themselves as conventional public schools. Ironically, the movement, which eventually became The

---

65   Samuel Butler, quoted in Percival, *Very Superior Men*, p. 45.

Graduated County Schools Association, illustrates the inveterate snobbishness of the public schools. The early schools failed to find social acceptance because their fees were too low. It is not a mistake made by many contemporary governing bodies.

There is one area in which Arnold did set the pace and the tone, and for which he deserves full credit. Prior to his time, most of the staff had been clergymen holding down curacies elsewhere and seeing their teaching duties as little more than pin money. Arnold increased staff salaries, but in return demanded a full-time commitment from staff, thus for the first time introducing what we would now call pastoral care into the public schools. He also encouraged masters to take in boarders, avowedly also to increase the quality of and opportunities for pastoral care, and thus laid much of the foundation for the boarding House system on which the boarding schools were to come to rest.

As a decaying 1960s liberal, I take against people who think they have God on their side, and at times I wonder if Arnold did not take that adage one stage further, and think that he *was* God. Yet in fairness there is another, probably more reasoned, view of Arnold:

> Arnold, then, was by no means the overwhelmingly successful reformer that popular convention has often made him out to be. Yet, when all is said, the popular view of him as a great educational figure . . . is true in substance. He tended to overdo the religious and moral pressure; he was not always practical; he lacked humour. But despite these defects, the tremendous force of his personality was thrown so firmly in the right direction – 'I believe that boys may be governed a great deal by gentle methods and kindness, if you show

that you are not afraid of them' – that he made it easier for such an approach to be followed by later teachers. He invented no new method, but the intensity of his personality gave his methods the stamp of novelty.[66]

The best thing about Thomas Arnold was that he was not John Keate. Ironically, the greatest evidence against him is in *Tom Brown's Schooldays*. Tom Brown may have been turned into a vision of Victorian sporting manliness by his mentoring of the weedy Arthur, but morally he is a baby. His values are desperately immature: 'I want to be A1 at cricket and football, and all the other games . . .' is his top priority, exactly the philosophy Young Brooke so proudly announced on Tom's arrival in School House. In other words, all the Doctor's preaching has had zero effect. Tom is blissfully unaware of any of the moral code Arnold spends so much time prosing about.

Tom's admiration for the man turns into blind hero worship. 'Had he returned to School again, and the Doctor begun the half-year by abolishing fagging and football and the Saturday half-holiday, or all or any of the most cherished school institutions, Tom would have supported him with the blindest faith. 'He is still in fact in that state of "moral childishness" which Dr Arnold had sought for fourteen years striven to eradicate.'[67]

George Cotton (1813–66)

My own personal hero among the 'great' Headmasters is one of the least-known. George Cotton had taught at Rugby under Arnold, and appears in *Tom Brown's Schooldays* in the penultimate

---

66 Lamb, *The Happiest Days*, p. 137.
67 Avery, *Childhood's Pattern*, p. 176.

chapter, talking to Tom and Arthur about cricket, which he admits he did not understand. He turned Marlborough round in a mere six years, after which he departed to become Bishop of Calcutta. He took over the headship in 1852. The school had been founded eight years earlier, and was already a lost cause, and dying. His extraordinary achievement in turning Marlborough into one of the best schools in the country rested on a number of pillars. Most importantly, he above all other Heads realised the importance of good staff, and replaced the ageing floggers of his predecessor's day with bright young men who actually appeared to like their pupils. He did this despite an almost permanent financial crisis that meant staff salaries were continually under threat. Cotton could talk to boys and understood them. He made brilliant and thoughtful use of prefects, but also realised that one way to bring the rebellious Marlburians to heel was to use organised games, even though he himself was no sportsman: '. . . [he] made games the outlet for the animal spirits that had hitherto expressed themselves in poaching.'[68]

As has been noted elsewhere, in this work and in others, the cult of the prefect and the cult of athleticism in the final count did damage to the public schools by being carried to excess. To blame Cotton for this is to miss the point. He was not responsible for the excesses caused by lesser brains. He was, in the best sense of the word, an opportunist. Great Heads make the best of the material they have to work with, or get rid of dead wood. Cotton managed the latter with his staff, and used the fact that older boys actually like to be given responsibility. He also used the addiction of the male of the species to organised sport to channel the energy and aggression that had hitherto gone in rioting into more amenable channels.

---

68 Ogilvie, *The English Public School*, p. 153.

Similar opportunism was shown in the 1980s by a very great state school Headmistress who took over a comprehensive school riven by violence and gangs. The bus queues were for some reason a flashpoint, and things became really serious when a new girl was seriously beaten up at the bus stop by other girls for the crime of handing her homework in. The Headmistress asked to see the girl who was the leader of the most notorious and influential gang in the school. She happened to have a younger sister who was the same age as the girl who had been hospitalised. Would she have liked her sister to be beaten up like that? the Head asked. The gangsta said no, of course she wouldn't. OK, said the Head, so if I put you in charge of the bus queue, will you be strong enough to stop the violence? The girl said yes. Violence at the bus queues stopped overnight.

A week later the gang leader asked to see the Head, and told her exactly where violence was most common in the school and when, and suggested a new form of staff supervision rota to help control things. At that point, the Head decided to offer her the post of Head Girl, which did not actually exist until that moment. The gang leader looked incredulous, then burst out laughing.

'Me, miss? You must be jokin'! What's in it for me?'

'You've been pleasing yourself for years in this school,' said the Head. 'Now it's payback time. Time you stopped being totally selfish and only working to protect yourself, and time you started protecting others.'

The poacher turned gamekeeper after a lot more words (the Head said it took her an hour and a half), and a year later the inspectors noted a remarkable turnabout in terms of behaviour and the pupils' attitude towards each other. Opportunism. The Head had spotted that adolescents get trapped by their own image, and frequently hide their yearning to break free. Trust is a great thing, but also a very dangerous and difficult thing to give. Cotton and that modern Headmistress were opportunists right enough, but they shared another invaluable feature in great Heads: the capacity to trust pupils, and indeed staff, to rise to a challenge and get it right.

Edward Thring (1821–87)

Edward Thring was an old Etonian who became Headmaster of Uppingham School in 1853, staying until 1887. An ordained clergyman and the son of a clergyman, Thring was arguably as powerful a preacher as Thomas Arnold but the fact that, unlike Arnold, Thring actually achieved something in educational terms has put his preaching power on the back burner. Yet Thring was just as bad as his contemporaries when it came to sermonising on the evil of masturbation:

> And so the poisonous breath of sin keeps tainting and corrupting all the freshness and purity of young life, and gets into the very soul, destroying all its power to do true work, and win even earthly credit; the face loses its frank and manly expression; and the poison begins to be seen outwardly; and after disappointing father and mother, and family, and himself most of all, the wretched victim either sinks down to a lower level [homosexuality] . . . or often finds an early grave, killed by his own foul passions.[69]

---

69 Hickson, *The Poisoned Bowl*, p. 14.

Thring is usually credited with forming the Headmasters' Conference, or HMC, the group (officially, it counts as a trade union) representing the 'top' public schools in England. It would be more accurate to say he claimed the credit. He capitalised on a meeting called by John Mitchinson, Headmaster of King's, Canterbury, in 1869, calling a second meeting for 21 December. Both meetings were fired up by the need to defend the old endowed grammar schools from government and outsiders, in the form of the Clarendon and Taunton Committees.

Thring's achievement has been eulogised, but in fact had one major element to it. He turned a small-town, sleepy grammar school in a most unlikely rural setting into a full-to-bursting public boarding school. In educational terms, Thring had a few ideas, but not many. It was his personality that put him among the great headmasters, not his ideas: '. . . Thring had in a high degree that quality which his own century might have described as "magnetic" and a later age "charismatic".'[70]

This is not a feature that recommends a Head to his Governors. Thring was a fighter, and like many such he did not always choose wisely those he fought: 'During the long years of his headship, he was at different times at conflict with his Governors (frequently), the Education Commissioners (fundamentally), the Town Authorities (critically), the parents (occasionally), the Masters (understandably) and even with his own creation, the Headmasters' Conference.'[71]

The most extraordinary chapter in the saga of Thring versus his Governors was the school's move to Borth in Mid Wales. The town water supply at Uppingham was contaminated. We were told as boys that cess pits drained directly into it. In

---

70 Percival, *Very Superior Men*, p. 190.
71 Ibid., p. 190.

any event, there was a typhoid outbreak in the 1870s and the Governors insisted on closing the school. Thring instead moved it to a Welsh hydro resort in Borth for a year, with absolutely no support from his Governors except to continue paying staff salaries; not one even visited the school in its temporary home. Thring returned in triumph to a cleaned-up Uppingham in 1877, after a year away. In the interim, Thring's bitterest foe on the town council, the Chairman of the Sanitary Committee, had himself died of the fever.

Clashes with Governors, as noted above, are as old as the public schools themselves, and almost the outward symbol of a successful headship. The great founding Head of Merchant Taylors' School, Richard Mulcaster (who went on to be a High Master of St Paul's), was reprimanded by the Court of the Merchant Taylors' Livery Company for losing his temper at their most recent 'visitation': they admonished him for 'his injurious and quarelinge speache as he used to the visitors'.[72]

The records of St Paul's School are full of the most poisonous rows between the Mercers' Company and the High Master. The London Livery Companies – The Mercers', Haberdasher Askes', Merchant Taylors', the Grocers' and so on – have played a major role in the development of the English public school, but it has sometimes been a strange marriage. A livery company may bring money to the relationship, but it is usually short on educational expertise and long on personality politics, with power struggles within the companies out of both the reach and the understanding of the schools they govern, but impacting on them directly. Similarly, as mentioned earlier, the relationship between the Dean and Chapter of cathedral schools has seen the death

---

72 Draper, *Four Centuries of Merchant Taylors' School*, p. 19.

or dismissal of countless Heads, and was a major feature in the decline of Westminster in the early 1800s. The basic truth is that it requires a very strong personality to run a school and a strong will to get one's way. Governors can react adversely to this, becoming obsessed with getting their way. Not infrequently in history, 'their way' has translated into saving money, or seeing that it went into areas not deemed beneficial to the school by the Head.

It is easy to underestimate the sheer force of character and determination a man such as Thring showed in the Borth exodus, and other achievements. He illustrates a basic truth about 'great' Headmasters, which is that their greatness usually derives not from their intellect or their business acumen, nor even their faith, but rather from the size of their personality. It is no wonder they clashed so often with their Governors, so many of whom were defined by their intellect (Oxford and Cambridge), their financial skills (successful merchants) or their faith (the Church). One historian commented about Dr Welldon, the outstanding Head of Tonbridge between 1843 and 1875,

> Welldon was not . . . a man of intellectual eminence, but he had in full measure the evangelistic fervour, the Roman 'gravitas' which was in those days, and perhaps always, a more important element in successful Headmastership.[73]

One problem facing the modern public school is the proliferation of Heads who are good at drawing up the timetable on a computer, but less good at getting pupils and staff to flock to the lessons it contains.

---

73 D. C. Somervell, quoted in Percival, *Very Superior Men*, p. 215.

Thring was remarkable in one other area: the curriculum. Moving away from the arid diet of classics, classics and more classics, boys at Uppingham were taught in the morning classics, scripture, mathematics, history, geography and English composition. In the afternoon they could choose from optional subjects – French, German, chemistry, drawing and carpentry. He brought music into the school with a vengeance, with one-third of boys learning an instrument. This was revolutionary at a time when music was seem as fit only for women. Thring paid a penalty in that '. . . it was said that parents sent their less able sons to Uppingham and the clever ones elsewhere.'[74]

It was unfair, as Uppingham produced more than its fair share of scholars, but certainly in my time Uppinghamians were renowned for making lots of money, rather than propping up the Common Rooms of Oxford and Cambridge.

W. H. D. Rouse of The Perse

The conventional histories of public schools tend to favour the more famous or eccentric Heads, but ignore some men of equal or greater merit. The story of Dr Rouse of Cambridge's Perse School is interesting partly because of Rouse himself, but also because its sequel illustrates the fact that pleasant or attractive personalities do not always make the most successful Heads. Rouse became Headmaster of The Perse in 1902. He was a classicist who invented the 'Direct Method' of teaching classics, which involved using Latin as a spoken medium of communication. Rouse in effect modernised classics' teaching, after centuries in which the mainstay of the curriculum had been beaten into pupils by rote

---

74   Ogilvie, *The English Public School*, p. 174.

learning and repetition. He amassed a brilliant staff and restored the fortunes of the school, but it appears his Governors thought him too 'soft'. He fell out with the inspectorate, who reported that certain forms had either not been filled in, or filled in incorrectly, for the 1922 inspection of the school by the Board of Education. No wonder. Rouse did not have an office, and spent most of his time in the classroom. He detested bureaucrats and politicians, and his governing body. Rouse's Direct Method imposed discipline through the personality of the teacher, not because of the office and its licensed authority to physically hurt the pupil: 'The Direct Method was not conventionally dignified. It brought the master down from the dais – indeed some of the Perse boys took the master's part in lessons, thus exposing both the intellectual and social aspects of his authority to risk.'[75]

In so many areas Rouse looked ahead, even to his facing the *eminence noire* of the modern public-school Head – the fact that, to keep their most gifted pupils interested, the school feels obliged to give them material normally reserved for university: 'Peckett [Old Persean], who won a scholarship to King's College in the 1920's, found that he had already read most of the passages which confronted him in his examinations there.'[76]

Rouse was both unique, and a symbol of the eternal conflict and contrasts epitomised by the English public school. He was the last of the great Victorian and Edwardian dictator-Heads, who brooked no disobedience and defined a school through the power of their own personality. Yet Dictator and Supreme Ruler though he was, he achieved his eminence through informality and delegation. In marked contrast to contemporary practice, Rouse trusted people – his pupils and his staff – to get it right,

75 Stray, *Living Word*, p. 59.
76 Ibid. p. 71.

until such time as they showed conclusively that they had got it wrong. He believed passionately in an outdated classics curriculum, yet revitalised and modernised that curriculum as well as manifesting a passionate and very modern commitment to music and drama. And, in an echo of so many other Heads, he achieved his success partly by defying his Governors, who nevertheless got him in the end, largely on the grounds that discipline in the school was slack.

When Rouse left The Perse, not altogether happily, the Governors appointed a man called H. A. Wootton, a martinet, as Head. The official school history describes him as 'incredibly rude'. He reversed the informality favoured by Rouse, preferring communication by typewritten note. *La plus ça change . . .* As I leafed though some dusty papers in my early days as Head of The Perse a handwritten letter fell out of a pile of ancient headed writing paper. It was from Rouse to one of his former pupils, who had invited his old Headmaster over to tea, presumably in response to one of the tea sessions that Rouse held on Sunday afternoons after his retirement in 1928 at Histon Manor. Thanking his former pupil for a very pleasant tea, in a brief note, Rouse made it clear that they had talked, understandably, about The Perse. Tagged on at the end of his note, Rouse had written, 'What can I say? They are ruining my lovely school.'

I gained a measure of Wootton's personality from a man who had joined the staff as a newly qualified young teacher in Wootton's last year. Early in his first term he was summoned to sit by Wootton's side for lunch at the table reserved for the Headmaster. The young man watched the Head angrily munch through his steak-and-kidney pie, not even turning his head, never mind exchanging a word of greeting. Having endured a silent lunch, Wootton turned to him at the end of the meal as he rose to leave and snarled, 'Young man! In my day a young teacher would have had the courtesy to exchange a few words with his Headmaster over lunch!'

Suitably chastened, the young teacher sat down at his next invitation, a week before the summer holiday, and asked brightly, 'Do you have any plans for the vacation, Headmaster?'

Wootton turned round and said, 'Young man! In my day a young teacher would have waited to be spoken to before conferring with the Headmaster.'

Nice man. But it was in Wootton's day that one of the few German bombs to land in Cambridge in World War Two landed slap bang in the middle of The Perse. One of the few other bomb hits in the war was on Wootton's lodgings, leading to the story that disaffected pupils had broken the blackout to guide the bombers on to Wootton's places of work and residence. Building materials were very scarce indeed at the time, and most contemporary commentators believe that the school was kept alive and rebuilt only through the force of Wootton's personality. He bullied Cambridge into rebuilding the school. This, perhaps, is another illustration of the contradictions that sum up the English public school: the appalling Head who saved the School.

Notorious and noble Headmasters

One of the strangest and perhaps saddest of all Headmagisterial sagas is that of the Victorian Headmaster C. J. Vaughan. Appointed to Harrow at the age of twenty-eight, he was widely credited with rescuing the school and seen as brilliantly successful. Harrow had 60 boys when he arrived, 469 when he left. All this made his sudden departure fifteen years later in 1859 all the more inexplicable. In 1863 he was offered and accepted a bishopric, and then a week later resigned. We now know that Vaughan wrote passionate letters to his pupils, and possibly more, a fact revealed only well into his headship, when one of Vaughan's boy partners wrote to an Old Harrovian telling the story. The Establishment decided Vaughan had to go, despite occasional semi-comic moments such as when his wife pleaded for mercy to his accuser: 'She had known of her husband's little weakness but it had never interfered with the running of the school.'[77]

The same accuser who did for Vaughan at Harrow threatened public exposure if he became Bishop of Rochester four years after Harrow, and so Vaughan remained Vicar of Doncaster. Not until his accuser died did Vaughan dare to become Dean of Llandaff. What is interesting also about this saga is the shakiness of the evidence against Vaughan: '. . . it must be remembered that the surviving evidence against him is derived from a document of "passionately partisan propaganda".'[78]

One is reminded of the fact that the historical judgement of Nicolas Udall may hinge on whether a medieval clerk's handwriting reads 'burglary' or 'buggery'. On such small things is history made.

The above reveals the truth that an allegation of sexual misconduct is far easier to make than to refute. Pendulums swing, but in doing so they frequently knock for six anyone standing beneath them. For years the silent victims were the abused children. Now the pendulum swings the other way, and the accused is like the medieval witch, guilty until proven innocent. At the time of writing I have been familiar with the story of a brilliant teacher accused of raping a pupil. The jury took less than half an hour to throw out the case, but the allegation ruined a

---

77 Gathorne-Hardy, *The Public School Phenomenon*, p. 81.
78 De Honey, *Tom Brown's Universe*, p. 190.

career and a marriage. The mere fact of an allegation renders the (innocent) accused unemployable. Is this justice?

Vaughan is seen as a hero in much of the writing on him and public schools in general, but, here again, commentators have looked at him through rose-tinted spectacles. He believed that masters supervising boys was tantamount to spying, and trusted his prefects too much, treating them as adult with all the judgement, wisdom and experience they did not have. In particular, by giving his prefects the official power to inflict corporal punishment he opened a can of worms that in its time did as much damage as the antics of Udall or Keate.

The doings of many of the early Heads of public schools make today's lot seem very dull by comparison. William Dugard, Head of Merchant Taylors' 1644–61, moonlighted as a printer and publisher. He was imprisoned in Newgate for trying to publish one pamphlet, and had another pamphlet burned in public. I am attracted to Dugard, because I too as a Head faced criticism for writing and publishing (the rather more illustrious John Rae may have lost his job for it, or possibly even for something his wife wrote), though in my case it was articles and not pamphlets, and I think I'd see it rather as a matter of distinction to have one of my books burned in public. It'd do wonders for the sales. One particular Governor proposed to the board that I should be allowed to publish only articles that had been approved by the governing body. It was turned down. William Page became Head of Westminster in 1815. Described as 'savage and ill-tempered',[79] he was not averse to lifting boys off the ground by their ears. Various Headmasters took their disputes with staff outside school, and assaulted colleagues in public.

---

79 Carleton, *Westminster School*, p. 46.

Mention should be made of Sanderson of Oundle, who is often cited as a revolutionary. He was highly unusual from the start. He was neither initially an Oxbridge graduate nor a classicist – he got a first in maths and physics from Durham, though he later took a scholarship in maths at Cambridge – whereas in 1914 a list of 114 Headmasters cited 92 as classicists. My predecessor at St Paul's was a classicist.

Sanderson established workshops and laboratories at Oundle, but the reason for his fame was the wrong one in a sense. He is well known because what he did was so rare, and his achievement does not exonerate the public schools from their shameful neglect of the sciences but rather emphasises it as the exception to the rule.

As well as great or notorious Headmasters, there were those who were just distinctly odd. David Whitehead Moss (1841–1917), Head of Shrewsbury from 1866–1908, did not partake of the cult of athleticism, and asked at a football match when it was time to draw stumps. When told a member of his Shooting VIII had hit the bull five times, Moss asked to be reassured that the farmer had been compensated for his loss. Almond of Loretto (over forty) preceded his request to a twenty-year-old lady to marry him by discussing the whole thing with his Head Boy (eighteen). When asked permission by four boys to go skating on a frozen lake, Selwyn of Uppingham deliberated lengthily, and said two boys could go. Two did, and got into difficulties. On their return, Selwyn tried to cover his back by saying he hadn't given his permission. The boys protested that he had said two of them could go.

'Ah yes,' Dr Selwyn replied hastily, 'but I didn't say *which* two.'[80]

---

80 Lamb, *The Happiest Days*, p. 146.

John Wesley

Perceptive readers may have sensed that, despite my own Anglicanism, I much prefer the French ideal of keeping religion out of education. I would take it one stage further and hope to found a society dedicated to barring all clergymen and women from serving on governing bodies. One reason is the saga of John Wesley, the founder of Methodism, who also founded Kingswood School.

I have to declare an interest here. I was once one of the final two candidates for the headship of a school based on a particular branch of Anglicanism. I was asked right at the end of one of the best interviews I have ever given, 'What do you think is the most important factor in the education offered at this school?' I had one of those awful moments that occur so often in interviews. The school at that time was being run by a saint of a man, who was no doubt a committed Christian but who was committed even more to the welfare and wellbeing of the pupils in his care. I knew what the serried ranks of dog collars assembled before me for the interview wanted me to reply: their branch of Anglicanism. The problem was that it wasn't true. It wasn't any one creed that made that school special at that time: it was simply love of its pupils. So I answered, 'It's love for its pupils,' knowing it was the wrong answer, and saw the shutters go down over the eyes interviewing me.

In a section on Heads, many of whom were monsters, it seems only right and proper to list one of the greatest monsters of them all, albeit he was founder of a school and not its Head. John Wesley founded Kingswood School in 1748 to educate young dissenting ministers. Put at its bluntest, Wesley was a complete control freak, who believed he could drive out all sin from his pupils by separating them completely from the world. To this end, he built his school 'in the wild', to free his children from the corrupting influence of other children. His pupils were taken in at twelve years old, and were not allowed to leave the school, even for a day, for the rest of their time there. Wesley held 'tender parents' in contempt, believing their care and concern merely served to deliver their children up to the Devil.

Six masters were engaged for fewer than thirty children, who were never allowed out of the presence of a teacher, even at night. No recreation, games or play time was permitted, and the children rose at four in the morning winter and summer alike. The chief item on the diet seems to have been gruel, but for those who despised their appetite there was the option of a fast on Fridays until midafternoon. This mixture of a man besotted by faith and obsessed by the corruption inherent in boyhood was the same poisonous blend that drove Thomas Arnold, though Arnold was a positive libertarian by the side of Wesley.

Wesley's school had other notable eccentricities. It had a communal clothing system, whereby any items of clothing needing washing or mending were put in a common area, and new clothes were drawn out from a mass jumble, apparently without a great deal of reference to the size of the child. In 1819 records show that sanitary arrangement were less than modern, though I suspect that in this area at least Kingswood may not have been untypical. It is stated that on Wednesday and Saturday the boys' faces and necks are washed, and their feet every other Tuesday. Every other Tuesday? I can still remember the smell of our changing room in the boarding House I attended at Uppingham, and nearly all of us would shower every day after sport. A hint of the old times was given in that we had to sign up for the luxury of a bath twice a week, and the list where one signed up for one of the four available baths was one of the most accurate guides to one's current popularity. Kingswood was reformed and returned to a great degree of normality midway through the nineteenth century.

Appointing the Head

One Head of a very well-known school was offered the job halfway through the interview process in the gentlemen's lavatory of a London club, while both men were about their business at the urinal. Another Head of a mid-range school was rung up at his desk by the Vice-Chairman of Governors of a famous school (this is in living memory), and was told that the Governors didn't think much of the five chaps they'd be interviewing on Friday for the post of Head of the famous school. Did he fancy throwing his hat into the ring? The Head, who was rather upper-class himself, intimated that he might be interested but wasn't prepared to go through the humiliation of a letter of application and interview. Good Heavens, no, said the Vice-Chairman, no need for that nonsense. Come to dinner at my club on Thursday night and meet a few of the other chaps. This he did, and after a convivial hour and a half talking about everything except the school the Vice-Chairman offered the Head the job, which he accepted. The next day five good men and true (but not good enough, apparently) were duly interviewed and turned down.

While being interviewed for a headship a good friend of mine had a very elderly old boy and governor wake up halfway through the interview, turn to the Chairman and say, 'John! Is this the man you said we were going to appoint?' It wasn't, as it turned out.

Perhaps my favourite story is the most-modern. A candidate applied to a highly regarded school, and, in the standard visit pre-interview to meet the current Head and ask questions, he received a great deal of support and help from him. The interviews were duly held, and the candidate thought he had done quite well. All the candidates were told on the Thursday evening of the interviews that the successful candidate would be rung up by a senior governor and given the news on the following Friday morning.

The candidate duly awaited the call, but none came, so he assumed the worst. He felt in some way he had let down the current Head, so late on the Friday afternoon he rang him up to say how sorry he was that it hadn't worked out, but that he was immensely grateful for the support and encouragement he had received. There was silence on the end of the line. Then the current Head barked, 'What?' The candidate repeated his disappointment and his thanks, to which the current Head replied, 'So no one's rung you?' The candidate said no, which was why he had rung to . . . The current Head barked again, 'Don't leave that phone!' and rang off.

Fifteen minutes later the phone rang. It was the Chairman of Governors, offering him the job. The Chairman had thought the Vice-Chairman was going to ring the successful candidate, and the Vice-Chairman thought the Chairman was going to ring. One is left wondering what would have happened if the candidate had not made to call to the current Head to apologise. Perhaps some weeks after the event a Governor would have growled into his gin, 'Surprised we haven't heard back from the chap we offered the post to . . .'

I could go on. One of the most frequent and often hilarious stories told at the annual meeting of the Headmasters' and Headmistresses' Conference was based on 'how I got my job'.

Earlier appointments had their notoriety as well. Take this from

T. W. Bamford, who says that, when the Warden of Bradfield, Thomas Stevens, appointed S. P. Denning, A. F. Leach gives the following account:

> It is said that his application was the first of several . . . that were opened by the Founder. When he read the words 'Stephen Poyntz Denning', he said, 'This is an omen. "Stephen appoints Denning." So he shall' and opened no more of the applications.[81]

Throughout history the Chair of the Governors has been the decisive factor in appointing a new Head. In one sense this is as it should be. There is no more crucial relationship than that between the Chair and the Head, and, if they do not get on, all hell breaks loose. There are many more safeguards than there used to be, but none that can stop a determined and/or unscrupulous Chair getting their man or woman. It is one of the undiscovered scandals of the public-school world just how much jiggery-pokery can go in the process that is undoubtedly the most important duty a governing body does. Of course, the vast majority of appointments are conducted entirely properly, but it still leaves too many cases where this has not been so. Nor does the appointment of an independent observer guarantee compliance with the will of the majority. In one case the clear first choice of the assembled governing body was overturned on a whim of the Chairman, and the third most popular candidate given the post.

Too many headships, and not just in the dim Victorian past,

---

81 Quoted in Bamford, *The Rise of the Public Schools*, p. 137.

have gone on the basis of whom you know rather than what you know: '. . . the way of the world is such that one lukewarm testimonial from an eminent man . . . is worth a dozen enthusiastic statements from unknown people'. Influence is always important and usually decisive . . .'[82]

The power of the Chairman is like all power, and can be used for good or evil. I owe my continued employment at St Paul's, I suspect, largely to a Chairman and Vice-Chairman who stuck by me when I had a major stroke. Yet, when it comes to the appointment of the Head, the Chair of Governors is almost the last residue of a culture in which decisions did not have to be transparent and those taking them were not accountable.

However, as a sign of changing times, I ought to give the very contemporary email correspondence between the male (gay) Head of a prep. school and his fifty-something female (mother of many) Chair of Governors.

> Dear Chair [real name redacted]: I've just had something happen to me for the first time. In the middle of an interview the prospective parent and mother of a three year-old started to breast-feed him in my study.

> Dear Head [real name redacted]: First time for me too. Hope it's a last time for you.[83]

If it had been John Keate, he'd probably have beaten her. Times *have* changed.

---

82 Bamford, *The Rise of the Public Schools*, p. 138.
83 Private email shown to the author.

Epitaph on a schoolmaster

Willie Michie was schoolmaster of Cleish, in Fifeshire:

> Here lies Willie Michie's banes:
> O Satan! When ye tak' him,
> Gi'e him the schoolin' o' your weans
> For clever de'ils he'll mak' 'em!

Robert Burns

10

MUTINY!: DISSENT IN THE ENGLISH PUBLIC SCHOOL

The boys at English public schools in the period we are covering [1800–64] were engaged in an irregular but continuous warfare against adult government.[84]

It is conventional to see the rise of rebellion in public schools as inspired first by the French Revolution, and then by the numerous revolutions in 1848 that redrew the map of Europe. In fact, the tradition of rebellion was far older than that. There was an ancient custom of 'barring out', whereby pupils barred the gate to their schoolmaster, a remnant of which is seen in Black Rod having to beat open the door at the opening of the UK Parliament. In 1690 the boys of The Manchester Grammar School disagreed with the timing of the Christmas holiday. They barricaded themselves in the school for a fortnight, receiving food and supplies from local townspeople, and presumably also the firearms and ammunition

---

84   Chandos, , *All Boys Together,* p. 167.

they employed to warn off invaders. George III used to ask any Etonians he met if they had had any rebellions lately. There was an even more remarkable rebellion at Merchant Taylors' School in the last quarter of the nineteenth century:

> This gave the occasion to the abolition of flogging in this school; for, the next time Lorde (the 'fourthe master') made the attempt, at a concerted signal (the rebellion had long been in preparation), all the boys, to the number of two hundred, rushed from the schoolroom into the lobby, where punishment was usually inflicted, hustled the pedagogue, rescued the victim, and scattered the birch into fragments, each one carrying off a twig in token of victory. We then returned into school with perfect coolness, having announced our determination *unâ voce* never to submit to such a degradation. To this arrangement the heads were compelled to submit; for so well was the spirited measure organised, and so completely carried into effect, that no ringleader could be pointed out as an example, and nothing short of the expulsion of the whole number could have been resorted to. The affair, therefore, was hushed up.[85]

It is tempting to believe that, with the advent of the Victorian era, all this ceased, and conformity became the norm. Yet in 1873 the very able John Mitchinson, Head of King's, Canterbury, and the actual founder of HMC, faced a rebellion that ended only because he was leaving the school. It included thirty-five boys preparing for a siege, the singing of 'The Marseillaise', much

---

85 Draper, *Four Centuries of Merchant Taylors' School*, p. 113.

hurling of missiles (albeit mainly at study doors) and public denial of the authority of the prefects. As boys we believed the militia had to turn out at Uppingham when the boys mutinied at the school's failure to mark the relief of Mafeking. Haileyburians took an unauthorised half-holiday to march through the streets of Hertford and Ware when Ladysmith was relieved (they thought the Master, Edward Lyttelton, was a secret, pro-Boer sympathiser). Seventy-two pupils were beaten for their involvement, including Clement Attlee.

At Uppingham again, I can't remember the exact date (for some reason it's not one the school seems to want to remember) but it must have been between 1962 and 1966 when Easter fell in term time, and the whole school was sent on a series of long walks on Good Friday. Some idiot had not ensured a staff presence to await the incoming tide of younger pupils at Seaton station, by the Seaton viaduct on the London main line (apropos of nothing, this was the station, now long closed, most of the attendees for the first meeting of the Headmasters' Conference came to). The result was carnage. A signal box was broken into, and the small explosive charges laid on the track to warn drivers of danger taken from it. At this distance I have no way of knowing if what we boys who were there at this historic event believed was true, but we genuinely thought that one charge meant watch out, two meant slow down and three meant emergency stop. We believed our heroic contemporaries laid ten charges on the line. To this day I believe when the police came they found a boy swinging from an old-fashioned signal arm, because I have the most vivid memory of such a boy, scratching his armpit, making monkey noises and asking for a banana. Reconstructed memory? I must ask my psychiatrist. In any event, the incidents were enough to make a good story in the *Daily Mail*. They were not a rebellion as such, more an illustration of the heaving tide of rebelliousness that lay under the calm surface of many 'modern' public schools.

Here in the issue of mutiny and rebellion, there was a graphic difference between the public schools of 1800–60, and the post-'Reform' and post-Clarendon Commission versions of those schools. Yet, even in their Victorian heyday, pupils at public schools were prone to mutiny and riot. Much of this was to do with the prefect system, whereby a school was in effect run by the pupils, which was a feature common to both the earlier and the later public schools. Any 'adult' interference was bitterly resented, up to the late-1950s. A future Warden of Winchester commented in 1776, 'They [the boys] have been taught to think that it was the duty of an assistant master by no means to interfere with the discipline of the foundation.'[86]

Winchester again features in the following incident. The first response to a questionnaire issued by the Headmaster in 1818, seeking to ascertain the reason for an insurrection, helpfully *gave* the reason: 'That you are ugly.' Helpful, innit?

The 'fags' rebellion' at Winchester in 1829 was highly unusual, in that it was boy against boy. The reason was interesting. The new Head Commoner Praefect in 1829 was a boy called George Ward. Though big of body and powerfully built, neither he nor any other of the senior praefects had any great athletic skill. The result appears to have been a decline in the moral (!) authority of the whole 'praefect' body, culminating in a rebellion led by one Arthur Malet. He defied Ward when commanded to undertake fagging duties. Ward tried to beat him with the ash rod that was the praefects' preferred method of torture at Winchester, but found himself buried under a writhing mountain of junior boys. Only his great strength allowed him to

---

86   Ibid., pp. 30–1.

emerge, albeit at the cost of his torn-off coat tails, with small boys hanging off his every extremity, trying to beat him to the ground, like a great bear dragging along the dogs baiting him.

Poor Malet! He and five further boys were expelled, but I think Winchester should have named a street after him. And I would love to present the Arthur Malet Prize at Winchester's equivalent of Speech Day. But how would it be decided which boy to offer it to?

Marlborough in flames

Arguably the most successful rebellion in the history of public schools, and one of the last major ones, was at Marlborough on 5 November 1851. Marlborough was one of a clutch of new public schools, founded in 1843 specifically for the sons of clergy. This was part of a trend to offer schools specialising in certain areas. University College School, London (1830), was in essence founded for, at the least, nonconformists, at best, those who distrusted the increasing dominance of Christianity and religion in the public schools. Epsom College (1855) was meant to be for doctors' sons, while Haileybury, partly because it was situated in the building of the old East India Company, disbanded after the Indian Mutiny in 1857, and, partly because it amalgamated with Kipling's old school, the Imperial Service College, was for many years perceived (actually rather wrongly) as specialising in those who wished to serve in the Empire.

Whatever the reason for the founding of Marlborough, by 1851 it was a seething if not boiling mass of discontent, partly because it was of its time and partly because of weak leadership and appalling conditions. The boys assembled a positive arsenal not just of fireworks but of gunpowder and other military-strength explosive. At 5 o'clock on 5 November the launching of a huge rocket from the centre of the school (fireworks had been banned) announced the start of the rebellion. The explosions carried on for two days. The Headmaster beat a hasty retreat when an improvised grenade burst behind him. On the third day, a staff assault party ventured out and captured five boys, who were expelled. This merely inflamed the situation, and after a week the Head caved in and granted all the school's requests, mainly the restoration of 'privileges' that had been taken away from them in an attempt to put some sort of order into the anarchy that was Marlborough. This revolt was the last fling of the old public-school ethos, in which the school was controlled and run by the boys and adults not expected to interfere, nor tolerated if they did so.

Esmond Marcus David Romilly (1918–41)

Romilly is proof that the spirit of rebellion was alive and well in public schools in the 1930s. His is a remarkable story, and it is surely only a matter of time before someone writes a musical around it. The son of an aristocratic and well-connected family (his father, a highly regarded figure in the Army, had been Governor of Galilee – now *that's* a job title to die for!), Esmond was nephew by marriage to Winston Churchill. He was a pupil at Wellington, but at Wellington of all places refused to join the OTC and distributed pacifist leaflets. Clever boy!

He ran away from what he saw as Wellington's oppression, and established a base in Parton Street in London for runaways from public schools, as well as issuing a revolutionary magazine called *Out of Bounds*. His activities were funded by means of milking anyone who could provide a service to the revolution, and then engaging someone else when demands for payment became too pressing. His organisation recruited 'agents' in public schools who then forwarded scurrilous or damaging stories to Romilly for publication. He visited schools himself to speak to his mission, and at various times was set upon by the OTC and hunted like a fox by boys.

His revolution, brilliant story though it is, barely dented the public-school monolith. His eventual fate was tragic. Though he was a pacifist by nature, the horrors of the Spanish Civil War saw him cycle to Marseilles to join one of the International Brigades. Most of those who joined with him were killed in action. He was invalided home with dysentery. He married Jessica Mitford when he was nineteen, and met his death after he joined the Royal Canadian Air Force and was shot down in 1941. His physical resemblance to Winston Churchill caused Jessica to suggest several times in her letters that he was Churchill's illegitimate son; his mother had been notoriously available to all comers.

Romilly was not everyone's cup of tea. T. C. Worsley was a disruptive and rebellious schoolmaster at Wellington, but he had little time for Romilly:

> He was not an attractive personality, a tough, ruthless, wholly unscrupulous, iron-hearted youth, practising already in his relentless fashion the Communist doctrine that the end justifies the means . . . He was a lone wolf with a wolf's bite for any hand that fed him, and a wolf's snarl for anyone who reasoned with him[87]

The public schools have produced more than their fair share of conformists, their problem being that, in promoting this type of boy to the top of the ladder in the schools, they gave an erroneous

---

87   Worsley, *Flannelled Fool*, p. 98.

impression of the degree of conformity among the masses. As a fairly terrified pupil at Uppingham, I started to smoke because it was the only way I could defy authority and still have a reasonable chance of not being found out. I hid my ten-pack of Benson & Hedges (all I could afford) in my CCF uniform, which produced a strange feeling when, many years later as a newly commissioned CCF naval officer at Haileybury, resplendent in my uniform, I was offered and smoked a duty-free cigarette in the wardroom of HMS *Devonshire*, and later on pulled out of my uniform my own pack of – yes – Benson & Hedges and offered it round. Wheels do come full circle.

There is usually a ludicrous footnote to everything relating to public schools. As regards mutiny, one of the best must be that Frederick Delius, a pupil at the now defunct International College in Isleworth, composed his first song while recuperating in the school sanatorium from having been hit with a cricket bat in the 'Great College Revolt' of 1879.

If . . . and *Bottoms Up!*

It may seem utterly perverse to compare a violent film with a serious anti-Establishment message shown in 1968 with a Jimmy Edwards black-and-white broad comedy film shown in 1959. Yet the two films have in common their depiction of a mutiny by the pupils in a public school, and they share one other feature, which is to reveal the public school simply as a mirror to nature, an institution that is always *reactive* rather than *proactive*. It shouldn't be too much of a surprise. The mass of schools founded from the sixteenth century onwards were a reaction to the crippling blow done to education in England by the abolition of the monasteries and all they offered in the way of education.

MUTINY!

If . . . shows an autocratic establishment of a school that has not changed much since the 1930s. Prefects still beat boys with obscene ritualised rites, and the fear in the eyes of the small boys as they hear the strokes of the cane delivered is a cinematic *tour de force*. The crime of the boys beaten is little more than 'having the wrong attitude', the right attitude being whatever conventional one the school demands of its pupils. I recognise that awful school from my own schooldays in the 1960s – *but I do not recognise it as the school I attended*. Rather, I recognise it as the school my older brother first attended in the 1950s, over a decade before I went.

If . . . is often seen as a depiction of life at a public school at the time it was made. It isn't. It's a film about growing rebelliousness in the 1960s among young people as manifested by the opposition to the Vietnam War, and the canonisation by poster of revolutionaries such as Che Guevara. As such it is a brilliant, if occasionally infuriating, film. What on earth, for instance, is the director trying to achieve by having the dead Chaplain emerge from a drawer opened by the Headmaster? Where has the token girl come from who appears fully armed on the parapet of the Chapel? But it is not about public schools. It simply uses an imaginary public school as the ideal setting to reflect the turmoil and discontent that was bubbling in society at the time.

Outwardly, *Bottoms Up!* could not be more different. It is set in a school where Matrons are there to be ogled, boys' bottoms are there to be caned and any semblance of learning or scholarship is there to be ignored. It is utterly and totally politically incorrect. Yet what it shows is 'the workers' (the boys) rebelling against 'the bosses' (the Headmaster and his staff) and negotiating a hilarious winning contract with the Headmaster. The rather small boy who leads the rebellion bears a passing resemblance to Che Guevara, in dress at least, while Jimmy Edwards's character fights the rebellion in a bomber jacket that would not have disgraced a Spitfire pilot (well, he had ended the war as Flight Lieutenant Edwards, DFC) and a General Montgomery beret. The film is no more about a real school than *If . . .* It simply uses the school as a set against which is played out the increasingly turbulent story of industrial relations in England at the time.

To believe that both films are about public schools is to believe that the film *Shakespeare in Love* is about Holkham beach in Norfolk, where the last scene was filmed. Public schools are brilliant at telling us what the values of our society are, in life and in films. They do little to tell us how that society came about.

And what of today's public schools? I used to have to face nearly a thousand thirteen-to-eighteen-year-old Mancunians on a regular basis for assemblies where there was no particular pressure on staff to attend, and, even if they had, there was little they or I could have done in the face of mass dissent. I know just how Keate must have felt when faced by the massed hordes of Etonians. Yet, though at such functions one sensed the rumbling potential for volcanic activity when a thousand feisty young men are gathered together in one space for an event they don't really want to come, it never erupted, and it certainly wasn't because I was wielding a birch. I'd like to think it was my charisma that did it, but it wasn't that, either. It was the sea change that had come over the relationship between a pupil, his school and his teachers since the mad, bad old days of Keate. Those young men might not have chosen in a free world to be at that assembly, but they had chosen to be at that school, and sensed its massive desire to do the right thing by them. Education had become a partnership between staff and student, not a war, and the public schools have never been given their due credit for bringing that revolution about.

Demon sex or demon drink?

As a footnote, much has been written about homoeroticism and public schools. Less has been written about public schools and alcoholism. Up until the 1860s, there was little adult supervision of pupils, and hence almost unlimited access to alcohol. Much of this was down to the fact that much of the water available to children was even less healthy than alcoholic beverages, their own water having been purified by the brewing process. Winchester took things one stage further. Beer was obligatory for the boys, and the devil was tea, condemned because it was unknown to the Founder.

In any event, it seems likely that many of the acts of mutiny and rebellion that pepper the history of public schools were fuelled by alcohol. Eton was not unusual in locking its boys in, but supplies were pulled up in baskets or smuggled in through side doors: "'The rioting, masquerading and drinking that took place in College after the doors were closed at night," said an old Etonian of the eighteen-twenties, "can scarcely be credited.'"[88]

Harrow had its Red Nightcap Club early in the nineteenth century, the prep. school for the Hellfire Club, while tradesmen at Winchester supplied the boys with brandy in ginger-beer bottles.

Did it all end when the Victorians held sway? One relic is end-of-term pranks, where pupils ran riot on the last night of the summer term or on the day that examination leave started for the Upper Sixth in the summer term. It has come to be known by its American term, 'Muck-up Day', but it was around long before anyone imported the Americanism. Sometimes, these pranks are funny. We turned up one morning at Sedbergh to find each

---

88 Lamb, *The Happiest Days*, p. 34.

of the glass-globe light shades in the library sporting a goldfish swimming round happily in half a bowl of water. At other times Sedberghians turned all the benches round in the Powell Hall to face the wrong way, and put rugby posts at the top of Winder, the hill that lowers over the town and the school.

Sometimes these pranks are plain dangerous, as witnessed by the preference for daubing offensive slogans on the tallest roofs overlooking the Westminster quadrangle, or the time boys put two lavatory bowls on top of the pinnacles at the end of the very, very tall Uppingham Hall. Sometimes they are offensive, as when pupils daub 'FUCK OFF' in weed killer on the main cricket pitch. They can cause deep offence to well-meaning teachers, as when one teacher found his pride and joy, a BMW sports car, with artificial turf glued all over it.

The truth is rarely reported, but quite a lot of schools face an outburst of anarchy or near-anarchy at the end of term or the start of exam leave that would not have disgraced the 1820s – superglue in all the locks, every fire extinguisher in the school set off, soapflakes in the fountain and clingfilm placed across the top of every lavatory bowl. Fireworks and stink bombs are old hat, as are leavers doing the conga round the school, but where it can turn very nasty is when the playing fields are full of vomiting, drunk young people, often semicomatose.

What is interesting is that there is no parallel history of mutiny in state schools, or, if there is, no one has written it. Should we take this to mean that there is less rebellion in children who attend state schools? Hardly likely. I prefer to think it illustrates the simplest law of physics: that for every action there is a reaction. The public schools placed the most intense pressure on their pupils to conform, and in turn produced pressure from the recipients to rebel.

I I

CHANGE AND DECAY: WHO NEEDS SCIENCE? AND DAISY PULLS IT OFF

Learning and the advent of coeducation

Public schools are kicked into change, frequently screaming, by threats to their existence. I believe there have been three radical, life-giving changes in the history of these schools. The first was the change from anarchy to some semblance of order, in the mid-nineteenth century. The other two were the ditching of classics in favour of a more modern curriculum and academic ambition, and the almost unbelievable willingness of these schools to take girls in as pupils.

A little learning: who needs science?

It was not unreasonable for schools often founded as 'grammar' schools in order to teach Latin grammar to continue to have it as their teaching and learning staple for so long. What was unreasonable was the inordinate length of time they clung onto this one-track curriculum, long after its sell-by date. Part of this harks back to one of their dominant features, a monumental conservatism uniquely allied to an evolved survival instinct that sees them hurl off their languor and leap into action at any real threat to their existence.

Whatever the reason, for the majority of their lives the public schools did very little indeed to advance learning. It was not that they taught only Latin and some Greek, largely ignoring maths, science and modern languages: it was more that they taught even these subjects extraordinarily badly. Of course, there were always some brilliant students who had been taught brilliantly who arrived at Oxford or Cambridge. More common was the young men who arrived markedly deficient in their vocabulary and grammar.

They hung on to the classics for a very long time indeed. Even when they did appoint teachers for science they were rather like the first engineering officers in the Royal Navy, deemed to be *infra dig* and rather working-class. There was also a vast ignorance (more often than not wilful, one suspects) about what science actually was and what it required. One late Victorian Head caused a total panic attack by telling a young teacher he would need to teach physics. The young man protested, to no avail, that he had no qualifications to teach physics. Two days before the start of term, and after much swotting-up, the Head told the teacher he was teaching chemistry. To the Head the two subjects were much the same thing.

There was, and is, one justification for teaching classics that was much used at the time, and probably still has some modern relevance. It is that it taught an approach to learning that could be applied to any other subject. I remember Toby Belk, the ancient librarian at Uppingham, telling me that the purpose of education was not to equip one with a given set of knowledge or facts, but to give one the capacity to *acquire* any set of knowledge or facts – in other words, to acquire the technique of learning.

There is a strange irony that the public schools roped themselves so firmly to two horses running at times in opposite directions. The classics – Latin and Greek – were frequently all they taught in what nowadays we would hesitate to call a curriculum. Yet these classic texts were pagan and pre-Christian, and at times in their hedonism and carnality, as well as their morality, in direct opposition to Christian teaching and values. It was a clash that seems to have gone largely unnoticed. In any event, the reason why the classics dominated was not their construction, beauty or content – though many public-school boys did gain a lasting love of the subject from having it beaten into them – but, as with so many aspects of the public school, a social issue.

A study of the classics may have led to an ordered mind and a wonderful supply of quotations to suit every need, but it did not qualify one for a job. Therein lay its beauty and attraction. If you sent your son to a school where he would learn only classics, you were both stating that he would never have to work for a living and buying him his ticket into membership of the gentry. The English are brilliant at 'placing' someone socially. A true member of the gentry will not tie his own bowtie, because in the past all gentlemen had valets who would hand-tie them. A true member of the gentry knows it is incredibly vulgar to arrive at a shoot wearing, driving or shooting anything new. A true member of the gentry knows it is bad form – 'ostentatious', in fact – to wear one's club tie while being interviewed on television, or indeed to wear it other than when going to the Club.

Just as in medieval times a smattering of the classics was the route to employment in the Church and a more lenient legal system, so in the eighteenth and nineteenth centuries a smattering was an essential attribute for anyone who wanted to be seen as a member of one of the greatest clubs of all time, that of the English gentleman. A major feature of the English gentleman was that he did not have to work. He might choose to do so, just as Dorothy L. Sayers's Lord Peter Wimsey (Eton and Baliol, and a brilliant cricketer) *chose* to solve crimes rather than *have* to do so. Contemporary society criticises the public schools for enabling their students to monopolise the top jobs. A hundred years earlier they were more likely to be criticised for preparing people for employment.

All this leads on to one of the major conclusions to be drawn about the English public school. Until very recently, these 'schools' had little or nothing to do with learning, or even the assimilation of knowledge.

> A boy when he leaves public school at the age of eighteen will very likely imagine that Michelangelo was a musician, or that Handel wrote comic verse . . . He can get in a Public School what he could not get anywhere else in the country . . . He will learn self-reliance, and will learn certain other moral qualities, a sense of duty and fellowship, a knowledge of how to command and obey.[89]

Nor, actually, is their major demerit the old school tie or network issue. Public-school boys and girls are not a variant of a Masonic Club, or a group who artificially arrange for their

---

89   Mack, *Public Schools and British Opinion*, p. 300.

alumni to gain the top jobs regardless of their ability – though this may have been the case in the past (see 'The old school tie – fact or fiction?' below). The reality is slightly more complex, but compelling. For most of their history the product of a public school was consciously or unconsciously tuned into a certain set of values, and, because of the intensive nature of boarding-school life in particular, those indentured to these schools were imprinted by the values of the hive. Prime among those values – and in the very air one breathes at Eton or Winchester – is the sense of one's fitness to rule and the sense of being a member of a highly elite club – a sense fostered even further in those who moved on to the even more elite clubs of Oxford or Cambridge, and the greatest clubs of all, the House of Commons and the House of Lords.

The public schools have always trained people for power, and political power in general. It is in their DNA. The Earl of Derby's Cabinet in 1866 had eleven of its sixteen members educated at public schools, nine of those from Eton. And, before the vultures swoop on this long-dead body, they might be surprised and annoyed to remember that this was the Cabinet that pushed through the Second Reform Act, hugely extending the right to vote of people who had not been at public school.

That sense of fitness to rule was there in the attitude and instincts of David Cameron and Boris Johnson, and, amusingly, in Tony Blair (Fettes College). It helped Clement Attlee (Haileybury) run a Labour government, and even in the actor and lovely man Simon McCorkindale (Haileybury), whose sense of effortless superiority wooed him into numerous parts much better actors pined for. Public-school boys and girls do not even have to recognise each other: they *sense* each other. The right to rule and to command is in the air they breathe, though more so at boarding schools.

That doesn't mean they relax. The top public schools are

intensely competitive, and public-school boys and girls will often circle warily round the campfire like two predators after the same piece of meat. They do not like each other, they may not even approve of each other, but above all they *understand* each other.

There is another feature of the public-school boy that first impressions suggest is being carried through to the new generation of new public-school girls: an enlarged sense of irony leading above all to self-deprecating humour. In the hothouse of the public school it is better to laugh at yourself before others start to laugh at you. It is a very cunning plan, and stands out well in comparison with certain politicians in particular who see life as a very serious business, and themselves the most serious thing in it. Self-deprecating irony is amusing, and disarming, as well as being an excellent cloaking device. It takes one to know one, and to know in particular that the public-school man who appears to be laughing at himself is in fact laughing at you.

All this, of course, means that for much of their time the curriculum was the most minor element of what a public school sought to achieve. It could be argued that the major reason public schools take examinations and Oxbridge success so much to heart nowadays (when A-levels were brought in, many leading public schools spurned and did very badly at them) is that these are now the crucial rungs on the ladder to power, in politics, in business and so on. As a footnote, *Country Life* magazine produced a glossy, full-colour 'Schools' supplement in 2016. These things are often ignored by historians, for the good reason that they are entirely pro-Establishment. Their aim is to sell advertising space to public schools, so it would be unreasonable to expect them to bite the hand that feeds them. What is interesting about these supplements is that they hold a mirror up to a certain part of nature. They do not tell us what public schools are actually like. They tell us how the public schools would like the readership to see them. It was therefore fascinating to read that the reason parents sent their children to public school was not any longer for them to have an old-school-tie network (Heaven forbid!), but rather because it gave the children a set of 'shared values'.

Like the great guns in Thomas Hardy's poem 'Channel Firing', the noise of this rolls down through the ages. Shared values? This was what Squire Brown was so concerned about when he sent Tom to Rugby. And what are those values? They were and are a shifting kaleidoscope of whatever it is the wealthy middle and upper-middle classes of the day have persuaded themselves they want for their children. At one stage it was 'manliness', whatever that is. And nowadays? Freedom from drug dependency; access to a top university as a means to a career in the professions or banking. Interestingly, it is still to keep their children away from the rough children down the road.

This is much scoffed at by the opponents of public schools, including leading figures in the Labour Party who chose to send their own children to them. Is it wrong to deride people who wish to keep their children away from the rough children down the road? Superficially, it is. Yet, as I write this, there has been in the news the tragic story of a fourteen-year-old murdered at school in a knife attack, and a piece on the state of Texas making it legal for students to bring concealed guns into classes. Interestingly, the ruling is binding on state but not private institutions, and the majority of the latter have rejected the ruling. Parents nowadays do not want to isolate their children in case they pick up a working-class accent or disease. They want to avoid the pupil who can single-handedly stop the rest of the children in a class learning anything in a lesson, to avoid violence and to see their child stretched and challenged. And who are we to blame them?

Fauntleroy pulls it offs

'The study led us to conclude that, despite schools' claims, prospectuses paint a picture of boys' schools which happen to have girls in them rather than of schools whose policies and practices have become genuinely co-educational.'[90]

So states a collection of academic essays published in 2002. Is the introduction of girls into the boys' public school actually a revolution, or is it simply a cosmetic fraud? The key to the comment above is its date. By 2002 a majority of boys' public schools had introduced girls into the Sixth Form, but a majority had not undertaken the follow-through, which was to go coeducational throughout. It was that latter change that started to produce real thought about the education of women, rather than the previous years, when it was assumed that girls would thrive on the leftovers from the men's table. Here again, public schools created nothing. They merely reflected what was happening in wider society.

Even if the early change to coeducational Sixth Forms did not stop the public schools from offering a primarily male culture, nothing illustrates the almost infinite flexibility and resilience of the English public schools more than the relative ease and speed with which these bastions of masculinity adapted to taking girls. It also, cynically, illustrates that sometimes they are best seen as a business rather than an institution devoted to education. For most of their history, the public schools had not only been proudly masculine, but positively *braggadocio*. All-male status was the equivalent of the Church's Thirty-nine Articles rolled into one. Yet, when the punters and the money got behind coeducational Sixth Formers, centuries of cant and unthinking

---

90 Walford (ed.), *British Private Schools*, p. 128.

humbug went out of one window while the cash and the cheques rolled in at the other.

And why not? Coeducation is not immoral, nor is it evil. It happens to be the way that most of the Western world educates its children. Which is better? To lament the passing of the dodo because it could not evolve, or admire it if it did? There was certainly a lot of cant and humbug that went into the justification of School Testosterone; there was nearly as much shown among those who criticised its end.

The revolution was started by Marlborough in 1968 with girls admitted to the Sixth Form, and it was followed by a horde of other major and minor public schools in the 1970s, including Rugby. No one has measured Thomas Arnold's grave to see if his turning increased its size. Inevitably, the schools that had started by taking girls only into the Sixth Form became in due course of time fully coeducational, in Marlborough's case in 1989. Among other momentous changes, this resulted in the HMC (the Headmasters' Conference) becoming HMC (the Headmasters' and Headmistresses' Conference), as public, former boys' schools started to contemplate the unthinkable and appoint a woman as their Head. It sounds easy as I write it. It wasn't. We were there, 'we' being Jenny and myself. We were asked to design, found and run the first Sixth Form girls' house at Haileybury, and Jenny subsequently went on to be one of the first female Heads of an HMC school.

The enormity of this change cannot be stressed too much. As the preceding chapters have shown, testosterone was the only aftershave used by the English public schools for most of their history. So why this change? There were supporting reasons, as given below. But the main one was very simple. The invention of the Pill in the 1960s for the first time in their history gave women control of their fertility, independent of men. From this grew feminism, and a much wider and softer change in popular culture that required men and women to be equal. And the public schools? As ever, they did not dictate change. They followed, slavishly, the cultural changes adopted by the social classes who could afford to pay twice over for education. All of a sudden, the moneyed middle classes wanted schools that could send their daughters as well as their sons to the best universities, where perhaps they might meet (and even marry?) a future Prime Minister or the Prince of Wales. And the dear old English public schools did what they have always done, which was to redefine their product along the lines the consumer demanded. All of a sudden, 'girls' were no longer conceived of as 'skivvies', 'hags' or maids, or Matrons or Dames, but as people who might gain an Oxbridge place. All of a sudden, they were valuable, bit players promoted to a leading part.

There is a different view of the change, favoured by the gay lobby, who see the admission of women into public schools as the final admission by those schools that there was no other way to banish homosexuality:

> But from the late 1960's several boys' schools . . . began to claim they had been won over by the logic of gender egalitarianism, though some members of staff continued to hint that they were rather more preoccupied with the 'unhealthy' atmosphere of their schools . . . But it is the more vociferous voice of many parents and boys that mixed education is more 'natural' which is the more revealing, hinting that homosexuality has played a considerable but unquantifiable role.[91]

---

91 Hickson, *The Poisoned Bowl*, pp. 94-5.

The move to 'coeducation' faced bitter opposition and criticism. I was vilified in the street for making The Perse Boys' School, Cambridge, coeducational. I was told I was destroying The Perse School for Girls. That genuinely wasn't my aim, though I didn't make many friends by pointing out that I'd been appointed to the post by The Perse Boys' School, and to run it in the interest of any other school would be like asking a Labour Prime Minister to enact no legislation that might hurt the Conservative Party. I recommended the change to the governing body because Cambridge's leading academic school took its colour and its culture from Cambridge's leading academic institution, and, when the University of Cambridge made the last all-male college coeducational, believed it sounded the death knell for all-boy education in Cambridge, and would put The Perse dangerously out of touch with its community. I noted two all-female colleges survived, and, yes, I was influenced by the fact that bright boys and girls wanted to be educated together. Fee-paying schools are a business, and a business that survives adapts to a changing market. My treatment was not untypical. Girls' schools, particularly middle-of-the-road girls' boarding schools, were stripped of their Sixth Forms, and even the best girls' schools, boarding and day, lost some of their brightest pupils.

My own experience suggests that the initial introduction of girls into the Sixth Form of boys' public schools (and early on it was only into the Sixth Form) was not only a cynical response to market conditions, but also the biggest kick in the pants ever issued to girls' schools, who had simply failed to respond to the market. This was not a simple issue. A basic reason for many girls to leave their existing girls' school was 'campus fatigue' – the tendency of the girls' schools to recruit their pupils at eleven or in many cases to an 'all-through' school starting at age five or seven, with the result that many girls simply became bored with the same surroundings. Girls at sixteen are and were far more mature emotionally than their male counterparts, and the girls' school in many cases made the fatal mistake of treating their Sixth Form pupils as if they had not grown up.

I shall probably get lynched for saying it, but our experience in the late 1970s and early 1980s was that much of the teaching in the girls' schools was not so much bad as repetitive, formulaic and risk-averse, whereas that in the boys' schools was simply more exciting. I was introduced to this very early on, when one of the first girls at Haileybury in my A-level English class came up to me and said she had finished reading one of the set texts, *The Revenger's Tragedy*. Without thinking, I said well done and suggested she read Webster's *The Duchess of Malfi*. 'You mean you don't want me to read *The Revenger's Tragedy* again?' she asked. It came out that, far from reading round her O-level set texts, she had been actively discouraged from doing so, and that she had been through *Julius Caesar* in minute detail in class three times, but neither seen nor read any other Shakespeare play. Times have changed.

The boys' school sometimes offered more exciting teaching, particularly in the sciences, and often offered much more in the way of sport, art, music and drama, if only sometimes because the boys' school tended to be larger than the girls' school. And, of course, they offered boys. Many a Headmistress would sniff disparagingly and say she knew *exactly* why the girls wished to be in a Sixth Form with boys. This always struck me as a bizarre criticism of motive. Why shouldn't a girl want to go to a school where she can meet boys? And why shouldn't a boy want to go to a school where he meets girls? Surely children need to learn how to live alongside the opposite gender as much as they need to learn mathematics?

It wasn't only the pupils who needed to learn. It was the staff. The arrival of girls terrified numerous of the born-again bachelor brigade of teachers so common in boys' public schools after the war. There was some heavy-handed humour – I remember the early report that read, 'Jane is not firing on all four cylinders – if girls have cylinders, that is.' Ho-ho! How very reassuring for Jane's parents to know the intuitive sympathy her teachers had for her.

My own most vivid memory of the clash of the news occurred when a girl in my house was sent home for a week, having been caught in a compromising position in a boys' study, which, had the member of staff come into the room half an hour later, would probably have resulted in her (and him) being expelled. At the time we had a number of daughters of very famous, high-profile people in the house. As a result, the gutter press was paying employees at the school to tip them off should anything juicy happen. When this story broke, a pack of journalists were lurking exactly on the boundary of the school's property, waiting to pounce on any emerging pupil. One such innocent was making his way to the shops in Hertford Heath when one of the nation's finest emerged from a hedge, notepad extended (I wonder if nowadays they use an iPad), and asked him, 'What about this Christine business, then?' (Let's pretend the girl was called Christine.) Haileybury may have had its problems coming to terms with girls, but, for better or worse, she was a Haileyburian, and there is no loyalty greater than that of a public-school boy to his own kind. Putting on his most innocent face (I'd taught the boy O-level English literature, and innocence was not what I saw as the dominant feature in his personality), he stared the journalist in the eye and said, 'Christine? No, I'm sorry, you've got it wrong. It was a boy, Christopher, and it was homosexual rape in the kitchens.'

The aftermath of this was the journalist in question seeing his future assured with the exclusive byline on the story 'Homosexual rape at *****'s daughter's school!' He forced his way into the Master of Haileybury's study with the immortal words, 'Right! I know all about this homosexual rape! What's your comment, then?' If you want to know why fewer and fewer people want to become Heads, imagine yourself facing that question knowing that tomorrow morning millions of people would be reading your answer, that answer being complicated somewhat by the fact that you didn't know what the hell the journalist was talking about. It's the adrenalin rush that makes us do it.

As it was, the story came out the next day under headlines along the lines of, 'GIRL SENT HOME FROM ****'S DAUGHTER'S SCHOOL IN KISS AND A CUDDLE IN A STUDY SAGA'.

In those days the fiercely bachelor Haileybury Common Room took the *Sun*. I walked in first thing to see one of the most confirmed bachelors of all reading the *Sun* open at Page 3. The beak in question looked like Friar Tuck, and was a delightfully benign teacher who would have left a room if a woman had walked in, not because he was a misogynist, but because he wouldn't know how to talk to her. He was one of the nicest men I've ever worked with. This morning he was clearly confused, looking at the biologically improbable Page 3 girl, alongside which was the 'GIRL SENT HOME FROM ****'S DAUGHTER'S SCHOOL IN KISS AND A CUDDLE IN A STUDY SAGA' story.

'What's wrong,?' I asked him.

'Martin,' said a clearly confused bachelor, 'does Christine *really* look like that?'

'Er ...,' I said, 'there's a clear and thick black line between the photograph and the story . . .'

The girls we had in our house at Haileybury were a brilliant bunch – intelligent, full of common sense and gloriously funny. They were also tough, and herein lies the key. We were able to choose the girls who came from as many as ten applicants for each place, and so were able to choose those with what we thought was the personality to cope. We were also able to house the girls in their own boarding House but integrate them very fully into the boys' Houses. What that meant was that the girls were able to build up their own group identity. This was crucial, because, while the boys were significantly less mature than girls of the same age at sixteen, the boys were past masters at hunting in packs. What I think very few people spotted in the early days was how much of a threat the girls were to boys.

The classic old-boy response to their school taking girls, if it wasn't apoplectic rage, was the heaviest nudge-nudge-wink-wink response – 'I wish I'd had [giggle] girls when I was at school.' But would they? The typical boy came into his public boarding school at thirteen years of age. As he was locked into close confinement with his year group, the pecking order was soon established, and for three years the boys would do what they have always done throughout history, and communicate affection by insulting each other often in the grossest terms, so that by the time they reached sixteen they were more or less armoured against any insult or attack. But then these girls turned up, with the capacity to hurt a boy somewhere much more important than the foot: his ego. If a girl, or the girls, didn't like you, you risked becoming the most terrible of things in a boarding school: unpopular. They were a status symbol, the prettier the better. But what if the potential status symbol said she didn't want to go out with you?

Also, these strange creatures didn't obey the same rules. When your closest mate let rip a ripe fart, you recoiled, you curled up your nose and said, 'God you're foul! You smell!' Tell a girl she smelled and there'd be trouble for weeks – and what the hell did you do when a girl farted, for God's sake? As well as throwing away the Social Interaction Handbook you'd sweated over so painfully for three years, these girl-things could make you look a fool. Result? An almost unconscious circling of the pack round the tribe of girls, the aim being to separate them out into individuals who could be picked off one by one, and made to conform to the image the boys wanted the girls to have.

If some of the girls' schools had only themselves to blame for the loss of their pupils, some of their complaints at what went on in boys' schools was justified. It was common in some schools, and still is in one of the best-known, for the boys to rank girls in numerical order on their sexual attractiveness as they entered the hall for the first time. School medical services simply did not adapt to the needs of girls, the Pill was expected to be used to avoid 'embarrassment' for the school, and various regions of the school were colonised by couples for the heaviest of petting and more.

The two that stick in my memory were the graveyard of a rural boarding school I had to walk back through in the early summer evening after giving a lecture (evidence suggested a flat tombstone was warm enough in summer to lie on) and the dimly lit crypt of a very famous school Chapel we were shown round at a divisional meeting of what was then the Headmasters' Conference. The poor prefect showing six Headmasters round got redder and redder as the moans and giggles emanating from the gloom made it clear what rite was being observed, but he stuck it out to the bitter end.

In the early days of coeducational Sixth Forms, many mistakes were undoubtedly made, the most common to ignore gender stereotypes, and blithely, if unconsciously, conform to them. Heads of schools could behave worse than their boys. I remember being at one of the first meetings held for housemasters and housemistresses of girls in boys' boarding schools. It was a strangely incompatible group of people. There were some schools that had taken the perhaps unwise decision to appoint to this post a man-hating (or at least a man-nervous) spinster lady. Others had appointed clearly unsuitable men who turned to the open window wistfully as the thwack of leather on willow permeated in from the cricket field. One of them sat bemusedly through the whole conference in silence, and blurted out at the end, 'Frankly, I don't know the first thing about girls!' Then there were people like Jenny and myself, who'd simply been standing in the wrong place at the wrong time, and the usual collection of brown-nosers who'd volunteer for anything if it meant promotion, up to and including forming a boarding House composed of rabbits. There we all were, sipping sherry nervously in the hall of the Headmaster's house, prior to going into dinner.

The Head was a larger-than-life figure, often drunk, who won his place in my heart by going up to a Housemaster who was a notorious beater and telling him that if he touched another boy he was out on his ear. That may have been his finest hour as a Head, but this evening wasn't. He'd been at an admissions conference at Oxford, in an age when Oxford didn't seem to mind admitting it took the occasional student from a public school, and he was well oiled. He followed his usual habit of not so much opening a door as walking into it, with the result of a very dramatic entry as the heavy piece of oak crashed back into the panelling. 'Christ!' he said. 'I've had a bad day! Give me a fag someone, will you?' At this, various spinster ladies started to look at the mullioned windows as a means of escape. By the time the Head, in a very loud voice, got into a discussion of how the Admissions Tutor for a leading college was the proud owner of the 'biggest pair of knockers' he'd ever seen in his life, all you could see through the mullions was vanishing, discreetly clad, ankles.

Yet for all the horror stories I and others can tell, I've yet to meet a girl who went to a boys' public school who seems to have lasting scars from the experience: the reverse is true, actually, and it's not because I spend my time at school reunions that tend by their very nature to attract only those who enjoyed or benefited from school. I hate reunions, or any going backwards in life. History throws a long shadow, and the advent of full coeducation has in many cases acted in a similar manner to the 'force quit' option on a computer. It has ended a bad programme and not saved any of it, and the schools that have emerged from the experience would, thank God, be unrecognisable either to Tom Brown or indeed to Tom Arnold.

12

EVOLUTION

These [the public] schools were lost to public
education, and went instead to form the nucleus of a
private, fee-paying system. Great national institutions
that should have formed the foundation of a national,
secondary education were given over to the 'higher
classes' who could afford to pay: it is as though
Buckingham Palace were sold to a hotel chain or the
Brigade of Guards sold off to Securicor . . . It is a sad
and savage irony that it is easier today for the son of a
South African millionaire or a wealthy African prince
to gain admission to an English public school than it is
for a poor child of English parents. . .[92]

These late-twentieth-century words reflect the hostility
towards English public schools that has always been a part
of English culture. A crucial key to the survival of these inherently

---

92   Shrosbee, *Public Schools and Private Education*, p. vii.

conservative institutions in this hostile environment has been their intuitive capacity to recognise when their survival was adversely affected by one of their hallowed traditions, and drop the tradition. In 1938, someone could write, 'The sight of small boys in top hats and morning coats riding in tubes and buses must cause foreigners and visitors to London some amazement. Every Londoner recognises them, however, as the boys of Westminster School wearing their traditional uniform.'[93]

The fact that no pupil would be seen dead in a top hat on the London Tube nowadays is not only linked to changing fashion. It shows the capacity of the sector to evolve in the face of threats to its existence. In 2004, when I arrived at St Paul's School as High Master, I was proudly told that the school encouraged the boys who walked to Hammersmith Tube station to be as scruffy as possible, this being deemed 'urban disguise' and a necessary defensive measure. The old attitude to uniform on the part of the school invited verbal and worse assaults on the pupils, who in the manner of boys throughout the ages handled this sort of thing remarkably calmly and sensibly. Not so their parents, and, as is the case with any other public school, St Paul's reacted to anything that might cause parents not to send boys to the school by adopting a remarkably pragmatic attitude to uniform.

Public schools love their traditions, but they love their fee income more. My case for this being a prime example of their evolutionary survival instinct is happy to rest on the fact that Etonians, who by and large do not travel to their school on public transport, have retained their traditional uniform (as have indeed their teachers), and are still inordinately (I refuse to use the word 'insufferably') proud of it. As an aside, my contribution at St

---

93 Rodgers, *Old Public Schools*, p. 27.

Paul's was to abolish uniform for the Sixth Form, as I believed sixteen-year-olds should learn to dress for the future they faced as adults and not the past they had occupied as schoolchildren for the past ten years.

The old school tie – fact or fiction?

One of the greatest criticisms levelled against the English public school is the concept of the old school tie, or the existence of a sub-Masonic cohort whereby those who went to public school receive unfair preferential treatment in jobs and advancement in general. If anyone is qualified to comment on the possession of an old school tie, it has to be I. I possess, and am authorised to wear, six of the things – Uppingham, Haileybury, Sedbergh, The Perse, Manchester Grammar and St Paul's. Forgive me if I point out that this surfeit of networks has made me neither rich nor famous.

Yet the existence of the old school tie as a network leading to success certainly used to be true, and in an earlier age the Establishment didn't see much wrong with it. Stanley Baldwin did more than many to fuel the concept in an address to the Harrow Association in 1923:

> When the call came to me to form a government, one of my first thoughts was that it should be a government of which Harrow was not ashamed. I remembered how in previous governments there had been four or, perhaps, five Harrovians, and I determined to have six.[94]

---

94 Quoted widely, but see, for example, Rodgers, *Old Public Schools*, p. 6.

I love the phrase 'the call' as being typically public-school. Baldwin was 'called' to be Prime Minister. It would have been such bad form to admit to lusting after it all his life. The important thing about Baldwin's fatuous comment is that the *quality* or suitability of those appointed is unimportant. What matters is that they went to Harrow.

We are all the prisoners of our history, and Eton did the image of the public schools no favours when it transpired that at one and the same time the Prime Minister of the UK, the Mayor of London and the Archbishop of Canterbury were all old Etonians. Never mind that two of them at least got there through raw ability. The fact of this *triumvirate* was meat and drink to the lobby, who believed the old school tie is alive and well, just a little bit more hidden than it needed to be in the past.

Is it?

Personally, I believe there is an old-school-tie network operating in Britain that exerts tremendous power and influence. It is formed of those who went to Oxford or Cambridge. Perhaps I feel it, like most of those who criticise networks, because I'm not a member of it. I went to the University of Leeds. That fact doesn't seem to have harmed me in my career. Yet the most common denominator in the truly powerful people I have met has been Oxbridge.

As for that network, it too is changing. We are seeing the last of the Etonians and Harrovians who got to Oxbridge as of right. You get there now, and have done so for very many years, by being very, very clever. Is it surprising that some of the cleverest people in the land get some of the best and most powerful positions? Is it even unfair? I remember a steaming debate with some hard-left thinkers in Manchester, just after Manchester United had won the triple of the Premier League, the FA Cup and the European Cup in the 1998–9 season. They were sounding off about the fact that disadvantaged children couldn't go to Oxbridge, and that they should be made to hold back places for such children. I suggested this was an excellent idea, but, to pave the way, which one of them would go to Sir Alex Ferguson and, on the same principle, suggest he hold open two places in the United team for young players who had been disadvantaged in their training? I forget what happened then. I think we retired to the pub.

The problem is that going to a public school used to more or less guarantee you a place at Oxford or Cambridge. It's not true now, but that's never stopped people believing it. It's a good story, and, as with believing in Heaven, we need it to be true. Parts of the media have never let the truth stand in the way of a good story. In fact the modern public school has been remarkably honourable in its attitude to university entry. A contemporary article stated the old lie that two-fifths of the students at Oxbridge were public-school-educated, yet only 7 per cent of children went to public schools. Why is this a lie? Yes, only 7 per cent of children of all ages attend public schools, but the percentage of young people in public or independent school Sixth Forms is near 20.

Public schools get more than 7 per cent of the places because they educate more than 20 per cent of the age cohort that goes on to university. They also get more Oxbridge places *because* they take getting to those universities seriously, whereas a survey in the *Times Educational Supplement* showed that well over half the teachers in state schools in England did not feel able to recommend Oxbridge to their pupils. The University of Bristol's answer is to officially offer lower grades to bad schools, thus rewarding them for *being* bad and removing a major incentive to improve. It's like offering cheaper funerals to cancer patients instead of spending the money on research. It also highlights the shameful neglect on the part of our universities of secondary education, which they have steadfastly refused to help improve. The one exception is the King's College London Mathematics School, which highlights how disgracefully hands-off our universities have been as regards their main suppliers. Instead of helping UK secondary education to improve, they have followed the money and taken more and more students from overseas countries that have sorted out their secondary schools.

In my experience public schools have always been very fair in their attitude to grade offers made to young people at bad state schools. When some years ago a girl from a bad state school gained a place at Cambridge and the papers found several public-school boys who had gained straight A grades and been rejected, none of the Heads I knew challenged the justice of the outcome. A girl who achieved three B grades at that school was likely to be every bit as good as the boy or girl who had been given all the help and support available at a good public school. I never doubted at St Paul's, The Manchester Grammar School or The Perse School that my boys needed to jump through few extra hoops to command their place. That wasn't discrimination. It was justice.

There is another aspect to the concept of the old school tie that suggests it might even be a disadvantage:

> When, later, at Cambridge and elsewhere, I got to know the products of public schools, the thing that struck me about them was their entanglement in their schooldays. At first I rather envied them this, and wished that I. too, had memories of famous cricket matches, a private, exclusive slang, and all the other outward

and visible manifestations of belonging to an inward and invisible *elite*, self-contained and economically and socially advantageous. On further consideration, however, I changed my attitude. It seemed to me that the great advantage of the sort of education I had was precisely that it made practically no mark upon those subjected to it. Scholastic and other deficiencies were more than compensated for by the fact that one's first vivid impressions of life were provided, not by a closed and essentially homosexual group of schoolboys under the direction of masters who had themselves been through the same process, but by men and women actually living and earning their livings. How much I preferred the ribald, noisy, dangerous world to any walled garden, however elegantly arranged and full of summer fragrance! No one ever seems to forget Eton. I easily forgot my Borough Secondary School.[95]

When I took my Diploma of Education the trendy belief was in the theories of Piaget, who postulated that the young child passed through several phases or stages in their development, and, if they failed to complete or froze at one, bad things happened. I've often wondered if secondary school is simply a phase one grows out of, and whether the public-school boy's development in some cases was stopped at adolescence by the intensity of the public-school experience, entangled in it rather than sent on life's journey by it. In this rendition I was one of the many scarred by it, but who made their way through the barbed wire to adult life beyond. But perhaps I'm fooling myself, and,

95 Malcolm Muggeridge, in Brian Inglis (ed.), *John Bull's Schooldays*, 1961, p.109

by returning to teach (albeit by accident) in that very same part of the front line, I simply revealed how entangled I had become, doomed to stay trapped in it all my working life.

Either way, the old-boy network becomes important because mixing with his own kind may not allow him to relive his boyhood, but at least it gives him the strongest possible reminder of it. Seen in that way, the old-boy network is not a means of advancement, but rather a passage backwards in time to a secure and certain world. I suggested earlier that Rupert Brooke welcomed World War One because it gave him release from thinking. I fear that public school served the same purpose for too many boys, reducing life's complexity to the safe certainties of Chapel, sport, house spirit and the continual battle for peer-group acceptance.

Against this one ought to set the story of the redoubtable Grimes, the total reprobate of a schoolmaster created by Evelyn Waugh:

> 'Is it quite easy to get another job – after you've been "in the soup?"' asked Paul.
>
> 'Not at first it isn't, but there's ways. Besides, you see, I'm a public school man. That means everything. There's a blessed equity in the English social system,' said Grimes, 'that ensures the public school man against starvation. One goes through four or five years of perfect hell at an age when life is bound to be hell, anyway, and after that the social system never lets you down ... They may kick you out, but they never let you down.'[96]

---

96 Evelyn Waugh, Decline and Fall, p. 28.

Such a network as exists now is a very different creature from Baldwin's day. Public-school boys and girls, if one can generalise, tend to have good academic results and be relatively at ease in a competitive environment. They know how to blend in and rub along, but are accustomed to individuality. They tend to be easy in their own skins, and hence make people easy in theirs. Their schools have made them get involved in activities outside the classroom, and as a result they are less likely than some others to be both bored and boring. Provided it has not grown into arrogance, they are confident and good communicators. They succeed because of what their schools have allowed them to become, not because of the *names* of their schools. Indeed, they have to work harder than ever before in the history of public schools to justify the privileged education they have received, and the value of having been at Eton or Harrow may even have slipped into negative equity.

The riddle of the English public school

The English public school is an infuriating beast, not least of all because its symbol could easily be Janus, because of its capacity to look (and go) in opposite directions at the same time. Yes, the Second Reform Act, which did perhaps more than any other to extend the franchise to 'common' people, was driven by a Cabinet dominated by Etonians, but it was an Etonian, Wellington, who opposed the First Reform Act. In a story that would be farcical if it were not so tragic, it was an Old Rugbeian, Lieutenant-General Arthur Percival, whose monumental incompetence was in large measure responsible for the fall of Singapore, the greatest defeat suffered by England in World War Two. Public-school generals lost two major battles in the Boer War, making it easy to believe

George Orwell when he wrote, 'Probably the battle of Waterloo was won on the playing fields of Eton, but the opening battles of all subsequent wars have been lost there.'[97]

Yet Wellington did win at Waterloo (even though he in all probability never said the battle was won on the playing fields of Eton, a comment of which there was no contemporary record and which was attributed to him only after his death), and a major cause of our winning World War Two was Old Sherbornian Alan Turing. Yet even here the ironies resonate and clash. Turing was nurtured by Sherborne, but it distrusted his interest in maths and tried to shunt him towards . . . Guess what. The classics. His housemaster wrote to his parents, 'I hope he will not fall between two stools. If he is to stay at public school, he must aim at becoming *educated*. If he is to be solely a *Scientific Specialist*, he is wasting his time at a public school.'[98]

In yet another irony, these schools, which for so long turned their heads away from teaching science, are now crucial suppliers of undergraduates to university physics and chemistry departments, many of which would collapse without this supply line.

The story of the public school is not a simple one. One of the more recent commentators gave as his verdict, 'Public schools in their present form do more good than harm.'[99]

In a lifetime of fighting people who want to abolish public schools, the thing I've found most irritating is the frequency with which those most committed to state education are those who have played the system one way or another, and got their own children into the very best state schools. Public schools survive because people who can afford it will do anything rather than send their

97 Orwell, *The Lion and the Unicorn*, p. 55.
98 Hodges, *Alan Turing*, p. 26.
99 Turner, *Old Boys*, p. 280.

children to a bad school, and too many state schools do not pass muster. Having seen it at first hand, I am uncertain whether schools ranked as 'good' by Ofsted are good in the sense *I* use the word, but still 1.25 million children in the UK do not attend schools with a 'good' or 'outstanding' ranking. I have occasionally cringed at the arrogance and complacency of those who justify public schools (the upper-middle-class version of 'I'm all right, Jack'), but I have met more hypocrisy in the ranks of those who are most vociferous about shutting them down. You do not improve an education system by abolishing the best schools in it.

The greatest threat to the continued existence of public schools is, of course, an improved state education system, and, perhaps, the growth of grammar schools. My own wish would be for the public schools to do everything in their power to nurture the very thing that could kill them off. How to do that is a subject for another book, and is as complex as the schools themselves. Yet it is clear to me that the aim of government should be to share the good news of public schools with those who cannot afford them from their own pocket.

The barrier is not only the obvious one that has killed off earlier schemes, namely the cost. Public support of the public schools would require a UK government to recognise the *real* cost of an outstanding education. From first-hand experience I can confirm that to provide a Sixth Form education of an equivalent quality to that found in a good public school costs no less than £1,500 per year per pupil more than the government is willing to provide. In 2016 the public schools offered yet again to educate ten thousand children, in exchange for the same money the government gives state schools per pupil. At the time of writing the most positive response was to damn the idea with faint praise, while the least positive was simply knee-jerk hysterical.

The other barrier that exerts a baleful influence is the failure to realise that it is not snobbish or divisive or socially unacceptable to recognise that more able students need to be taught in a different way from the normally gifted. One size does not fit all. Albert Einstein and Lionel Messi, and Stephen Hawking and Wayne Rooney, did not need the same secondary education. When I wrote a book based on a year's research on how the world educates its more able pupils, it was clear that a different philosophy in the classroom was needed to educate the more able, a philosophy more commonly found in the independent sector than in the maintained sector. Interestingly, what the research also showed was that you did not need selective education or grammar schools to bring the best out of the most able. You simply needed the right attitude.

Governments have consistently shown themselves unwilling to bite the financial or the philosophical bullet that support of public schools demands, and even when they have tried, as with the ill-fated Assisted Places Scheme, they have done it in such a cack-handed way as to mean the schemes carried the seeds of their own destruction. The Direct Grant Scheme produced schools that have probably done more for social mobility than any other single type of school, but were killed off largely as a result of government demands that they be funded from local rather than national sources.

Yet, if the public schools are indeed highly resilient, they are not immortal. There are two threats to their existence that seem to me to be crucial. The first is the increase in fees that has placed a public-school education beyond the reach of the middle-class families that have been their bedrock for most of their history. The greed that has driven fee increases lies at the door of poor governance, and too many governors whose eyes rarely take in more than the good lunch they get at a Governors' meeting. Greed is not a new feature of the governance of public schools, though in earlier times the greed was associated with a corruption and a desire to line one's own pockets that no longer applies. The greed nowadays is justified by the statement that the schools need to provide state-of-the-art-facilities, but it is greed nonetheless – the greed of those who see a market and people willing to pay more and more for their child's education without asking too many questions.

Private greed has been replaced by corporate greed. Helping schools raise fees to astronomical heights has been the overseas market. When the pound is low, the market is even brighter, but currencies rise as well as fall, and the overseas market is a fickle partner. Charity and the survival of public schools probably both begin at home.

The real killer blow to public schools would not be loss of charitable status (it actually confers a relatively small financial advantage to the schools), but the application of quotas for university entrance, where universities would face restrictions on the number of public-school pupils they could admit. There are very practical reasons why this will not happen, not least of all that it would close many departments of physics, chemistry, modern languages and maths. The moral objections are even stronger. Is it fair to punish a child for the school their parents have chosen for them? Do we really want a society in which we discriminate against those whose crime is to have done too well?

There are at least another couple of nasties that would not kill off public schools, but would greatly reduce their number. Yet why seek to damage the best schools in the world rather than share what they do for the greater good? The way to stop an act of educational vandalism is to make a majority of the British populace see public schools as giving to them more than they take away. Bursaries and free places are an obvious route, and, if state schools object because it is taking away their best pupils, then it's a challenge to them to make their schools so much better that children do not want to leave. But there are many, many other ways that the public schools could make themselves indispensable to UK Education PLC. Sadly, that is off topic for this book. One example, to stand for many? To the chagrin of many in the teaching establishment, public schools have been more successful in attracting graduates as teachers than the state sector in the UK, which suffers from a crippling shortage of maths, science and modern-languages teachers in particular. The reason is that many graduates simply wish to teach their subject to a level and with a frequency they cannot find in the state sector. So why not establish joint appointments, whereby recruits are given a soft landing by teaching half the time in a public school but in a state school for the remainder of the week? The public school pays half its normal salary, similarly the state school. New teachers are brought into the profession and the state sector has the best possible chance of setting out its market stall. The teachers might well learn a lot to tell their public schools about mixed-ability teaching, and their state schools about how to create an ethos in which it is normal to gain an A*.

The way ahead

I think the new dawn for the English public school is already up and running. It's just that no one has quite recognised it yet. Leicester Grammar School was founded in 1981, in a straight response to the local populace's despair about all the educational opportunities available to them. It is an affordable, independent day school serving its local people by giving them what they want for their children. Arnold at Rugby and Thring at Uppingham did not invent a system of education, any more than Wykeham at Winchester or Colet at St Paul's. They responded to a need.

The postwar 'new' schools in England – Leicester Grammar, Yarm School, the Grange School, Birkdale School – are the modern equivalent: affordable day schools in the spirit of the old direct-grant schools, offering both academic rigour and traditional discipline and structure. They are not particularly selective, but demand from students the best results it is in their capacity to obtain. In other words, they are not frightened to challenge their students to aim high. At the same time, they believe in the whole man and the whole woman, and place a significant emphasis on what a pupil does and achieves outside the classroom. They are the classic symbol of the independent sector's greatest strength: its ability to reinvent itself for a new generation of parents and children.

And it is here that the 'great' schools that have featured so largely in this book need to step aside. Eton, Harrow, Winchester, Westminster, St Paul's and the rest are brilliant schools that have survived civil war, the execution of the monarch, plague, fire, great depressions, world wars, the blitz and continual attacks on their existence and their independence. Nothing will destroy those schools, and good luck to them. Yet in our present time they are acting like huge and ancient trees blocking out the light to the green shoots that have the chance to reinvent independent education for modern times.

There are new kids on the block, and, though their grandparents were and are mighty patriarchs, the puppy needs to be let off the leash (forgive a classic mixed metaphor). However wrongly or rashly, the mere mention of Eton or

Harrow conveys an image of social elitism and privilege. The 'great' schools that have been so great an influence in English history and culture have become like a coat that is too heavy to take off. It is time for those schools to resign their position as the symbol of the English public school. When the Headmaster of Leicester Grammar School was elected Chairman of Thring's HMC, he was asked by journalists how he would measure his success. One of his answers was that it would be when journalists would cease referring to Eton and Harrow, and refer instead to Eton, Harrow and Leicester Grammar School. He was laughed at. Those journalists were not laughing at the school, but at the conjunction of two schools so associated with social privilege with one so clearly *not* so associated.

The English Public School has forever been based on snobbery, because the society it served was itself so intimately based on snobbery and class. Thring hesitated to meet his fellow Heads for fear they might not be the right 'type' of men. We have not removed class distinctions from our society. We probably never will. What we have produced is new schools in the spirit of the greatest school in my life, The Manchester Grammar School. It was not perfect; no school ever is. Yet it had and still has one overwhelming virtue. It was colour-blind, and class- and money-blind. It wasn't that it didn't care (and forgive a double negative) about its pupils' racial, religious, social or economic standing. It just didn't see them. All it saw was a child's ability, and whether that child wanted to go to university. That was all it cared about and all it wanted to know. In so doing, it knocked every -ism you can think of into touch. The Manchester Grammar School was not one of the Clarendon Commission's nine 'great' schools. As a day school sending literally hundreds of poor children to Oxford and Cambridge, it wouldn't be, would it? Yet such a school lit a torch, and the heirs and inheritors of that tradition are Leicester Grammar School, Yarm and The Grange.

Schools that give parents what they want, not what government thinks they need – that is the proudest tradition of the English public school. In terms of leadership, the schools that once simply served the parent body have by default been left holding the baton, and they need to pass it on to those, often new, schools that cannot pick and choose their pupils, and that of necessity have to serve their community if they are to continue to exist. Schools that simply do not notice the race, colour, creed or social and economic standing of their pupils or parents – that is the proud tradition of English independent schools that we must fight to preserve. And, like all truly good things, it's not new. Look at The Manchester Grammar School. The mention of Manchester Grammar reveals another beacon of light, The London Academy of Excellence, a state sixth-form college based in London's Newham that is now sending more than twenty of its students annually to Oxford and Cambridge. The Academy is the product of a brilliant co-operation between a number of public schools, including Eton, and the state sector. LAE shows just how much can be achieved if rather than being endlessly threatened public schools are used for the greater good. And politicians please note: the public schools suggested this brilliantly successful partnership entirely on their own initiative, without an Act of Parliament in sight.

AFTERWORDS

'Since public schools are basically run by people brought up to different codes of behaviour from what is often accepted today, they become rather out of touch with the world that surrounds them. Public schools were originated to turn out educated gentlemen; the trouble is that they still do even when gentlemen are in small demand.'[100]

— Radley pupil, writing in the mid-1970s

* * *

La plus ca change! The following was written in 1959:

'. . . All kinds of schools today are suffering from lack of funds . . . The sinister feature in the case of the public school is . . . the

---

100 Heale, *School Quad*, p. 111.

fact that they are being forced, by sheer economics, to become increasingly the preserve of the high salary earner . . .'[101]

* * *

'They were great days and jolly days
At the best school of all.'
— Sir Henry Newbolt

* * *

'The blackest and most odious period of my life arrived – I was sent to St Paul's School.'
— Serjeant Ballantine

* * *

'O the great days, in the distance enchanted,
Days of fresh air, in the rain and the sun.'
— Edward E. Bowen

* * *

'My whole time at Wellington was so disgusting and useless that I find myself hardly able to write about it without nausea.'
— Lord Grantley

* * *

---

101 Snow, *Public Schools in the New Age*, p. 115.

'The schoolmaster, it is sometimes said scathingly, is a man among boys and a boy among men. What the scoffer has failed to realise is that the schoolmaster is too often a boy among boys.'[102]

* * *

'It is perhaps ironical that the first specific reference to any school game is not to cricket but to a relative of its humble summer rival. A phrase book published in 1519 by the former Master of Eton (a Wykehamist) contains the revealing sentence, "He hit me in the eye with a tennis ball".'[103]

---

102 Lamb, *The Happiest Days*, p. 223.
103 Ibid., p. 229.

SELECT BIBLIOGRAPHY

have not listed here the vast number of histories of individual schools. Every school has its own book and many have several. Some are excellent, most are dire. I do list volumes I have quoted from in the text, and ought to record my thanks to the East India Club, to whose library I resorted in many a dull moment in HMC meetings, there to immerse myself in its remarkable collection of histories of individual schools.

Avery, Gillian, *Childhood's Pattern: A Study of the Heroes and Heroines of Children's Fiction 1770–1950* (London: Hodder and Stoughton), 1975.

Bamford, T. W., *The Rise of the Public Schools: A Study of Boys' Public Boarding Schools in England and Wales from 1837 to the Present Day* (London: Nelson), 1967.

Barnett, Correlli, *The Collapse of British Power* (London: Faber & Faber), 1972.

Benson, Steve, with Martin Crossley Evans, *I Will Plant Me a Tree: An Illustrated History of Gresham's School* (London: James & James), 2002.

Betjeman, John, *Summoned By Bells* (London: John Murray), 1960.

Bradby, G. F, *The Lanchester Tradition* (Saxmundham: John Catt Educational Press), 2003.

Campbell, Michael, *Lord Dismiss Us* (London: William Heinemann), 1967.

Carleton, John D., *Westminster School. A History* (London: Rupert Hart-Davis), 1965.

Champneys, Arthur C., *A Soldier In Christ's Army: An Explanation of Confirmation and the Catechism for Public School Boys* (London: George Bell & Sons), 1900.

Chandos, John, *Boys Together: English Public Schools 1800–1864* (London: Hutchinson), 1984.

Clarendon Commission, *Report of Her Majesty's Commissioners Appointed to Inquire into the Revenues and Management of Certain Colleges and Schools, and the Studies Pursued and Instruction Given Therein* (London), 1864.

Copley, Terence, *Black Tom: Arnold of Rugby: The Myth and the Man* (London: Continuum), 2002.

Cooper, Rev. William M., *Flagellation & The Flagellents. A History of the Rod in All Countries from the Earliest Period to the Present Time* (London: William Reeves), no date.

Craig, Patricia (ed.), *The Oxford Book of Schooldays* (Oxford: Oxford University Press), 1994.

Dancy, John, *The Public Schools and the Future* (London: Faber & Faber), 1966.

Delderfield, R. F., *To Serve Them All My Days* (London: Coronet Books), comprising Book 1, *Late Spring*, and Book 2, *The Headmaster*, 1980.

Draper, F. W. M., *Four Centuries of Merchant Taylors' School 1561–1941* (London: Oxford University Press), 1962.

Farrar, F.W., *Eric, or Little by Little* (Amazon Paperback Book Edition), no date.

Gathorne-Hardy, Jonathan, *The Public School Phenomenon* (London, Hodder & Stoughton), 1977.

—, *The Rise and Fall of the British Nanny* (London, Hodder & Stoughton), 1972.

Heale, J (ed.), *School Quad; Being a Word-Picture of the English Public School in 1974, Created from the Writings of Pupils from Bradfield College, Cranleigh School, Radley College and Sutton Valence School* (Tunbridge Wells: Fenrose Ltd), 1974.

Heward, Christine, *Making a Man of Him: Parents and Their Sons' Education at an English Public School 1929–1950* (London: Routledge), 1988.

Hickson, Alisdare, *The Poisoned Bowl: Sex and the Public School* (London: Duckworth), 1996.

Hidden, Norman, *Dr Kink & His Old Style Boarding School* (London: Workshop Press), 1973.

Hilton, James, *Goodbye, Mr. Chips* (London: Hodder & Stoughton), 1934.

Hodges, Andrew, *Alan Turing: The Enigma* (London: Burnett Books), 1983.

Honey, J. R. de S., *Tom Brown's Universe: The Development of the Victorian Public School* (London: Millington Books), 1977.

Hughes, Thomas, *Tom Brown's Schooldays* (Ware: Wordsworth Classics), 1993.

Hurst, Steve, *The Public Schools Battalion in the Great War: A History of the 16th (Public Schools) Battalion of the Middlesex Regiment (Duke of Cambridge's Own), August 2014–July 1916* (Barnsley: Pen & Sword Military), 2007.

SELECT BIBLIOGRAPHY

Irvine, Rebecca, *A Girl's Guide to the English Public School Boy* (London: Enigma/Mandarin), 1990.

Kipling, Rudyard, *Stalky & Co.* (Harmondsworth & London: Puffin Books), 1987.

Lamb, G. F. (ed.), *The English at School* (London: George Allen & Unwin Ltd), 1930

—, *The Happiest Days* (London: Michael Joseph), 1959.

Lambert, Royston, *The Hothouse Society* (London: Weidenfeld & Nicolson), 1968.

Lunn, Arnold, *The Harrovians* (Los Angeles: Viewforth Press), 2010.

McConnell, James, *English Public Schools* (London: Herbert), 1985.

MacDonald, Lynn (ed.), *1914–1918: Voices and Images of the Great War* (London and Harmondsworth: Penguin), 1988.

Mack, Edward C., *Public Schools and British Opinion Since 1860: The Relationship Between Contemporary Ideas and the Evolution of an English Institution* (New York: Columbia University Press), 1941.

Marples, Morris, *Romantics at School* (London: Faber & Faber), 1967.

May, Trevor, *The Victorian Public School* (Botley, Oxford: Shire Publications), 2011.

Moynihan, Michael (ed.), *People at War: 1914–1918* (Newton Abbot: David & Charles), Battle Standards Series, 1988.

Mumford, Alfred A, *Hugh Oldham 1452[?]–1519* (London: Faber & Faber), 1936.

Musgrave, P. W., *From Brown to Bunter: The Life and Death of the School Story* (London: Routledge), 1985.

Nicolson, Harold, *Some People* (London: Faber & Faber), 2010.

Ogilvie, Vivian, *The English Public School* (London: Batsford), 1957.

Ollard, Richard, *An English Education: A Perspective of Eton* (London: Collins), 1982.

Panichas, George A. (ed.), *Promises of Greatness: The War of 1914–1918* (London: Cassell), 1968.

Parker, Peter, *The Old Lie: The Great War and the Public School Ethos* (London: Constable), 1987.

Parkin, G. R., (ed.), *Edward Thring, Headmaster of Uppingham School: Life, Diary and Letters* (London: Macmillan), 2 vols, 1898.

Percival, Alicia C., *Very Superior Men: Some Early Public School Headmasters and Their Achievements* (London: Charles Knight & Co.), 1973.

Quick, Anthony, *Charterhouse: A History of the School* (London: James & James), 1990.

Rae, John, *The Old Boys' Network: A Headmaster's Diaries 1970–1986* (London: Short Books), 2009.

Raven, Simon, *The Old School: A Study in the Oddities of the English Public School System* (London: Hamish Hamilton), 1986.

Rich, P. J., *Elixir of Empire: The English Public Schools, Ritualism, Freemasonry, and Imperialism* (London: Regency), 1993.

Richards, Jeffrey, *Happiest Days: The Public Schools in English Fiction* (Manchester: Manchester University Press), 1988.

Rodgers, John, *Old Public Schools of England* (London: Batsford), 1938.

Seldon, Anthony, and David Walsh, *Public Schools and the Great War: The Generation Lost* (Barnsley: Pen & Sword Military), 2013.

Shrosbree, Colin, *Public Schools and Private Education: The Clarendon Commission 1861–64 and the Public School Acts* (Manchester: Manchester University Press), 1988.

Snow, George, *The Public School in the New Age* (London: Geoffrey Bles), 1959.

Sorley, Charles Hamilton (ed. W. R. Sorley), *The Letters of Charles Sorley* (Cambridge: Cambridge University Press), 1919.

Stray, Christopher, *The Living Word: W. H. D. Rouse and the Crisis of Classics in Edwardian England* (Bristol: Bristol Classical Press/ Duckworth), 1992.

Turner, David, *The Old Boys: The Decline and Rise of the Public School* (New Haven and London: Yale University Press), 2016.

Wakeford, John, *The Cloistered Elite: A Sociological Analysis of the English Public Boarding School* (London: Macmillan), 1969.

Walford, Geoffrey, *Life in Public Schools* (London: Methuen), 1986.

— (ed.), *British Private Schools: Research on Policy and Practice* (London: Woburn Press), 2003.

Waugh, Alec, *The Loom of Youth* (London: Methuen), 1984.

—, (Fillquarian Publishing LLC/Qontro), no date.

—, *Public School Life: Boys, Parents and Masters* (Leopold Classic Library), internet download, no date. Originally published by William Collins, Glasgow, 1921.

Waugh, Evelyn, *Decline and Fall* (London: Penguin), 1987.

Weinberg, Ian, *The English Public Schools: The Sociology of Elite Education* (New York: Atherton Press), 1967.

Woolf, Leonard, *Sowing – An Autobiography of the Years 1880–1904* (London: Hogarth Press), 1960.

Worsley, T. C, *Flannelled Fool* (London: Hogarth Press), 1985.

APPENDIX A

Ten ways to identify a public-school man

1. He would never dream of appearing on TV wearing his club tie.

2. He will habitually use self-deprecating irony to lull you into a false sense of security. He will laugh at himself; but God help you if you laugh at him in public.

3. He does not need to tell you what school he attended. You will sense it instinctively if you went to one, and if you didn't you don't really matter anyway.

4. He will cultivate probably no more than one eccentricity, often of dress, just to show you that he doesn't really care.

5. He will walk towards glass doors talking to you with his back

towards the door, secure in the knowledge that someone will open it for him.

6. He will not invite you to or show off his home; he will assume you know it's magnificent.

7. He will want to down his food as if the rest of the boarding House were still waiting to pounce on every morsel.

8. He will want to invite his Housemaster to his wedding, but never his Headmaster.

9. He will not need you to flatter him. He knows he's good.

10. Very little about him – clothes, briefcase or car – will be brand-new. When you (or your parents) buy things at such an extortionate price you expect them to last.

APPENDIX B

Random examples of public-school slang, mostly historical

WINCHESTER SLANG (1930S)

SWEAT: fagging

TEGE (pronounced 'teejay'): a 'one-year man' or boy who has been at college for a year, allocated to a new boy to initiate him into the mysteries of Winchester 'Notions'

PITCH-UP: parents

TART: favourite or popular boy

CATHEDRAL: top hat

COW-SHOOTER: bowler hat

THE ENGLISH PUBLIC SCHOOL

CONTINENT: sick house

THOKE: holiday

TOYE TIME: prep

TOYES: wooden compartments for study

WORDS USED TO DESCRIBE A NEW BOY'S GUIDE OR MENTOR

SHEPHERD (Osbert Sitwell's prep. school)

SUBSTANCE (Westminster: the new boy was a shadow)

FATHER (Charterhouse)

FAG MASTER (Uppingham)

BIOLOGICAL FUNCTIONS

GO FOR A REAR: to go for a shit (Uppingham)

SEXUAL

FLOG: masturbate (Uppingham and generic)

QUEER: homosexual (generic)

LITTLE BOY: object of sexual desire (generic)

RISE: erection (generic)

APPENDIX B

OBSCURE

POLLY: school prefect (Uppingham)

LICK: cane or beat (generic)

SACK: expel (generic)

INDEX

The names of fictional characters and institutions are set within inverted commas, as are titles of poems and songs. Page references in **bold** type indicate a chapter or section within a chapter.

Abbotsholme School, 92

Abbott, Diane, MP, 11

Addis Ababa, 174

Alcoholism, 243–4

Aldis, Dr, 42

'Algie', 190

Almond, of Loretto 224

Ampleforth College, 15, 139

Anglicanism, 118

Anzio, 160

Archbishop of Canterbury, 2, 17, 96, 266

Archer, Jeffrey, Lord, 89

Arkwright, Richard, 93

Arlington House School, 106, 107

Arnold, Dr Thomas, 84, 114, 115, 117, 122, 123, 128, 129, 150, 174, 176–8, 179, 180, 194, **205–11,** 214, 226, 253, 262, 277,

'Arthur', 212

ASDIC, 94

Assisted Places Scheme, 10, 274

'As The Team's Head Brass', 166

Attlee, Clement, 235, 249

Ayckbourn, Alan, 100

Ayrton, A. S., 80

Bailey, Ian, 142, **189**

Baldwin, Stanley, 265–6, 271

Ballantine, Serjeant, 282

Balliol College, Oxford, 4, 104, 106, 173, 248

Balston, Edward, 83

Bamford, T. W., 229

Barnard Castle School, 16, 209

Barnett, Correlli, 94

'Bash Street Kids', 137

Baxter, R. S., 131

Bazalgette, Joseph, 125

BBC, 201

Beano, The, 137, 138

Bedales School, 16, 92

Bedford School, 16

Bedford Modern School, 16

'Beetle', 179, 180

Belfast, HMS, 152

Belk, Toby, 246

Bell, Canon G. C., 198

Benn, Tony, 11

'Bernard', 101

Betjeman, Sir John, 99, 121, 139

Bideford, 179

'Billy Bunter', 17, 24, 102, 141, 178, **180–2**

Bishop of Calcutta, 212

Bishop of Rochester, 222

Bisley Shooting Competition, 158

Blair, Tony, 249

Block Club, The, 145

Blundell's School, 16, 40

Blunden, Edmund, 107

Boer War, 173, 271

Bofors gun, 152

Bonhote, Revd Canon Edward, 127

Borth, 42, 215, 217

Bottoms Up!, 139, **187,** 240–2

Bowen, Edward E., 282

Boys' Club Movement, 110

Bradby, E. H., 199

Bradby, G. F., **173–6**

Bradfield College, 16, 73, 134, 229

Braithwaite, John, 197

Brereton, Revd J. L., 209

Brighton College, 15, 58

Bristol, University of, 267

Britannia Royal Naval College, 157

British Empire, 24, 108–9, **168–70,**

Broadcasting Complaints Commission, 197

Brooke, Rupert, 107, 161, 162, 170, 270

'Brookfield School', 188

Brunel, Isambard Kingdom, 93

Bryanston School, 16

Buchan, John, 108

'Bulldog Drummond', 108

Burns, Robert, 231

Busby, Revd Dr, 196–7

Butler, Montagu, 65, 83

Butler, Rab, 10

Butler, Samuel, 84, **202–5**

Byron, Lord, 107, 161

INDEX

Cambridge University Library, 114

Cameron, David, MP, 208, 249

Canford School, 16

'Carruthers, Gordon', 184

Catholic Church (Roman), 69

Chadwick, Catherine, 206

Champneys, Arthur C., 114

Chancellor of the Exchequer, 2

Chancery, Court of, 80

Chandos, John, 36, 207

'Channel Firing', 251

Charles II, King, 196

Charterhouse School, 6, 10, 14, 15, 36, 78, 83, 105

Chatham Naval Dockyard, 152

Chaucer, Geoffrey, 21

Cheltenham College, 12, 16, 78, 83, 97, 209

'Chiltern School', 173

'Chislehurst College', 139, 187

'Chowdler', 175

Christ Church, Oxford, 195

Christ's Hospital School, 16, 48, 49, 94, 145, 146, 147

Churchill, Sir Winston, 94, 196, 238

Cinderella, 177

City of London School, 78, 83

Clarendon Commission, 14, 45, 63, **75–87,** 92, 93, 94, 99, 137, 146, 195, 199, 203, 215, 236, 278

Clarendon, Lord, 76, 83

Cleese, John, 90

Clifton College, 16, 66, 97, 108, 168, 198

Clockwise, 90

Clive of India, 169

Coleridge, Samuel Taylor, 49

Colet, Dr John, and Foundation, 78, 79, 80, 114, 123, 124, 144, 202, 277

Combined Cadet Force (CCF or 'Corps'), 66, 72, 120, 151–2, 153, 158, 159, 184, 238, 239, 240

Community Service, 110

Conrad, Joseph, 62

Conservative Party (and 'Tory'), 19, 76, 89, 118, 255

Contemporary Review, The, 96

Cooke, A. M., 106

Coote, Lieutenant-General Sir Eyre, MP, 145, 146

Cotton, George, **211–4**

Country Life, 250

County Schools, 209

Cranleigh School, 16, 209

Crapper, Thomas, 125

Crayford, 196

Crommelin-Brown, J. L., 167

Cryer, Barry, 200

Curraghmore House, 145

Daily Mail, The, 235

Dartington Hall School, 92

Darwinian Evolution, 14

'Dead-Beat, The', 164

Dean of Llandaff Cathedral, 172, 222

Death of a Salesman, 101
Delderfield, R. F., 175, **190–2**
Delius, Frederick, 240
Dell, William, 196
Denning, S. P., 229
'Dennis the Menace', 137
Derby, Earl of, 249
Derbyshire, 166
Devon, 179
Devon, Earl of, 83
Devonshire, HMS, 240
Dickens, Charles, 50
Direct Grant Scheme, 274
Direct Method, the, 218, 219
Dobson, Christopher, 97
'Doctor Who', 12
Doncaster, Vicar of, 222
Down with Skool, 5, 49
Dreadnought, HMS, 94
Duchess of Malfi, The, 256
Dugard, William, 223
'Dulce et Decorum Est', 161
Dulwich College, 15
Durham, University of, 224

'East', 169
East India Club, 283
East India Company, 168
Edinburgh Review, The, 60
Edwards, Jimmy, 89, 139, 187, 241
Einstein, Albert, 274
Elegy in a Country Churchyard, 90
Eliot, T. S., 165
Elizabeth I, Queen, 120
Elwyn, Richard, 83

Endowed Schools Commission
    and Bill, 80, 86
Epsom College, 16, 42, 237
Eric, or Little by Little, 176, **178–9,**
    180
Eton College, 3, 8, 9, 10, 12, 14, 15,
    19–20, 25, 27, 28, 29, 39, 40, 43,
    47, 51, 54, 55, 56, 60, 67, 71, 75,
    76, 78, 83, 84, 87, 88, 91, 97, 98,
    99, 105, 107, 122, 128, 145, 146,
    147, 157, 158, 195, **199–202,**
    208, 214, 234, 242, 243, 248,
    249, 264, 266, 269, 271, 272,
    277, 279, 282
Eyebrook Reservoir, 158

Fagging, **32–7,** 211
'Fagin', 48
'Falstaff', 180
Farrar, Revd Canon William, 178
Felsted School, 16
Ferguson, Sir Alex, 267
'Fernhurst School', 100, 184
Fettes College, 113
Fielding, Henry, 53
Financial Times, 173
'Flaggon, Mr', 174
Flannelled Fool, **172–3**
'Flashman', 169
Flecker, James Elroy, 107
Fleming Committee, 10
Foreign Secretary, 2
Framlingham College, 209
Fraser, George McDonald, 169
French Revolution, 233

Friar Tuck, 258
Fry, Revd T. C., 56
Fry, Stephen, 174

Gandhi, 169
Gathorne-Hardy, Jonathan, 63, 69, 86, 151
George III, King, 234
Gill, Alexander, 197
Goodbye, Mr. Chips, 48, **188–90,** 192
Goodbye To All That, 6
Goodford, Charles Old, 128, 129
Golding, William, 60
Gonville & Caius College, Cambridge, 9, 78, 196
Gore, S. W., 32
Governance and Governors, 91, **202–4,** 207–8, 215, 216, 219, 220, 229, 230, 274–5
Graduated County Schools Association, The, 210
Grant Duff, Mr, 79
Grantley, Lord, 282
Grange School, The, 12, 277, 279
Graves, Robert, 6, 107
Gray, Thomas, 90
Gresham's School, 16,
'Greyfriars School', 17, 178, 181
Griffiths, George, 196
'Grimes', 270
Grocers' Livery Company, The, 216
Guevara, (Ernesto) Che, 187, 241

Haberdashers' Aske's Livery Company, The, 216
Haberdashers' Aske's School, 15
Haileybury College, 15, 26, 41, 46, 53, 58, 63, 67, 68, 71, 78, 100, 119,122, 127, 138, 150–1, 168, 173, 180, 199, 209, 235, 237, 240, 253, 256, 257, 258, 267
Hammersmith, 123, 264
Handel, George Frideric, 248
Hardy, Thomas, 251
Harrovian, The, 118, 176, **181–2**
Harrow School, 12, 14, 15, 23, 32, 41, 61, 65, 67, 83, 86, 88, 94, 97, 99, 105, 107, 146, 147, 157, 158, 168, 182, 198, 221–2, 243, 265, 271, 277, 278
Hattersley, Roy, MP, 186
Hawking, Stephen, 274
Hawtrey, Charles, 145
Hellfire Club, 243
Hertford, 59, 235
Hertford Heath, 257
Hessey, J, 83
Hidden, Norman, 142, 143
Highfield House, Uppingham, 7, 31
Highgate School, 16
Hill, Geoffrey, 191
Hills Road, Cambridge, 209
Histon Manor, 220
HMC (Headmasters' and Headmistress's Conference), 5, 10, **87–93,** 134, 215, 228, 223, 253, 260, 283

Holkham Beach, 242
Homerton College, 209
House of Commons, 76, 249
House of Lords, 76, 89, 249
Hughes, Thomas, 179, 205
Hullah, Revd Peter, 197
Hurstpierpoint College, 198

If . . . (film), **187,** 200, 240–2
Internet, 44
Ivy League, the, 105
Imperial Service College, 150,
    157, 180, 237
Imperial War Museum, 152
Independent Schools' Council
    (ISC), 152
Indian Civil Service, 168
International College, Isleworth,
    240

James, Lord (Eric), 197
James, Dr Herbert, 72
James, Thomas, 206
'Jeeves', 156
Jeudwine, John, 204
John Lyon School, 86
Johnson, Boris, 249
John Colet Foundation, 10, 79
Jones, I for (or Evans?), 136
Joseph Andrews, 53,
Journey's End, 154
Julius Caesar, 256
Jutland, Battle of, 152

Kazan, University of, 37

Kaufman, Gerald, MP, 186
Keate, John, 51, 84, 145, 147, 193,
    199–202, 201, 211, 223, 230, 242
Kennedy, Benjamin, 83
Keynes, John Maynard, 143, 144
'King', 179
King James Bible and Book of
    Common Prayer, 121
King's College, Cambridge, 195,
    219
King's College London
    Mathematics School, 268
King's College School,
    Wimbledon, 15, 83, 91
King's Lynn, 39
King's School, Canterbury, 13,
    15, 88, 122, 196, 215
King's School, Chester, 16
Kingswood School, 225–7
Kinsey, Alfred, 82
Kipling, Rudyard, 157, 179–80
Kynaston, Herbert, 83

Labour Party, 76, 251
Ladysmith, Relief of, 235
Lambert, Royston, 45, 70
Lancing College, 16, 122, 126,
    197
'Lanchester, Dr Abraham', 174,
    175
Lanchester Tradition, The, **173–6**
Latymer Upper School, 16, 79
Laxton School, 86
Leach, A. F., 229
Leeds, University of, 191, 266

Leeds Grammar School, 16,
Lee-Enfield rifle, 160
Leicester Grammar School, 12,
   276–7, 277, 278, 279
Lenin, Vladimir, 37
Liberal Party, 76
Life and Correspondence of
   Thomas Arnold, The, 206.
Livery Companies, 202, 203
'Loman, Biff', 101
'Loman, Willy', 101
London Academy of Excellence,
   8, 279
Long Chamber (Eton), 28, 60
Loom of Youth, The, 100, 176,
   181, **183–7**
Lord Dismiss Us, 48
Lord of the Flies, 14, 60
Lord of the Rings, 104
Loretto School, 224
'Lucifer', 181
Lunn, Arnold, 118, 130, 176,
   182–3
Lyttelton, Edward, 235
Lyttelton, Lord, 83

Mafeking, Relief of, 235
Magdalen College School,
   Oxford, 15
Magnet, The, 24, 180
Malet, Arthur, 236–7
Malvern College (Boys), 16
Manchester, 266
Manchester Cathedral, 123, 132
Manchester Grammar School,
   5, 9, 15, 20, 89, 110, 114, 123,
   142, 189, 197, 233, 267, 268,
   278, 279
Manchester United FC, 266, 267
Marquis's Eye, The, 173
Marlborough College, 10, 12, 15,
   38, 51, 83, 96, 99, 107,121,153,
   172, 178, 209, **212–4, 237–8,**
   253
Marshalsea Prison, 55
Mayfair, 120
Mayo, C. H. P., 23
Mayor of London, 17, 266
McCorkindale, Simon, 249
Melville House (Haileybury) 53
Mercers' Company, 10, 77, 79, 80,
   202, 216
Merchant Taylors' Livery
   Company, The, 216
Merchant Taylors' School, 14, 15,
   78, 80, 83, 223, 234
Mertens, Revd Frederick, 198
Messi, Lionel, 274
Methodism, 118, 225
Michelangelo, 248
Miller, Arthur, 101
Milton, John, 181
Mitchie, Willie, 231
Mitchinson, John, 88, 215, 223
Mitford, Jessica, 239
Moberly, George, 83
'Molesworth', 5, 49
Montague, Bernard, 83
Montgomery, Field Marshal, 139,
   242

Mosquito aircraft, 94

Moss, David Whitehead, 224

'M'Turk', 179, 180

Muck-Up Day, 243

Mulcaster, Richard, 216

National Youth Orchestra, 101

Nelsonian navy – *see* Royal Navy

Newbolt, Sir Henry, 108, 149, 282

Newham, 279

New College, Oxford, 1, 3, 195

New Statesman, 173

Nicolson, Harold, 28

Niven, David, 6, 139–40, 141

Norwich, Bishop of, 39

Nuremberg, 160

O'Keefe, John, 65

Oakham School, 16, 27

Oerlikon gun, 152

Ofsted, 84, 273

Oh What a Lovely War!, **187**

Oldham, Hugh, 114

'Olive Oyl', 103

Oliver!, 48

Oliver Twist, 50

Orwell, George, 181, 272

Oundle School, 15, 56, 84, 86

Out of Bounds, 238

Owen, Wilfred, 4–5, 161, 164, 165, 166, 191

'Oxbridge' (Universities of Oxford and Cambridge), 4, 14, 17, 68, 95–6, 97, 100, 106, 170, 195, 196, 202, 203, 218, 224, 246, 249, 250, 254, 261, 266, 267, 278, 279

Oxenholme Station, 70

Oxford Book of Modern Verse, 165

Page, William, 223

Parton Street, 238

Peckett, 219

Pennell, 198

Percival, Lieutenant-General Arthur, 271

Percival, John, 66, 198

Perse, Dr Stephen, 78, 196

Perse School, 5, 9, 15, 132, 194, 196, 202, **218–21**, 255, 267, 268

Perse School for Girls, 255

Philby, Kim, 19

Piaget, Jean, 269

Pilkington, Canon Lord (Peter), 197

Pitt, William, the Elder, 39

Polo Mints, 117

Pontius Pilate, 117

'Popeye', 103

'Potter, Harry', 122

Potts, Dr, 113

Powell Hall, 46, 244

'Powlett-Jones', 190–1

Prime Minister, 2, 17, 208, 254, 266

'Prout', 179

Public Schools Act, 1868, 76, 77

Purdey shotguns, 62

Putin, President, 8,

'Quelch, Mr', 181

Radley College, 15, 89, 98, 281
Rae, John, 204, 223
Raven, Simon, 61
Red Nightcap Club, 243
Repton School, 16, 166
Revenger's Tragedy, 256
Reynolds, Frederick, 38
Richard III, 178
'Roger the Dodger', 137
Romilly, Esmond Marcus David, **238–40**
Ronald, C. J., 163
Rooney, Wayne, 274
Rosenberg, Isaac, 166, 191
Rossall School, 16, 209
Rothschild, Baron, 79–80
Rouse, W. H. D., **218–21**
Roxburgh, J. F., 140
Royal Grammar School, Guildford, 15
Royal Grammar School, Newcastle, 15
Royal Navy, 139, 152, 246; Nelsonian, 27
Royds, Revd John, **127–8,** 174
Rugby School, 14, 15, 26, 31, 66, 72, 78, 83, 84, 105, 115, 157, 161, 173, 177, **205–11,** 253, 271, 277
Russell, John, 36
Rwanda, 120

Saffron Walden, 120

St John's College, Cambridge, 204
St Paul's Cathedral, 115, 122,123, 125, 132
St Paul's School, 5, 10, 14, 15, 20, 54, 78, 79, 80, 81, 83, 89, 91, 106, 114, 122, 123, 144 , 147, 189, 197, 202, 216, 224, 230, 264–5, 267, 268, 277, 282
St Peter's School, 97
Sanderson, F. W., 84, **224**
Sandhurst, Royal Military Academy, 83, 157
Sassoon, Siegfried, 107, 164, 166, 191
Sayers, Dorothy L., 156, 248
Scott, Charles, 83
Scott, Sir Peter, 29
Seaton Station, 235
Secondary Heads' Association, 92–3
Sedbergh School, 16, 45, 46, 66, 70, 85, 102, 103, 129, 130, 134, 168, 243–4, 267
Seldon, Sir Anthony, 81
Selwyn, Revd Dr Edward Carus, 224
Sevenoaks, 16
Shakespeare in Love, 242
Shakespeare, William, 17, 121, 178, 181, 256
Sheffield, 50, 119
Shepherd, Jonathan, 81
Sherborne, 16, 83, 88, 94, 100, 184, 272

Sherriff, R. C., 154

Shoreham College, 198

Shrewsbury School, 14, 15, 78, 83, 105, **202–5,** 224

Silk, Dennis, 89

Singapore, 271

'Sir Humphrey' (*Yes, Minister*), 25

Smith, Sydney, 59–60

'Soldier, The', 161

Sorley, Charles Hamilton, 30, 107, 153, 170

Spanish Civil War, 173, 239

Spender, Stephen, 173

Spitfire aircraft, 94, 242

'Stalky', 179, 180

Stalky & Co, 157, **179–80**

Stanley, A. P., 206

Stephen, Sir Andrew, 11

Stephenson, George, 93

Stevens, Thomas, 229

Steward, Revd Alan, 119

Stewart, William, 68, 138

Stonyhurst College, 16

Stowe School, 67, 139, 140

Stuka aircraft, 190

Summerhill School, 92

Summerscale, David, 68

Summoned by Bells, 99, 121

Taunton Report and Commission, 10, 85, 87, 88, 215

Temple, Frederick, 83, 84

Thomas, Edward, 107, 166

Thorpe, Ian, 9,

Thring, Edward, 27, 39, 42, 60, 84, 88, 95, 174, 202, **214–8,** 277

Times, The, 176

Times Educational Supplement, The, 267

To Serve Them All Our Days, 175, **190–2**

Tolstoy, Leo, 37

'Tom Brown', 122, 161, 169, **176– 8,** 179, 191, 251, 262

Tom Brown's Schooldays, 17, 40, 98, 104, **176–8,** 180, 183, 191, 194, 205, 206, 211

Tommy, 69

Tonbridge School, 16, 217

Tower of London, 115

Trebor Mints, 117

Trinity College, Cambridge, 209

Trollope, Anthony, 40

Turing, Alan, 94, 272

Tusser, Thomas, 54

Twistleton, Edward, 83

Udall, Nicholas, **54–5,** 67, 222, 223

United Services College, 102, 179

University College, School, London, 16, 237

Uppingham School, 16, 18, 20, 27, 28, 31, 58, 60, 71, 74, 84, 88, 95, 97, 101, 103, 110, 116, 122, 127, 136, 146, 158, 174, 186, **214–8,** 224, 226–7, 223, 235, 240, 244, 246, 265

Vaughan, C. J., 66–7, 198, **221–2**

INDEX

Vaughan, Henry, 83

Victoria, Queen, 81

Vietnam War, 241

Vitaï Lampada, **108–9,** 149

Wall Street Crash, 165

Wallis, Sir Barnes, 94

Ward, George, 236

Ware, 235

Warre, Dr, 55

Waste Land, The, 165

Waterford, Lord, 145

Waterhouse, Alfred, 122, 123

Waterloo, Battle of, 98, 155, 272

Waugh, Alec, 100, 118, 176, 182

Waugh, Evelyn, 183, 270

Webb, Thomas, 99

Webster, John, 256

Welldon, J. I., 217

Wellington aircraft, 94

Wellington College, 12, 16, 53, 78, 81, 83, 96, 158, 172, 238, 239, 282

Wellington, first Duke of, 98, 271

'Wendover', 187, 200

Wesley, Revd John, **225–7**

Westminster School, 11, 12, 14, 15, 28, 34, 35, 38, 39, 40, 54, 78, 83, 91, 105, 146, 195, 197, 204, 217, 223, 244, 264, 277

Westward Ho!, 179

West Kensington, 123

Whacko!, 139, 141, **187,** 200

Whitgift School, 16

Who, The, 69

William of Wykeham, 1, 2, 114, 277

Williams, Rowland, 41

Wilson ('Ten Mile) Run, 46

'Wimsey, Lord Peter', 156, 248

Winchester College, 1, 2, 3, 6, 12, 13, 14, 15, 39, 40, 59, 78, 83, 91, 105, 114, 131, 141, 146, 147, 157, 195, 236, 243, 249, 277

Winder (Hill), 244

Woodard, Canon Nathaniel, 117, **125–6**

Woodard Schools, 198, 209

Woodbine Willie (Revd Geoffrey Studdert Kennedy), 164

Woolf, Leonard, 106

Woolwich, Royal Military Academy, 83

World War 1, 4, 6, 18, 42, 44, 72, 73, 107, **149–67,** 183, 191, 270

World War 2, 25, 37, 189, 190, 271

Worsley, Ben, 173

Worsley, T. C., 96, **172–3,** 239

'Wooster, Bertie', 156

Wootton, H. A., 220–1

Yarm School, 277, 279

Yeats, W. B., 165

Yes, Minister, 25

York, University of, 197